# PRENUPTIAL AGREEMENTS
## Second Edition

**Iain Harris and Rachel Spicer**

First Edition

by
**Iain Harris and Rachel Spicer**

**Foreword by the
Rt. Hon. Lord Justice Wilson**

NOVA
LAW AND FINANCE

Published by
Nova Law and Finance Ltd
18b Charles St
London W1J 5DU

www.nova-legal.com

ISBN 978-1-908013-18-7



Printed and bound in Great Britain by
Marston Book Services Ltd, Didcot, Oxon

# About the Authors

**Iain Harris** has been as a solicitor since 1977 with a significant part of his practice being concerned with matrimonial matters in particular prenuptial agreements and financial relief. He has sat regularly as a deputy district judge on the South East circuit since his appointment in 1998.

**Rachel Spicer** is a barrister at 1 Hare Court. She specialises in all aspects of family finance including financial provision on divorce and child support. She is a member of the Family Law Bar Association.

# Contents

# Foreword to 1st Edition

### THE RIGHT HON. LORD JUSTICE WILSON

For a number of reasons the law of ancillary relief in England and Wales has been slow to give effect, even in principle, to pre-nuptial agreements. Forty years ago, when I started in practice, the law was (can one credit it?) exceedingly wary of all agreements, even if reached with legal advice following the breakdown of the marriage, whether as to the basis of its dissolution, or to finance or even as to children; such agreements had to be presented to the court with respectful diffidence, ideally (so I considered) by young and inexperienced barristers. In particular, however, our law has long been proud to stand as a bulwark for the protection of wives from overbearing husbands; and the foundations of the bulwark have been driven deep. The philosophy has also been that, if you elect the status of marriage, you accept the whole package of legal consequences which attend it. There has also been distaste for the practice of catering for the breakdown of your marriage before you have even articulated your mutual vows. Finally our law of ancillary relief has been chauvinistic and thus poorly reactive to the general respect given to pre-nuptial agreements in other jurisdictions.

Now, however, the general approach of family law towards agreements has changed 180 degrees. The social and financial emancipation of women has made the bulwark cast around them by the law generally redundant. The philosophy has become that marriage is more made for man than is man for marriage, with the result that, within limits, people should be allowed to pick out the bits they want. The distaste to which I referred has given way to a perception that entry into a marriage in a romantic haze, oblivious to its likely difficulties ahead, to their capacity often to prove terminal and to the legal consequences which may then follow, is positively conducive to its failure. And the chauvinism of our law has had to be tempered by increasing international mobility and by our membership of the E.U.

In this book Iain Harris and Rachel Spicer have brilliantly charted the law's fitful movement so far towards recognition of pre-nuptial agreements. The movement will surely continue in the same direction and pick up speed. It would be probably be better if the criteria for their recognition were to be spelt out in an amendment to s.25 of the Matrimonial Causes Act 1973 but, in the absence of any current appetite on the part of government to promote or even support reform of s.25, the more realistic hope is for an authoritative pronouncement in the Court of Appeal or, better still, in the future Supreme Court. But the problem for practitioners is that, however the law be finally cast, there will presumably have to be some facility for the court's departure from the terms of the agreement in a residue of cases (and here for convenience I use the label which Baron J recently commended) of "manifest unfairness". I suspect that, where the terms of a pre-nuptial agreement provide a result far removed from that which the principles of ancillary relief would otherwise yield, family judges may fall into two camps as to whether the case should fall into the residue, whatever its label; and it may arguably prove important for the courts to keep the residue within narrow bounds. Otherwise the tail will wag the dog. If the pre-nuptial agreement yields a result reasonably correlative to that provided by the general law, there is of course scant need to recognise it anyway; so principles of recognition have significance only where there is no such reasonable correlation.

Equally the law will need to develop clear principles which govern the circumstances pre-requisite to validity which must obtain at the time of entry into the agreement. I note with interest, for example, the suggestion of the authors that mutual disclosure might best be achieved by the swearing of affidavits in Form E. I can foresee a challenge for the courts in achieving a balance between insistence on truthful disclosure and a refusal to allow trawls through ancient affidavits in Form E which catch only trivial, unintentional error.

The subject of this book is therefore of the greatest topicality and interest for all of us who practise, in one way or another, in the field of family law. Having read it in proof, I am resolved to use it myself; and hope that you who have been kind enough to read this foreword may find it helpful to do likewise.

**1 April 2008** **Nicholas Wilson**

# Table of Cases

*Barrett v Barrett* (1981) 11 Fam Law 178
*Brockwell v Brockwell* [1975] Court of Appeal Transcript 468
*C v C (Divorce: Stay of English Proceedings)* [2001] 1 FLR 694
*Camm v Camm* (1983) 4 FLR 577
*Charman v Charman* [2007] EWCA Civ 503
*Crossley v Crossley* [2008] 1FLR 1467
*Dart v Dart* [1996] 2 FLR 286
*Dean v Dean* [1978] Fam 161
*Edgar v Edgar* [1980] 1 WLR 1410
*Ella v Ella* [2007] 2 FLR 35
*F v F (Ancillary Relief: Substantial Assets)* [1995] 2 FLR 45
*H v H* [2007] EWHC 459 (Fam)
*Hughes v Hughes* [1929] P 1
*Hyman v Hyman* [1929] AC 601
*J v V (Disclosure: Offshore Corporations)* [2004] 1 FLR 1042
*K v K (Ancillary Relief: Pre-nuptial Agreement)* [2003] 1 FLR 120
*M v M (Pre-nuptial Agreement)* [2002] 1FLR 654
*MacLeod v MacLeod* [2010] 1 AC 298
*Miller v Miller*; *McFarlane v McFarlane* [2006] 2 AC 618
*N v N (Divorce: Ante-Nuptial Agreement)* [1999] 2 FCR 582
*N v N (Foreign Divorce: Financial Relief)* [1997] 1 FLR 900
*NA v MA* [2007] 1 FLR 1760
*Radmacher (formerly Granatino) v Granatino* [2010] UKSC 42
*Royal Bank of Scotland v Etridge* [2001] UKHL 44
*S v S (Divorce: Staying Proceedings)* [1997] 2 FLR 100
*Smith v McInerney* [1994] 2 FLR 1077
*X v X (Y and Z Intervening)* [2002] 1 FLR 508
*White v White* [2001] 1 AC 596
*Wright v Wright* [1970] 3 All ER 209
*Wyatt v Goldsmith* Unreported

# Table of Statutes

Children Act 1989
  Section 15
  Schedule 1
Divorce Law Reform Act 1969
Divorce (Religious Marriages) Act 2002
Domicile and Matrimonial Proceedings Act 1973
  Section 5(6)
Inheritance (Provision for Family and Dependants) Act 1975
Law of Property (Miscellaneous Provisions) Act 1989
Lord Hardwicke's Marriage Act 1753
Maintenance Agreements Act 1957
Manx Matrimonial Proceedings Act 2003
  Sections 49–51
Married Women's Property Act 1882
Matrimonial and Family Proceedings Act 1984
Matrimonial Causes Act 1857
Matrimonial Causes Act 1973
  Section 10A
  Section 23(1)(d)
  Section 25
  Section 34(2)
  Section 35
Matrimonial Proceedings Act 1973
  Sections 34–36
Matrimonial Property and Proceedings Act 1970
Supreme Court of Judicature (Consolidation) Act 1925
  Section 190
Trusts of Land and Appointment of Trustees Act 1996

# Introduction

Enthusiasm for the institution of marriage remains keen notwithstanding the current levels of breakdown.

In 2006, 2007 and 2008 (the most recent year for which statistics have been published) there were 239,454, 235,370 and 232,990 marriages respectively.[1] This equates to about 21.8 men marrying per 1,000 unmarried men aged 16 and over and 19.6 women marrying per 1,000 unmarried women aged 16 and over.

In the years 2006, 2007 and 2008 there were 147,236, 136,187 and 128,837 petitions for divorce filed. Although between 2007 and 2008 the number of divorces granted in the UK decreased by 5 per cent from 128,232 to 121,779 the simple fact is that one in three marriages will end in divorce. This is one of the highest rates in the European Union.

Divorce brings with it significant problems for the spouses and children. Not least are the problems of disentangling the former spouses' financial affairs, doing what may be necessary to enable each to have a fair share of the family assets and to be able to meet their continuing financial responsibilities for each other and any children.

Many spouses are able to resolve their financial issues by agreement, often led or brokered by lawyers and/or mediators. A significant number, however, are unable to achieve such resolution by agreement. They need to ask the courts to resolve their differences and adjudicate upon asset and income division.

The courts have extremely wide powers to vary financial arrangements between parties on or at any time after pronouncement of a decree of divorce or nullity. The legislature has added to and developed these powers over the years since their introduction. The courts have interpreted them in a manner consistent with changing social and moral attitudes. For present purposes it is not necessary to go back to earlier than the last thirty years of the twentieth century.

1 National Statistics Online.

In terms of exercise of their legal powers the courts currently have an unfettered discretion. Until the changes introduced by the Matrimonial and Family Proceedings Act 1984 the courts were required to exercise their discretion in order to place the parties, so far as practicable and, having regard to their conduct, just to do so, in the financial position in which they would have been if the marriage had not broken down and each had properly discharged his or her financial obligations and responsibilities towards the other.[2]

That direction, as to the manner in which the court was to exercise its discretion, was abolished by the Matrimonial and Family Proceedings Act 1984. It had been criticised in *Barrett v Barrett*[3] where Cumming-Bruce LJ in the Court of Appeal said:

> "The court is enjoined, so far as practicable, to put the parties back into the situation they would have been in if the marriage had not broken down. That direction in the statute of the legislature creates for the court exactly as simple a situation as the direction in the nursery rhyme after Humpty Dumpty had tumbled off the wall – to 'put him together again'. It simply is not on and all that one is doing really is trying to produce an admittedly unsatisfactory situation that minimises as far as is sensible the real hardship to the loser."

Upon its abolition in 1984, Parliament did not put anything in its place. The court's discretion to adjust the financial affairs of former spouses simply has to be exercised fairly having regard to all the circumstances of the case. As Lord Nicholls said in *Miller v Miller*[4]

> "Fairness is an elusive concept. It is an instinctive response to a given set of facts. Ultimately it is grounded in social and moral values. These values, or attitudes, can be stated. But they cannot be justified, or refuted, by any objective process of logical reasoning. Moreover, they change from one generation to the next. It is not surprising, therefore, that in the present context there can be different views on the requirements of fairness in any particular case."

There is presently a significant degree of uncertainty amongst advisers as to how the court would be likely to divide assets in any particular case. As

2 Matrimonial Causes Act 1973 s.25(2).
3 (1981) 11 Fam Law 178 CA.
4 Miller v Miller; McFarlane v McFarlane [2006] 2 AC 618.

there is such a wide discretion it is to be expected that its exercise will differ between different judges and courts. No two adjustments on any set of facts by different tribunals are likely to be exactly the same.

Whilst this is clearly one of the strengths of the present discretionary system it is also one of its weaknesses in that it is impossible to predict the exact asset division a court will impose in any particular case. All that can be anticipated is a solution within broad parameters. So long as any division falls within such parameters it will be unappealable.

It is said that the "yardstick of equality of division"[5] is a key and fundamental directive. But there can be departure from that yardstick and, in particular, the treatment of certain assets brought into the marriage remains uncertain.

Although the government attaches great weight to the importance of the family as a social unit it has indicated it has no present intention of reviewing the law in relation to asset division on marriage breakdown.[6] This remains the position subsequent to the 2010 general election.

In *Charman v Charman*[7] the Court of Appeal took the unprecedented course of including a 20 paragraph postscript to its judgment headed "Changing the Law." This is set out in full at Appendix B. It calls for a review of the law, endorsing, at paragraph 121, Lord Hope's speech in *Miller* identifying the need for reform of Scottish law and saying that arguably the English statute is in equal need of modernisation.

That call has not gone entirely unheeded. The Law Commission announced in June 2008 that it would examine the status and enforceability of marital property agreements. The Commission is due to publish a consultation paper in early 2011 when it will review the eventual timing for publication of a report and draft bill.

The most significant development since the publication of the first edition of this book in April 2008 has been the Supreme Court decision in *Radmacher*.[8] The essential proposition handed down in that decision is that "the court should give effect to a nuptial agreement that is entered

5 First mentioned by Lord Nicholls in *White v White* [2001] 1 AC 596 at 605.

6 On 6 June 2006 Baroness Ashton, Parliamentary Under Secretary of State at the then Department of Constitutional Affairs, answered the question whether in the light of the House of Lords judgment in *Miller* and *McFarlane* the government had any plans to introduce legislation to reform divorce and maintenance law by saying that the government had no plans for such reform: *Hansard*, 6 June 2006, column 1136.

7 [7][2007] EWCA Civ 503.

8 See Chapter 3.

into by each party with a full appreciation of its implications unless in the circumstances prevailing it would not be fair to hold the parties to their agreement".[9]

It therefore comes as no surprise that an increasing number of prospective marriage partners are seeking professional advice as to what steps they may take in order to mitigate the uncertainties of the courts' approach to asset division and to bring, if they can, a degree of certainty to their own circumstances if their relationship should break down.

The vehicle for this purpose is the prenuptial agreement. This book, intended for the practitioner, examines the prenuptial agreement, its origins, purposes, enforceability and future uses. It contains practical advice as to best practice and gives guidance upon the appropriate form for prenuptial agreements.

9 [2010] UKSC 42 at paragraph 75.

# Chapter 1

# Introduction to the prenuptial agreement

There are a number of different types of agreement in relation to the financial aspects of marriage.

## Prenuptial agreement

A prenuptial or ante-nuptial agreement (the prefixes are interchangeable) is an agreement by which a man and a woman, prior to marriage, seek to regulate their financial liabilities and responsibilities the one towards the other in the event of a divorce.[1]

Such agreements are to be distinguished from maintenance agreements and ante-nuptial settlements.

## Maintenance agreement

By virtue of the definition in Section 34(2) of the Matrimonial Causes Act 1973 a maintenance agreement is:

> "any agreement in writing made, whether before or after the commencement of the Matrimonial Causes Act 1973, between the parties to a marriage, being –
>
> (*a*) an agreement containing financial arrangements, whether made during the continuance or after the dissolution or annulment of the marriage; or
>
> (*b*) a separation agreement which contains no financial arrangements in a case where no other agreement in writing between the same parties contains such arrangements."

1 Although a prenuptial agreement can only be between a man and a woman parties to a civil partnership are covered by the same legal principles set out herein and may enter into pre civil partnership agreements.

## Ante-nuptial settlement

An ante- or post nuptial settlement is a settlement made in contemplation of or during the marriage of the husband and wife whose marriage is in question.

## Post nuptial agreement

A post nuptial agreement is one entered into by the parties following their marriage to regulate their financial affairs. It may be made before or after a breakdown in the marriage, or in contemplation of proceedings.[2]

None of these agreements is inherently unlawful. They vary in their effectiveness, usefulness and enforceability. The only type of agreement which was (pre *Radmacher*[3]) considered to be unlawful was one that contemplated or provided for the separation of a husband and wife at a future time.[4] In *Radmacher*, the Supreme Court comprehensively swept away this 'public policy' rule in relation to both pre and post nuptial agreements.[5]

These types of agreement need to be considered in the context of marriage. Anthropologists have not been able to trace the origin of marriage. In the twenty-first century we understand marriage as the relationship between man and woman recognised by civil authority and often bound by religious belief. In Western society marriage is a monogamous union.

Although it was not always so we now enter into the marriage bond with expectations of a happy familial and fiscal union. Trevelyan, in his *English Social History* described the view of medieval marriage:

> "Love might chance to grow out of marriage, as doubtless it often did. If it did not, the wife tried to assert her rights by her tongue, sometimes with success. But the lordship was held to be vested in the husband, and when he asserted it by his fist and stick, he was seldom blamed by public opinion. In this unequal struggle, the woman also laboured under the handicap of constantly bearing children – most of whom soon died and had to be replaced. Such

2 For an example see *NA v MA* [2006] EWHC 2900 where the parties agreed a reconciliation on the basis that the wife signed a post nuptial agreement setting out the financial division that would be given effect if the marriage subsequently broke down.

3 [2010] UKSC 42.

4 *N v N (divorce: ante-nuptial agreement)* [1999] 2 FLR 745.

5 *Radmacher* at paragraph 52.

> marriage was not an ideal state of things, but for centuries it served to people England, a difficult task in those days of plague and medical ignorance."

In England the church claimed jurisdiction over marriage and divorce. Until the 1750s marriage was largely a private matter between two individuals and their families. Although divorce by Act of Parliament was available it was not until the Matrimonial Causes Act 1857 that civil divorce was available. Some religious authorities permitted a marriage to be terminated.

Prior to 1753 clandestine marriages were valid in the eyes of the church and the law. Lord Hardwicke's 1753 Marriage Act vested control over marriage in the hands of the state. Marriages which had not taken place in the Church of England or a synagogue were invalid.

Diverse interest groups had problems with this. The Quaker, Daniel Defoe, considered it testimony to the increasingly successful alliance between property and patriarchy. In other words, the interests of the state and the landed gentry coincided with those of the established church. Although mere consent, as the basis for matrimony, created significant problems, their resolution in the form of the Marriage Act provoked enduring ill-will.

The resentment generated by the established church's 'ownership' of marriage is evident in the historical record. Owing to the Act's requirements – for the reading of banns, a ceremony carried out in public and the signing of the parish register – large sections of the population ended up with informal ways of living together rather than in meeting the requirements of the Act.

"Living tally" was the phrase for a permanent and respectable relationship outside formal marriage, when such a marriage might be avoided because of a woman's wish to retain personal and financial autonomy. After marriage a woman's right of settlement was removed to her husband's parish. If he deserted then it was possible neither of the parishes would be obligated to take responsibility for her.

The act of marriage had been caught up in the wider social movement in so far as it was coming to be considered in terms of contract rather than as status. Status is fixed and unchanging but contract is dissoluble. This was the start of the perception that marriage altered status permanently but that such status could be altered again by marriage termination on divorce.

From the mid nineteenth century the state gave the courts increasingly wide powers to regulate arrangements between parties who had married and who subsequently wished to terminate their marriage contract.

Few areas of the law are quite as entwined with social and political mores as those that regulate the making and breaking of marriage. The law has developed over many centuries. In the late sixteenth and seventeenth centuries, where the poor were unable to afford a written deed of separation, they adopted a type of self divorce, namely wife sale. This entailed literally a sale of a wife on market day.

The process is described in the *Laws Respecting Women* (1737) in the following terms:

> "Among the common people, a method is sometimes practised of dissolving a marriage, no less singular than compendious. When a husband and wife find themselves heartily tired of each other, and agree to part; if the man has a mind to authenticate the intended separation by making it a matter of public notoriety, thinking, like Petruchio, that his wife is his goods and chattels, he puts a halter about her neck, and thereby leads her to the next market place, and there puts her up to auction to be sold to the best bidder, as though she was a brood mare or a milch-cow.[6]"

The law has developed significantly over the last three centuries. For example, for many centuries a woman lost any right to have contact with her offspring if she was guilty of adultery. Now, rather than needing to identify a wrongdoer, the law regards the breakdown of a marriage as a misfortune to all involved. The parties have equal rights over children and division of assets, albeit, it may be suggested, this latter right has only been recognised since the seminal House of Lords decision in *White*.[7]

Prospective marriage partners now turn more frequently for legal advice, prior to their marriage, as to whether they may regulate their financial relationship in the event of it subsequently breaking down.

It is not difficult to assess what may have led to this demand for advice. One factor is the concern as to the uncertainty of outcome of any judicially imposed division of assets. There are many references in recent

6 *The Laws Respecting Women* (Anon, London, 1737) p 55.

7 *White v White* [2001] 1 AC 596.

judgments to such uncertainties and the desire for parliamentary intervention.[8] The government has made it clear that no such intervention can be expected in the foreseeable future.[9]

Another factor is the prevalence of ante-nuptial agreements in other jurisdictions. They are commonplace in the United States, where it appears to be comparatively rare for wealthy individuals to marry or re-marry without such agreements. They are similarly a regular feature in countries in the European Union and those in the Commonwealth.

Against the background of increasing recognition being given to negotiated arrangements made between prospective and actual spouses, the main concern of this book is with prenuptial agreements, their drafting and enforceability. In order to secure an adequate understanding the draftsman will need to be aware of the likely approach of the court to such agreements. As can be seen from the case analysis in Chapter 2 there has been an incremental acceptance that regard will be had to the terms of any agreement and that in the right circumstances it may ultimately carry considerable, or even decisive weight.

The incremental approach of the courts to the treatment of prenuptial agreements has progressed significantly since publication of the first edition of this book in April 2008 in two key decisions, namely *MacLeod v MacLeod*[10] and *Radmacher (formerly Granatino) v Granatino*.[11] The Supreme Court decision in *Radmacher* has moved the law to the position in which the court will give effect to a prenuptial agreement that is freely entered into by each party with a full appreciation of its implications unless in the circumstances prevailing it would not be fair to hold the parties to their agreement.

In addition, the Law Commission is currently examining *Marital Property Agreements*. Its project will examine the status and enforceability of agreements made between spouses or civil partners (or those contemplating marriage or civil partnership) concerning their property and finances. As the Law Commission states:

> "Such agreements might regulate the couple's financial affairs during the course of their relationship; equally they might seek to

---

8 For example *Cowan v Cowan* [2001] EWCA Civ 679, *Charman v Charman* [2007] EWCA Civ 503.

9 See Introduction, n 6.

10 [2010] 1 AC 298.

11 [2010] UKSC 42.

> determine how the parties would divide their property in the event of divorce, dissolution or separation."

The Law Commission project, which states that "The legal recognition of marital property agreements is of great social importance", commenced in late 2009. The Commission plans to publish a consultation paper in early 2011, at which time it will review the eventual timing for publication of a report and draft Bill. Prior to the Radmacher decision it had indicated it would publish its report and draft bill in late 2012.[12]

12 http://www.lawcom.gov.uk/marital_property.htm

# Chapter 2

# Analysis of case law prior to *MacLeod* and *Radmacher*

In modern case law the starting point for the traditional analysis of the enforceability of agreements between husband and wife is *Hyman v Hyman.*[1] This House of Lords case is the authority for the proposition that a husband and wife cannot make an agreement not to invoke the jurisdiction of the court or to control the powers of the court when its jurisdiction is invoked.

In view of the importance of the proposition of law established by *Hyman* it is appropriate to set out its facts and the approach of the court to the issues raised in it in some detail.

Maurice and May Hyman married on 14 September 1912. They did not have children and by 1919 their relationship had deteriorated to the extent that they executed a deed of separation. They agreed to live apart. Maurice agreed to pay May £20 every Monday for "her separate use and maintenance". She also agreed not to compel Maurice "to allow her any maintenance further than the weekly sum of £20".

In January 1926 May presented a divorce petition. A decree was duly pronounced and in February 1927 she sought maintenance, contrary to her earlier agreement not to do so. At first instance, in what was then the Probate Divorce and Admiralty Division of the High Court, Mr Justice Hill held, on a preliminary issue, that May was not prevented from seeking increased maintenance.

Maurice appealed. His appeal was heard over four days during May and June 1928 by a six-judge Court of Appeal. Interestingly it was heard at the same time as the case of *Hughes v Hughes*[2] in which the President, Lord Merrivale, had, on 26 March 1928, held that the wife was not precluded from seeking maintenance where she had covenanted not to claim maintenance.

1 [1929] AC 601.
2 [1929] P 1.

The Court of Appeal held, in both cases, that the wives were not bound by their promises not to seek an increase in maintenance. There were, however, two strong dissenting judgements in the Court of Appeal, from Lawrence and Russell LJJ and Maurice duly appealed to the House of Lords.

So important was the appeal to the parties that the husband was represented by a Leader and two juniors and the wife by two Leaders and two juniors, who in the event were not called on.

The thrust of the husband's argument was that:

> "In the absence in a statute of any express provision against contracting out, a free citizen is at liberty to barter away his rights as he pleases, unless he is prevented on some ground of public policy. No question of public policy arises here. Public policy requires that contracts should be kept and covenants fulfilled, and the Appellant Husband is merely seeking to keep a lady to her bargain."

This fell on deaf ears in the House. The Lord Chancellor, Lord Hailsham, delivered the leading opinion and all the other members, bar one, gave full agreeing opinions. The ratio of the decision is as follows:

> "Before 1857 it was not competent for any Court to dissolve a marriage validly contracted; in order to effect such a dissolution it was necessary to have recourse to an Act of Parliament. In 1857 the Legislature for the first time gave to the courts the power to dissolve the marriage tie by a decree of divorce …the Court may compel the husband to make adequate provision for the support of the wife. … the parties cannot validly make an agreement either
>
> (1) not to invoke the jurisdiction of the Court, or
>
> (2) to control the powers of the Court when its jurisdiction is invoked."

This ratio was based upon the construction of statute. The relevant provision from the Matrimonial Causes Act 1857 was re-enacted in the Supreme Court of Judicature (Consolidation) Act 1925 of which Section 190 is in the following terms:

> "(1) The court may, if it thinks fit, on any decree for divorce or nullity of marriage, order that the husband shall, to the satisfaction of the court, secure to the wife such gross sum of money or annual sum of money for any term, not exceeding

> her life, as having regard to her fortune, if any, to the ability of her husband and to the conduct of the parties, the court may deem to be reasonable … and may, if it thinks fit, suspend the pronouncing of the decree until the deed or instrument has been duly executed.
>
> (2) In any such case as aforesaid the court may, if it thinks fit, by order, either in addition to or instead of an order under sub-section (1) of this section, direct the husband to pay to the wife during the joint lives of the husband and wife such monthly or weekly sum for her maintenance and support as the court may think reasonable.'

There follow provisos for the variation or discharge of such order and then Section 190(4) is in the following terms:

> 'Where any decree for restitution of conjugal rights or judicial separation is made on the application of the wife, the court may make such order for alimony as the court thinks just.'

Lord Hailsham LC made the following observation at page 609:

> "this by no means implies that, when this application is made, the existence of the deed or its terms are not the most relevant factors for consideration by the court in reaching a decision."

The decision of the House of Lords has subsisted to this day but the above observation has paved the way for significant developments in subsequent case law. Even though the decision was based on the interpretation of a specific statutory provision it has been argued in support of the proposition that the parties to a marriage cannot contract out of the court's jurisdiction to impose upon them a financial regime, even though they may have agreed their own arrangements before they were married.

In 1970 the Court of Appeal decided *Wright v Wright*.[3] This was the first reported case after *Hyman* in which the court had to consider the effect of an agreement by a spouse not to seek financial support. As one of the terms upon which a defended divorce was compromised the wife indicated that it was her "present intention not to apply for further maintenance, unless there is any unforeseen circumstance making it impossible for her to work at all or otherwise to maintain herself".

The wife subsequently applied for maintenance. The Court of Appeal held that the wife was not entitled to apply for maintenance. It held her to her agreement, Sir Gordon Wilmer saying, at page 214:

3 [1970] 1 WLR 1219.

> "that the existence of this agreement, having regard to the circumstances in which it was arrived at, at least makes it necessary for the wife, if she wants to justify an award of maintenance, to offer prima facie proof that there have been unforeseen circumstances, in the true sense, which make it impossible for her to work or otherwise maintain herself."

Whilst *Wright* was concerned with a post nuptial situation it was the first reported case in which the court had held a spouse to an agreed financial arrangement.

*Brockwell v Brockwell*,[4] decided in 1975, was the next significant step on the route to acceptance by the court that a party to a marriage might be held to a commitment in relation to financial issues. Mrs Brockwell agreed not to claim a lump sum. Ormrod LJ suggested that such an agreement should be taken into account under the heading of conduct and added:

> "when people make an agreement like this it is a very important factor in considering what is the just outcome of the proceedings."

The cases of *Hyman*, *Brockwell* and *Wright* were considered in detail in the seminal Court of Appeal decision of *Edgar v Edgar*.[5] In this case the court held the wife to her agreement not to seek a capital payment.

The husband and wife had executed a deed of separation in April 1976, which was negotiated by the parties each being represented by solicitors. In fact the wife was firmly advised by both solicitors and counsel not to enter into an agreement to forgo her further claim for a lump sum. The husband was a multi-millionaire and the wife agreed not to seek a capital payment.

When she subsequently petitioned for divorce in 1980 she claimed a capital payment. At first instance the husband was ordered to make the wife a lump sum capital payment of £670,000. The husband appealed to the Court of Appeal where he succeeded. Whilst the Court indicated this was a "wholly exceptional case on the facts" it decided that the parties should be kept to their agreement.

Oliver LJ said, at page 1420,

> "Men and women of full age, education and understanding, acting with competent advice available to them, must be assumed to

4 Court of Appeal Transcript 468.
5 [1980] 1 WLR 1410.

> know and appreciate what they are doing and their actual respective bargaining strengths will in fact depend in every case upon a subjective evaluation of their motives for doing it."

Further on, at page 1424, he said:

> "... in a consideration of what is just to be done in the exercise of the court's powers under the Act of 1973 in the light of the conduct of the parties, the court must, I think, start from the position that a solemn and freely negotiated bargain by which a party defines her own requirements ought to be adhered to unless some clear and compelling reason, such as for instance, a drastic change of circumstances, is shown to the contrary."

The effect of the decision in *Edgar*, in July 1980, was that the court appeared willing to keep parties to agreements they had reached on financial matters within marriage, provided that each party had received competent legal advice and there were no good and substantial grounds for concluding that an injustice would be done by holding the parties to the terms of their agreement.

On one analysis of *Edgar* it can be treated as a conduct case. Ormrod LJ referred, at page 1417, to his judgment in *Brockwell* and said:

> "I suggested in my judgment that an agreement not to claim a lump sum should be taken into account under the heading of conduct, and added, 'when people make an agreement like this it is a very important factor in considering what is the just outcome of the proceedings.' I see no reason to resile from that statement."

On another analysis it can be treated as an example of freedom to contract, as per Oliver LJ's observation above, that "a solemn and freely negotiated bargain by which a party defines her own requirements ought to be adhered to".

When the court came to consider the prenuptial agreement in *F v F (Ancillary Relief: Substantial Assets)*[6] in October 1994, in the first reported case directly concerning such agreements, it gave no weight to the prenuptial agreement the parties had made. The principle of keeping parties to "a solemn and freely negotiated bargain" did not arise.

The parties were of German origin. At the time of divorce the husband was 50 and the wife 36. They had been married for eleven years. The husband said he had capital assets of not less than £150 million.

6 [1995] 2 FLR 45.

Prior to the marriage prenuptial contracts were executed, the primary one in Germany regulating arrangements in accordance with German and Swiss Law and a second one in England intended to be governed by US Law. The prenuptial agreement confined the wife to a sum equivalent to the pension of a German judge. The parties had three children.

Thorpe J dealt with the prenuptial agreement in the following somewhat dismissive terms:

> "The other special condition which has to be considered in this case, albeit briefly, is the existence of the antenuptial contracts. It is not in dispute that contracts of this sort are commonplace in the society from which the parties come. They are much emphasised by the husband in his affidavits, since if strictly applied they would have the ridiculous result of confining the wife to the pension of a German judge, whatever that may be. Equally, in the affidavits the wife is urgent in protesting the circumstances in which they came to be signed. I regard the protestations of both in relation to these contracts as having an urgency that the documents themselves do not demand. In this jurisdiction they must be of very limited significance. The rights and responsibilities of those whose financial affairs are regulated by statute cannot be much influenced by contractual terms which were devised for the control and limitation of standards that are intended to be of universal application throughout our society. It is said that these contracts would be strictly enforced against the wife in Germany. I have declined to enlarge the arena to allow evidence from German experts in that field. I cannot think that even in Germany the wife would not have the right to deploy a case either that there was some inequality of bargaining power, alternatively undue influence, or that they are inconsistent with social policy in Germany. For the purposes of my determination I do not attach any significant weight to those contracts."

The next case in which the courts considered the relevance of a prenuptial agreement was *N v N* (*Foreign Divorce: Financial Relief*),[7] decided by Cazalet J in December 1996.

This was a case in which Swedish nationals had executed a prenuptial agreement prior to their marriage in 1967. The agreement was entered into in Stockholm and the parties then married at the Swedish Embassy in Paris.

---

7 [1997] 1 FLR 900.

They were divorced in 1993 by agreement in Stockholm. In 1996 the husband issued proceedings seeking financial provision in England, the wife having moved to London.

Cazalet J. considered that the prenuptial agreement had a bearing on the question of whether the husband should be given leave to pursue his applications for relief in the English courts. He found that overall the husband had not made out substantial grounds for making the application in England.

Although Cazalet J. did not need to rule on the enforceability of the prenuptial agreement he said, *per curiam*, at pages 912/913 as follows:

> "Furthermore the Swedish Court, in my view, is the appropriate Court in which to decide the effect of the prenuptial agreement. It would be binding in Sweden as against being no more than a material consideration in this Court under Section 25 of the Matrimonial Causes Act 1973. Indeed, by coming to this Court, the husband may obtain an advantage in that the Court here in considering its award can step outside the constriction of the prenuptial agreement and may grant the husband more than his entitlement under Swiss law by taking into consideration the wife's overall assets, including her inheritance from her father, a matter expressly excluded from the husband's reach by the prenuptial agreement."

In March 1997 Wilson J, as he then was, gave some encouragement to those concerned with prenuptial agreements in *S v S (Divorce: Staying Proceedings)*.[8]

The husband and wife had met in 1983. The husband had been twice married and the wife once. The husband was not prepared to marry again without the protection for him and his children of a prenuptial agreement. The wife conceded that she knew he would not marry her without such an agreement.

A prenuptial agreement was executed. The parties were advised by independent New York based lawyers. Wilson J. found that the wife's evidence that the prenuptial agreement was never fully explained to her was "not very convincing". He also found that:

> "there is no doubt that the wife would undergo a period of painful adjustment in creating her future life upon assets of perhaps little more than £1m"

8 [1997] 2 FLR 100.

if she were confined to the provision under the agreement. Whilst there was a dispute as to the value of the husband's assets his evidence was that

> "he and trusts set up by him own shares currently worth only $84m. Additionally there are, at least, the real properties and the chattels".

The wife issued proceedings in England on 15 November 1996. The husband issued proceedings in New York on 21 November 1996 and subsequently applied for a stay of the wife's English proceedings.

After a hearing of about five days (Wilson J. said "... at times I wondered whether I was allowing it to proceed for too long") he held that the wife's English proceedings should be stayed because New York was

> "clearly more appropriate than England as a forum for the proceedings for divorce and for the determination of financial issues between the parties".

Wilson J. indicated, at page 114, that:

> "but the provisions of the prenuptial agreement, both the substantive financial provisions and in particular the provisions as to forum, have weighed heavily with me. Even if (which I doubt) this agreement were to be of limited significance in any substantive analysis by this Court of the wife's financial claims pursuant to Section 25 of the 1973 Act, it in no way follows that it must be of very limited significance in the dispatch of the current application. Fairness requires otherwise".

Wilson J. also indicated at page 102 as follows:

> "I am aware of a growing belief that, in the dispatch of a claim for ancillary relief in this jurisdiction, no significant weight will be afforded to a prenuptial agreement, whatever the circumstances. I would like to sound a cautionary note in that respect. No-one could have more profound respect than I for the observations of Thorpe LJ. In *F v F (Ancillary Relief: Substantial Assets) [1995] 2 FLR 45*, 66G he said:

'In this jurisdiction [prenuptial agreements] must be of very limited significance. The rights and responsibilities of those whose financial affairs are regulated by statute cannot be much influenced by contractual terms which were devised for the control and limitation of standards that are intended to be of universal application throughout our society.'

There is a danger that these wide words might be taken out of context. There is no doubt that, where the English court proceeds to determine an application for ancillary relief, Section 25 of the 1973 Act precludes any choice of foreign law, however vividly circumstances of the case might protest its relevance. So the application is of English law and under Section 25(1) regard must be had to all the circumstances of the case. In *F v F* itself, the results of a strict application of the effect of the prenuptial agreements would have been, as the judge said, 'ridiculous'. In those circumstances, they inevitably constituted circumstances of negligible significance. But there will come a case – were I to refuse a stay, might this be it? – where the circumstances surrounding the pre-nuptial agreement and the provision therein contained might, when viewed in the context of other circumstances of the case, prove influential or even crucial. Where other jurisdictions, both in the USA and in the European Union, have been persuaded that there are cases where justice can only be served by confining parties to their rights under pre-nuptial agreements, we should be cautious about too categorically asserting the contrary. I can find nothing in Section 25 to compel a conclusion, so much at odds with personal freedoms to make arrangements for ourselves that escape from solemn bargains, carefully struck by informed adults, is readily available here. It all depends.

The matter must be left open and on the footing that, were she to be unable to claim ancillary relief in England, the wife *might* secure an award of substantial further provision. In what follows my duty is to appraise the relevance of the pre-nuptial agreement to the determination not of the wife's potential application of ancillary relief but of the entirely different issue as to forum".

The next key reported case was the first one between parties who had entered into their prenuptial agreement in England. It was *N v N (Divorce: Ante-Nuptial Agreement)*,[9] decided by Wall J, as he then was, in July 1999.

The husband and wife were Orthodox Jews who entered into an ante-nuptial agreement. This was made three weeks before they married and contained provisions that would have effect in the event of the breakdown of their marriage. Inter alia it was recorded that neither party would make any financial claims of any kind on the other. Any dispute would be determined by the Court of the Chief Rabbi, the London Beth Din, and both parties would comply with instructions of the Beth Din.

9 [1999] 2 FCR 582

The wife complained to the court that the husband did not comply with the Beth Din's instructions because he took no steps to procure the writing of a Get.

Wall J. indicated, at page 590, that three questions arose:

1. Are ante-nuptial agreements as a class specifically enforceable?
2. If the answer to the first question is no, are particular and severable clauses of an otherwise unenforceable ante-nuptial agreement specifically enforceable?
3. If the answer to 1 and 2 is no in each case, can an ante-nuptial agreement or particular clauses in an ante-nuptial agreement be enforced by other means?

In his judgment, pages 590–595, Wall J. answered each of these questions. This judgment contains a useful analysis of the law as it then stood.

In response to the first question Wall J. said, at the foot of page 592:

> "Leading Counsel for the wife did not cite to me any case in which an ante-nuptial agreement had been specifically enforced. The reason he was unable to do so, in my judgment, is that there is no such case and that, as a class, ante-nuptial agreements are not specifically enforceable in English law".

Speaking to the second question Wall J. referred to the provision in the agreement that the invalidity or unenforceability of any provision of the deed "shall not affect the validity or unenforceability of any other provision and any invalid or unenforceable provision will be severable".

He said

> "even if one divides up the ante-nuptial agreement in this case, and looks at the individual clauses separately, one cannot, in my judgment, avoid the fundamental proposition that each is part of an agreement entered into before marriage to regulate the parties' affairs in the event of divorce. The public policy argument, therefore continues to apply".

Speaking to the third question Wall J. concluded that in the particular circumstances of the case the clauses could not be enforced by other means. He said

> "it follows therefore, despite the fact that I reach the conclusion with considerable reluctance, that the wife's Summons must be dismissed".

*N v N* is clear recognition of the proposition that prenuptial agreements are agreements that, as a class, are not specifically enforceable. It also recognizes the fact that there were no reported cases to that date in which the provisions of such an agreement had been enforced.

However, it is important to note that the issue in *N v N* was not concerned with the attempt of one party seeking to hold the other to the financial terms of a prenuptial agreement from which the other was seeking to renege. It was the wife's attempt to force the husband to apply for a Get, which application he had agreed to make in the prenuptial agreement. Under Jewish law only a husband may make such application and, as the English law then stood, (it has since been changed by the enactment of the Divorce (Religious Marriages) Act 2002 which has inserted Section 10A into the Matrimonial Causes Act 1973) the only route available to the wife was for her to attempt to enforce the husband's agreement in the prenuptial agreement. It was for this reason that Wall J indicated that he reached his conclusion "with considerable reluctance."

In May 2000 Johnson J heard and determined *C v C (Divorce: Stay of English Proceedings)*.[10]

This was another case concerning non-UK nationals. The husband and wife were both French nationals. They had entered into a prenuptial agreement under French law executed on the day of their marriage. They had also executed mutual wills in France reaffirming the prenuptial agreement.

Following the breakdown of the marriage the wife issued divorce proceedings in England and the husband issued divorce proceedings in France. The husband applied for a stay of the wife's English divorce proceedings.

The prenuptial agreement was executed in circumstances of formality before a notary. It was the notary's duty to ensure both parties understood the significance of the document. The wife said she did not truly understand the significance of what she was signing and that the notary failed to perform his duty of ensuring that she did. Johnson J. was not asked to hear oral evidence relating to that issue but he said

> "it seems to me to be doubtful, to say the least, that the wife's account of that is correct".

10 [2001] 1 FLR 694.

Johnson J granted the husband's application for a stay of the wife's English proceedings. He considered that under Section 5(6) of the Domicile and Matrimonial Proceedings Act 1973 the balance of fairness was in the issues between the parties being resolved in the French courts.

One of two particular factors that weighed heavily in his balancing exercise was the

> "positive and joint decision to execute the pre-marital contract in France according to French law in terms which envisaged issues, such as those presently arising being resolved according to the French Civil Code."

In July 2001 Connell J decided *M v M (Pre-nuptial Agreement)*.[11] This is a particularly important case in that it demonstrates a judge giving significant weight to the provisions of a prenuptial agreement in the context of the quantum of an ancillary relief award.

Again this case involved non-UK nationals. The husband and wife were both Canadians who entered into a prenuptial agreement shortly before their marriage in Vancouver.

The judge described the characteristics of the case as unusual. At the hearing the wife was 39. She had previously been married, which marriage was childless. The husband was 55. He had three children from his first marriage.

The wife fell pregnant and claimed this was accidental. The husband claimed it was deliberate. Whilst the wife considered an abortion the husband was adamantly opposed. The wife insisted on marriage because she was not prepared to contemplate bringing up a child as a single mother. The husband, still very bruised as a result of his expensive and hostile litigation relating to his first marriage was not prepared to marry the wife unless she entered into a prenuptial agreement.

The husband's lawyers produced a prenuptial agreement. The wife sought legal advice. The first two lawyers she approached refused to represent her insisting financial disclosure from the husband was essential before they could give proper advice. The wife eventually received advice from an experienced Canadian lawyer who advised that she should not sign the agreement because he thought it was fundamentally unfair. His attempts to negotiate with the husband's lawyer produced cosmetic adjustment

11 [2002] 1FLR 654.

only. The wife insisted on signing the agreement because this was the only way she could ensure the marriage went ahead. She duly did so.

The agreement provided that after a marriage of five years the wife would be entitled to a capital payment of £275,000. The husband contended that the wife should be held to the contractual bargain in the agreement. The wife contended that the agreement was, at most, a material circumstance, an aspect of conduct for the court to bear in mind. It should not determine the wife's application. She claimed a once and for all lump sum payment of £1.3 million.

Connell J considered the prenuptial agreement as one of the circumstances of the case. He said, at page 661:

> "Sometimes such an agreement is considered by the court as part of the conduct of each of the parties which it would be inequitable to disregard under section 25(2)(g) of the Act. In my view it matters not whether the court bears such an agreement in mind as part of the circumstances of the case (a very important factor) or as an aspect of the parties' conduct. Under either approach the court should look at any such agreement and decide in the particular circumstances what weight should, in justice, be attached to it. Given that a significant percentage of marriages these days end in divorce, it is understandable that mature adults, and in particular those who have been married before, might wish to agree what should happen in the event of a breakdown. The desire for certainty, or the wish to know where you stand, is not unusual. It is clear, of course, that the existence of such an agreement does not oust the jurisdiction of the court and leading counsel has not argued in this case that the court has no jurisdiction to entertain this claim. The public policy objection to such agreements, namely that they tend to diminish the importance of the marriage contract, seems to me to be of less importance now that divorce is so commonplace."

The judge went on to refer to *F v F* and *S v S*. He then considered the terms of the agreement and said at paragraph 26:

> "On the one hand this husband would not have married the wife unless she signed the agreement. On the other hand this wife signed the agreement because she was pregnant and did not relish single parenthood either herself or for her child and because she wanted to marry the husband. In my view it would be as unjust to the husband to ignore the existence of the agreement and its terms

> as it would be to the wife to hold her strictly to those terms. I do bear the agreement in mind as one of the more relevant circumstances of this case, but the court's overriding duty remains to attempt to arrive at a solution which is fair in all the circumstances, applying section 25 of the Matrimonial Causes Act 1973."

The judge concluded by awarding the wife a lump sum of £875,000. She had contended for £1.3 million and the husband had contended for the £275,000 as per the prenuptial agreement.

The husband's net worth was about £7.5 million. Clearly in his award the judge, as he indicated, had regard to the prenuptial agreement, but in his view this would not have adequately provided for the wife's needs, to which he was obliged to have regard, and therefore would have been unfair. He awarded the wife more than the provision in the agreement, but less than he would have been likely to have awarded had there been no agreement.

In July 2002 came the case of *K v K (Ancillary Relief: Prenuptial Agreement)*[12] decided by Rodger Hayward Smith QC sitting as a deputy High Court judge. This was (pre *Radmacher*) often described as the high-water point in the reported cases in relation to enforcement of prenuptial agreements.

The parties separated after fourteen months of marriage. They had entered into a prenuptial agreement. They had each received independent advice. Their agreement provided that if the marriage was dissolved within five years the wife would receive £100,000 and the husband would make reasonable provision for any children.

The wife sought for herself a lump sum payment of £1.6 million and periodical payments of £57,000. The husband proposed payment to the wife of £120,000 plus £600,000 in trust to provide a home for the wife with their child until he finished his education with reversion to the husband. He offered no periodical payments to the wife. They had agreed the husband would pay £15,000 per annum for the maintenance of the child.

The judge summarised the circumstances surrounding the marriage and the prenuptial agreement. The pregnancy of the wife was a serious shock to both parties. The wife did not wish to be a single mother. She wanted to

12 [2003] 1 FLR 120.

marry or she would have had the pregnancy terminated. The husband did not approve of abortion and was wholly against termination but he did not feel that he and the wife were ready to marry.

They did eventually agree to marry but the husband called the engagement off. The wife's family intervened and the wife's mother told the husband that he should either agree to marry the wife or she (the wife's mother) would take her to have the pregnancy terminated.

In the course of a discussion between the husband and the wife's father the possibility of a prenuptial agreement was raised. The judge found that at no time did the husband tell the wife that he would not marry her without a prenuptial agreement.

It appears that the wife's father advanced the matter of the prenuptial agreement; he made an appointment with his solicitors and they eventually prepared a draft of the pre-nuptial agreement which they sent to the husband. The prenuptial agreement was eventually settled and signed by both parties. In the ensuing litigation the husband relied on the agreement and the wife did not.

This issue for the judge to consider was whether the agreement was "binding or influential" in respect of the decisions he was required to make. Taking as his reference points the cases of *Edgar*, *F v F*, *S v S*, *M v M* and the unreported case of *Wyatt v Goldsmith*, he compiled a list of pertinent questions to which he then addressed himself.

His analysis on pages 131–132 is set out in full as follows:

> "(1) Did she understand the agreement?
>
> > Yes.
>
> Was she properly advised as to its terms?
>
> > Yes.
>
> Did the husband put her under any pressure to sign it?
>
> > No.
>
> Was there full disclosure?
>
> > No. There was disclosure of assets, but the decision not to press for values came from the wife's side and it was known that the husband was very wealthy; figures of up to £150 million were mentioned by the wife's father.
>
> Was the wife under any other pressure?

> The circumstances in which she found herself put her under pressure and there was pressure from her own family but she was not under pressure to sign the agreement. The husband too was under pressure. He was being pressed by the wife's family to enter into a marriage about which he had serious misgivings. The wife says in one affidavit that she signed the agreement in a hurry the day before the marriage. But the terms of the agreement had been discussed and agreed before then and she had had plenty of time to consider it. Having heard her evidence I do not accept that she felt under any pressure at the time she signed the agreement.

Did she willingly sign the agreement?

> Yes

Did the husband exploit a dominant position, either financially or otherwise?

> No

Was the agreement entered into in the knowledge that there would be a child?

> Yes

Has any unforeseen circumstance arisen since the agreement was made that would make it unjust to hold the parties to it?

> No

What does the agreement mean?

> It is suggested on behalf of the wife that cl 4 is so vague as to render the whole agreement bad. I consider the agreement is clear as to the capital provision to be made for the wife if the marriage broke down within 5 years. Clause 4 means that provision for the child was to be either agreed or adjudicated upon by the court bearing in mind that such provision would have to include the mother as full-time carer for the child.

Does the agreement preclude an order for periodical payments for the wife?

> I think not. If the agreement had meant to bar any claim by the wife for periodical payments, it would surely have said so. It does not. It refers to 'property' which I interpret as capital. But if I am wrong see para [16] below.

Are there any grounds for concluding that an injustice would be done by holding the parties to the terms of the agreement?

> My answer is no; not insofar as capital for the wife is concerned. On the contrary, I think an injustice would be done to the husband if I ignored the agreement

Is the agreement one of the circumstances of the case to be considered under s 25?

> Yes

Does the entry into this agreement constitute conduct which it would be inequitable to disregard under s 25(2)(g)?

> Yes

Am I breaking new ground by holding the wife to the capital terms of the agreement?

> No. Pre-nuptial agreements have been regarded as influential by Wilson J in *S v S (Divorce: Staying Proceedings)* [1997] 1 WLR 1200, [1997] 2 FLR 100 and by Connell J in *M v M (Pre-nuptial Agreement)* [2002] 1 FLR 654.

Insofar as maintenance for the wife is concerned, if I am wrong in my interpretation of the agreement as above, and if the agreement does preclude a maintenance claim, would it be unjust to hold the parties to that aspect of the agreement?

> My answer is yes, it would be unjust to the wife but not to the husband. The wife has a child to bring up. Although this was a short marriage with no contribution by the wife to the acquisition of the husband's wealth, I must have regard under s 25(2)(f) to the contribution that the wife has made and is now making and is likely for the next 18 years or so to be making in caring for their child. That is an enormous contribution. The wife is now 28. When the child has finished full-time education the wife will be approaching 50. Furthermore, any earning capacity she may have is clearly prejudiced by the time she must invest in bringing up their child. I accept that, but for the child, the wife would not have been financially prejudiced by this short marriage, but to suggest that in the circumstances as they are, she should have no maintenance, either because of the shortness of the marriage or because of the pre-nuptial agreement strikes me as wholly unjust to her. On the other hand her maintenance claim in my judgment should be in her capacity as a mother and to enable her to live as mother to a reasonable standard commensurate with the wealth of the husband/father.

> In my judgment, therefore, the wife should receive a lump sum of £120,000 in accordance with the agreement and the husband's offer. She should have no further capital claims upon him for herself, apart from a canteen of cutlery, which I will come to later."

As indicated at the conclusion of the above extract the judge held the wife to the capital provisions of the agreement and awarded the wife a lump sum of £120,000.

This case helpfully sets out the questions that need to be addressed in deciding what relevance should be attached to a prenuptial agreement entered into by the parties to a marriage. The practitioner needs to have the issues these questions raise at the forefront of his mind when advising upon and drafting a prenuptial agreement. The extent to which these questions (and the importance of the various answers) give a blueprint for drafting prenuptial agreements will be discussed in the following chapters.

There are three further reported cases worthy of mention. The first is *J v V (Disclosure: Offshore Corporations)*[13] decided by Coleridge J on 16 December 2003.

The report of this case notably contains no detail of the terms of the parties' prenuptial agreement. Coleridge J dealt with it in somewhat dismissive terms at paragraph 41:

> "I should also, as a preliminary point, deal with the prenuptial agreement. I mention it only to put it to one side in this case. Nowadays, occasionally, their existence can be of some significance but not in this case. This contract was signed on the very eve of the marriage, without full legal advice, without proper disclosure and it made no allowance for the arrival of children. It must, in my judgment, therefore, in this jurisdiction fall at every fence, quite apart from the fact that the terms were obviously unfair, preventing the wife from claiming against the husband's assets."

Whilst recognising that the existence of a prenuptial contract " occasionally ….can be of some significance", it was not so here. The judge addressed four of the cardinal questions set out in *K v K*, namely timing, independent legal advice, full disclosure and the effect of the arrival of children.

13 [2004] 1 FLR 1042.

The second is the decision of *Ella v Ella*[14] in which judgment was given in the Court of Appeal on 17 January 2007.

This was another case involving non-UK elements in that the parties both had dual Israeli and British nationality, had married in Israel and immediately before the marriage had entered into a prenuptial agreement there. This recorded that the provisions of Israeli law should apply on any question affecting their property.

The husband obtained a stay on the wife's application that the English court was the appropriate venue for the determination of the case. The wife appealed against that stay. She contended that the first instance judge had attached too much significance to the prenuptial agreement.

The Court of Appeal concluded that the first instance judge was correct to regard the prenuptial agreement as a major factor in her decision. The prenuptial agreement was a contract that, in the jurisdiction of Israel, was of considerable effect and led to the conclusion that Israel was the more appropriate forum for resolution of the parties' dispute.

The concern of leading counsel for the wife was that, given the significance attached to the existence of the prenuptial agreement, the court was not prepared to make a "profound investigation of vitiating factors or circumstances surrounding its creation which would reduce its validity and effect". It was brought into the equation at face value notwithstanding the wife's arguments as to lack of legal advice, timing and pressure.

The third and final case was *NA v MA*[15] heard in October and November 2006 in which Baron J handed down a long reserved judgment on 24 November 2006. This case concerned a post nuptial agreement, the first one to appear in the reported cases. The husband had discovered the wife had committed adultery with his best friend. He agreed to a reconciliation upon the basis that the wife agreed a post nuptial settlement setting out the financial division that would be effective if the marriage subsequently broke down. It did thereafter breakdown; the wife applied for ancillary relief and the husband contended she should be kept to the agreement.

The court did not hold the wife to the agreement but Baron J set out, albeit *obiter*, her understanding of the "current legal position in relation to contracts between spouses". It is a useful summary of the law as it stood at that time:

---

14 [2007] EWCA Civ 99.

15 [2006] EWHC 2900.

"12) It is an accepted fact that an agreement entered into between Husband and Wife does not oust the jurisdiction of this Court. For many years, agreements between spouses were considered void for public policy reasons but this is no longer the case.[16] In fact over the years, prenuptial "contracts" have become increasingly common place and are, I accept, much more likely to be accepted by these Courts as governing what should occur between the parties when the prospective marriage comes to an end. That is, of course, subject to the discretion of the Court and the application of a test of fairness/manifest unfairness. It may well be that Parliament will provide legislation but, until that occurs, current authority makes it clear that the agreements are not enforceable per se although they can be persuasive (or definitive) depending upon the precise circumstances that lead to their completion.

13) In *Edgar v Edgar [1980] 1 WLR 1410*, as Ormrod LJ, with whose judgment Oliver LJ agreed, said, at 1417C:

'To decide what weight should be given in order to reach a just result, to a prior agreement not to claim a lump sum, regard must be had to the conduct of both parties, leading up to the prior agreement, and to their subsequent conduct, in consequence of it. It is not necessary in this connection to think in formal legal terms, such as misrepresentation or estoppel, all the circumstances as they affect each of two human beings must be considered in the complex relationship of marriage. So, the circumstances surrounding the making of the agreement are relevant. Undue pressure by one side, exploitation of a dominant position to secure an unreasonable advantage, inadequate knowledge, possibly bad legal advice, an important change of circumstances, unforeseen or overlooked at the time of making the agreement, are all relevant to the question of justice between the parties. Important too is the general proposition that, formal agreements, properly and fairly arrived at with competent legal advice, should not be displaced unless there are good and substantial grounds for concluding that an injustice will be done by holding the parties to the terms of their agreement. There may well be other considerations which affect the justice of this case; the above list is not intended to be an exclusive catalogue.'

Oliver LJ similarly enunciated the general principle at 142E-F:

16 The authors questioned the correctness of this proposition at the time but the proposition has now been confirmed by decisions of the Privy Council in *MacLeod* and the Supreme Court in *Radmacher*.

'... in a consideration of what is just to be done in the exercise of the court's powers under the Act of 1973 in the light of the conduct of the parties, the court must, I think, start from the position that a solemn and freely negotiated bargain by which a party defines her own requirements ought to be adhered to unless some clear and compelling reason, such as, for instance, a drastic change of circumstances, is shown to the contrary.'

14 I accept that these are succinct and proper formulations of the test to be applied.

15) Munby J in *X v X (Y & Z Intervening)* [2002] 1 FLR 508 at page 536 summarised the following propositions as relevant [17]

'• In exercising its duty under s 25 the task of the court is to reach a just result, what Lord Nicholls of Birkenhead in *White v White* [2001] 1 AC 596, [2000] 2 FLR 981 at 599H and 983H respectively called the "fair" outcome ...

• The fact that the parties have made their own agreement is a "very important" factor in considering what is the just and fair outcome. The amount of importance will vary from case to case.

• The court will not lightly permit parties who have made an agreement between themselves to depart from it. The court should be slow to invade the contractual territory, for as a matter of general policy what the parties have themselves agreed should, unless on the face of it or in fact contrary to public policy or subject to some vitiating feature of the type referred to by Ormrod LJ, be upheld by the courts.

• A formal agreement, properly and fairly arrived at with competent legal advice, should be upheld by the court unless there are "good and substantial grounds" for concluding that an "injustice" will be done by holding the parties to it (I adopt Ormrod LJ's formulation in preference to that of Thorpe J: his references to "the most exceptional circumstances" and "overwhelmingly strong considerations" seem to me, with respect, to put

17 These are principles derived from a case concerned with a separation agreement rather than a prenuptial agreement.

the matter perhaps a little too high).

- The mere fact that one party might have done better by going to court is not of itself generally a ground for permitting that party to resile from what was agreed.
- The court must none the less have regard to all the circumstances. The circumstances are to be judged in their totality and with a broad perspective rather than individually one by one.
- In particular the court must have regard to the circumstances surrounding the making of the agreement, the extent to which the parties themselves attached importance to it and the extent to which the parties themselves have acted upon it.
- The relevant circumstances are not limited to the purely financial aspects of the agreement: social, personal and, I would add, religious and cultural considerations, all have to be taken into account.
- The court should bear in mind the undesirability of stirring up problems with parties who have come to an agreement.
- On the contrary the court should if possible, and consistent with its duty under s 25, seek to bring about family peace and finality.'"

Finally, before moving to the next chapter it is appropriate to refer to the Court of Appeal decision in *Crossley v Crossley*,[18] which was heard in December 2007. It was an appeal by a wife against case management directions given by Bennett J in October 2007 but the Court of Appeal made a number of *obiter* observations upon the weight to be afforded to prenuptial agreements.

In *Crossley* the parties had entered into a prenuptial agreement, with the benefit of advice from experienced lawyers. The husband and wife respectively declared assets of £44 million and £18 million. They agreed that neither party should apply to the court in any jurisdiction for any order for financial provision of any kind based upon their marriage.

The wife applied to the court for ancillary relief. An important plank of her case was that the husband had not made full disclosure in the

18 [2007] 1 FLR 1467, CA.

prenuptial agreement. The husband required the wife to show cause why her claims should not be resolved in accordance with the prenuptial agreement.

Bennett J directed a hearing at which the parties would explain in their Forms E why the prenuptial agreement was of such great importance or, from the wife's point of view why it was not and that there should be a full investigation and a full hearing.

The Court of Appeal dismissed the wife's appeal. Thorpe LJ indicated at paragraph 17 that:

> "Bennett J's management of this case in the orders which he made, so far from being questionable in my eyes, seem to me an admirable illustration of judicial initiative and good sense."

Thorpe LJ observed that the existence of a prenuptial agreement cannot oust the court's obligation to apply Section 25 and such an agreement is one aspect of a case.[19]

He went on to indicate at paragraph 15 that:

> "All these cases are fact dependent and this is a quite exceptional case on its facts, but if ever there is to be a paradigm case in which the court will look to the prenuptial agreement as not simply one of the peripheral factors in the case but as a factor of magnetic importance, it seems to me that this is just such a case."

Thorpe LJ referred to the principle of contractual dealing at paragraph 17 where he observed that:

> "It does seem to me that the role of contractual dealing, the opportunity for the autonomy of the parties, is becoming increasingly important."

At paragraph 17, in commenting on the approach that Bennett J had taken at first instance, Thorpe LJ referred to the fact that it seemed to accord with

> "a developing view that prenuptial contracts are gaining in importance in a particularly fraught area that confronts so many parties separating and divorcing."

Finally Thorpe LJ commented upon the argument for legislative reform at paragraph 17 where he said:

19 Paragraph 14.

> "There is in my judgment an even stronger argument for legislative consideration, given the resolution of the European Union to formulate some regulation to tackle the difficulties that arise from different approaches in the member states. There is an obvious divide between the provisions of the civil law jurisdictions and the absence of any marital property tradition in the common law systems. Undoubtedly there would be some narrowing between this European divide if greater opportunity were given within our justice system for parties to contract in advance of marriage, to make provision for the possibility of dissolution."

This was the state the law had reached by the end of 2007. There have been two subsequent key decisions, *MacLeod* in December 2008 and *Radmacher* in October 2010, which are considered in detail in the next chapter.

# Chapter 3

# Analysis of *MacLeod* and *Radmacher*

Since the publication of the first edition of this book, in April 2008, there have been two decisions of seminal importance in the field of prenuptial and nuptial agreements.

The first, on 17 December 2008, was *MacLeod v MacLeod.*[1] The second, on 20 October 2010, was *Radmacher (formerly Granatino) v Granatino.*[2]

Summaries of each of these cases are set out in the Case Digest. Given that *MacLeod* was a Privy Council decision and has been substantially overtaken by the Supreme Court decision in *Radmacher*, there is limited usefulness in a detailed analysis of it. *MacLeod* was, however, concerned with the validity and effect of a post nuptial agreement made between husband and wife whilst they were still living together. It was not about the validity and effect of prenuptial agreements as such.

The judgment of the Lords of the Judicial Committee of the Privy Council was delivered by Baroness Hale. It made a distinction between pre and post nuptial agreements. It held that it could not reverse the longstanding rule that prenuptial agreements were contrary to public policy and thus not valid and binding in the contractual sense. Any change to this rule should be made by legislation rather than judicial development.

However post nuptial agreements were in a different category. There was nothing to prevent a married couple entering into such an agreement. It would be governed, in the case of *MacLeod* by Sections 49 to 51 of the Manx Matrimonial Proceedings Act 2003, which is equivalent to Sections 34 to 36 of the Matrimonial Proceedings Act 1973, which would empower the court to vary it.

In setting out why the Court had concluded that it could not reverse the rule that prenuptial agreements were contrary to public policy and not valid and binding in the contractual sense Baroness Hale said, at paragraphs 33–35:

---

1 [2010] 1 AC 298.

2 [2010] UKSC 42.

"33 It is said that calls for the legislative recognition of ante-nuptial agreements appear to have increased with the development of more egalitarian principles of financial and property adjustment on divorce, following the decisions of the House of Lords in *White v White* [2001] 1 AC 596 and *Miller v Miller, McFarlane v McFarlane* [2006] UKHL 24, [2006] 2 AC 618. If such calls are motivated by a perception that equality within marriage is wrong in principle, the more logical solution would be to examine the principles applicable to ascertaining the fair result of a claim for ancillary relief, rather than the pre-marital attempt to predict what the fair result will be long before the event. If such calls are motivated by a fear that people who feel threatened by what might happen in the event of divorce will not get married at all, there is a need for serious research and consideration of the extent of and reasons for the reduction in marriage rates over recent decades. It certainly cannot be demonstrated that the lack of enforceable ante-nuptial agreements in this country is depressing the marriage rate here as compared with other countries where such agreements can be made.

The Board notes that the Law Commission for England and Wales, in their 10th programme of Law Reform, have declined to embark upon a review of the principles governing ancillary relief on divorce. But they have announced their intention to examine the status and enforceability of agreements made between spouses and civil partners (or those contemplating marriage or civil partnership) concerning their property and finances: see 2008, Law Com No 311, paragraph 2.17.

In the Board's view the difficult issue of the validity and effect of ante-nuptial agreements is more appropriate to legislative rather than judicial development. It is worth noting, for example, that in the Florida case of *Posner v Posner*, where such agreements were recognised, attention was drawn to the statutory powers of the courts to vary such agreements. The Board is inclined to share the view expressed by Baron J in *NG v KR* [2008] EWHC 1532 (Fam), at paragraph 130, that the variation power in section 50 of the 2003 Act (section 35 of the 1973 Act) does not apply to agreements made between people who are not yet parties to a marriage. Yet it would clearly be unfair to render such agreements enforceable if, unlike post-nuptial agreements, they could not be varied."

In relation to post nuptial agreements the judgment accepted that this was a case in which the agreement was valid and enforceable subject to the power of the court to vary the agreed arrangements. It set out the test for variation at paragraph 41 as follows:

"41. The question remains of the weight to be given to such an agreement if an application is made to the court for ancillary relief. In *Edgar v Edgar*, the solution might have been more obvious if mention had been made of the statutory provisions relating to the validity and variation of maintenance agreements. One would expect these to be the starting point. Parliament had laid down the circumstances in which a valid and binding agreement relating to arrangements for the couple's property and finances, not only while the marriage still existed but also after it had been dissolved or annulled, could be varied by the court. At the same time, Parliament had preserved the parties' rights to go to court for an order containing financial arrangements. It would be odd if Parliament had intended the approach to such agreements in an ancillary relief claim to be different from, and less generous than, the approach to a variation application. The same principles should be the starting point in both. In other words, the court is looking for a change in the circumstances in the light of which the financial arrangements were made, the sort of change which would make those arrangements manifestly unjust, or for a failure to make proper provision for any child of the family. On top of that, of course, even if there is no change in the circumstances, it is contrary to public policy to cast onto the public purse an obligation which ought properly to be shouldered within the family."

*Radmacher v Granatino* was heard at first instance by Baron J who handed her judgment down on 28 July 2008. The facts of this case are rehearsed at first instance, in the Court of Appeal and in the Supreme Court. They are of course germane to the issues determined and so it is appropriate that they be repeated here.

Nicolas Granatino, the husband, was French, born in Antibes on 22 July 1971. He had Italian ancestry and his father was an extremely successful businessman. Karin Radmacher, the wife, was German, born on 25 April

1969. She came from a very rich family whose wealth was derived from two successful commercial ventures.

The parties met in November 1997 in London where they were both living. At that time the husband was working for JP Morgan as an investment banker. The wife had been operating a boutique in Beauchamp Place, which was to prove unsuccessful.

They became engaged in June 1998 and began to live together. Upon their engagement they agreed to enter into a prenuptial agreement. This was prepared for them by Dr Magis, a German notary based in or near Düsseldorf upon whom, in relation to this matter, the wife's mother had first attended. Dr Magis had previously undertaken work for the wife's family.

The broad effect of the prenuptial agreement, which the parties executed on 1 August 1998, was that the marriage would confer upon neither party any interest in property brought into it by the other. Resources that accrued to each party during the marriage would remain owned by that party alone. In the event of divorce neither party would have any claim against the property or income of the other. The waiver of claims in respect of maintenance was expressed to apply:

> "to the fullest extent permitted by law even should one of us – whether or not for reasons attributable to fault on that person's part – be in serious difficulties."

The parties married on 28 November 1998 in London where they continued to live until April 2000 when the husband was posted to New York. After a period there, the family returned, in October 2001, to London.

The parties had two daughters, Chiara born on 4 September 1999, and Chloe, born on 25 May 2002. The marriage became increasingly unhappy and the parties finally separated in October 2006 when the wife moved into separate accommodation with the two girls.

Following upon the issue of divorce proceedings in 2007, in which cross decrees were duly pronounced in July, the husband, notwithstanding the terms of the prenuptial agreement, applied for ancillary relief. The matter was heard by Baron J between 23 June and 2 July 2008 and judgment was delivered on 28 July 2008.

The basis upon which the husband put his case was that he should be awarded a sum based upon his needs. He did not seek a percentage of the wife's wealth, which he put at £100 million, but argued that the prenuptial agreement should be disregarded entirely because he did not receive independent advice before signing, the wife did not give any disclosure of her wealth, it made no provision in the event of the birth of children and it was manifestly unfair because it made no provision at all for either party in the event of divorce. He asked the court to award him a capital sum of £9.009 million.

The wife's primary position was that the husband should have a property in England for £1 million for his life to enable him to provide a home for the children, a property in Düsseldorf of up to Euros 500,000 which he could occupy until the girls reached majority, and periodical payments for the benefit of the girls of £18,000 per annum per child until completion of secondary education.

In all other respects the husband "should stand on his own two feet". His claim should be so limited because he willingly signed the prenuptial agreement in August 1998.

Baron J concluded, at paragraph 137 that:

> "As I find the PNC is defective under English Law for the following reasons:
>
> a) The Husband received no independent legal advice.
>
> b) It deprives the Husband of all claims to the *'furthest permissible legal extent' even* in a situation of want and that is manifestly unfair.
>
> c) There was no disclosure by the Wife.
>
> d) There were no negotiations.
>
> e) Two children have been born during the marriage.

Baron J continued, at paragraph 139, that the award to the husband should be:

> "circumscribed to a degree to reflect the fact that at the outset he agreed to sign the prenuptial agreement. Of course, from an English perspective the agreement was flawed and I take full account of the fact that the Husband's agreement was tainted because he did not know what his future wife was worth and did not have independent legal advice about the ramifications of the deal. Nevertheless, he understood the underlying premise that he was not entitled to anything if the parties divorced. In essence, he accepted that he was expected to be self-sufficient. As a man of the

> world that was abundantly clear. His decision to enter into the agreement must therefore affect the award."
>
> Her award, at paragraph 141, was as follows:
>
> "In total therefore the Husband's needs are

| | | |
|---|---|---|
| (a) | Housing | £2,500,000 |
| (b) | Debts | £ 700,000 |
| (c) | Additional Capital | £ 25,000 |
| (d) | Duxbury Fund | £2,335,000 |
| | | **£5,560,000** |

> In addition the Wife will provide €630,000 (£504,000) for housing in Germany and she will pay periodical payments totalling £70,000 per annum for the girls as outlined above.

It is not clear from the judgment to what extent the learned judge did circumscribe the award to the husband to reflect the fact that he had agreed to the prenuptial agreement at the outset.

The only specific reference is in paragraph 140 d) (b) where the judge indicated that it could be argued that £125,000 net spendable per annum is not unreasonable which she then discounted "to produce a result which takes into account the PNC" to a "needs" figure of £100,000 per annum.

In October 2008 the wife was given permission to appeal to the Court of Appeal. Her appeal was heard in April 2009 and judgments were delivered on 2 July 2009.

By the time of the hearing in the Court of Appeal the Privy Council judgment in *MacLeod* had been delivered. There is a deal of interesting material in the judgments, in particular those of Thorpe and Wilson LJJ, as to where and why the Court of Appeal differed from the views in the Privy Council about prenuptial contracts and what were the drivers for a change in the law and how that could or should be brought about.

What was clear in the decision was the unanimous view that the prenuptial agreement should have been given decisive weight albeit that there is a tension between the fact that a prenuptial agreement is invalid and the proposition that it should potentially be given decisive weight. Rix LJ put this position, at paragraph 64 in the following terms:

> "It follows that pre-nuptial agreements are at one and the same time *both* unenforceable and invalid as being against public policy

> *and* matters which the court is prepared to take into account (and possibly decisively) for the purposes of its section 25 jurisdiction. That is a situation which has been criticised as 'the worst of both worlds' (see Hoffmann LJ in *Pounds v Pounds* [1994] 1 WLR 1535 at 1550/1, cited by Baroness Hale in *MacLeod* at [29]) and has on the contrary been described by Mr Todd QC in this case as reflecting the 'genius' of section 25. Be that as it may, it strikes me as anomalous, albeit plainly the present state of the law. On the one hand the pre-nuptial agreement is invalid as being contrary to public policy, and on the other hand it may be and is taken into account by the court. No doubt the court is *obliged* under section 25 to have regard to all the circumstances of the case (see the language of section 25 cited at paragraph [120] in the judgment of Wilson LJ below). Nevertheless, there is a problem in having regard to an agreement which is contrary to public policy. Mr Mostyn QC made submissions to this effect, but, in the present state of the law, forlornly."

In failing to give the prenuptial agreement the decisive weight she should have done, Baron J had erred in her judgment. Wilson LJ considered Baron J's concerns as to the prenuptial agreement and dismissed them all. Having done so the Court of Appeal substituted its own award the effect of which was to provide for the husband as follows:

(a) £2.5 million for accommodation as a base for the husband and children, on trust to revert to the wife once his home making duties have ceased to subsist, thereafter to revert to the wife.
(b) £700,000 in respect of the husband's debts.
(c) £25,000 additional capital for a car.
(d) A Duxbury fund.[3]
(e) A sum to be determined by Baron J to enable the husband to purchase property convenient to him and the children having regard to the fact that the wife and children have now moved to Monaco.
(f) Periodical payments for the girls of £70,000 per annum.

The husband appealed to the Supreme Court. His appeal was heard on 22 and 23 March 2010 by a nine-judge court which included Baroness Hale and Lord Walker who had heard the *MacLeod* appeal in the Privy Council.

3 Baron J had awarded a capitalised figure in respect of the husband's maintenance entitlement of £2,335,000. At paragraph 156 of his judgment Wilson LJ proposed that the court would fix a sum in substitution and gave directions to enable this to be settled. The report does not identify the figure.

Judgment was delivered on 20 October 2010. There are three opinions, one from seven of the justices, one from Lord Mance, which concurs with the majority conclusion but addresses three specific areas, and one from Lady Hale which is a dissenting opinion.

The majority opinion sets out a statement of the law and its development over time. It is appropriate to make the opening observation that the Supreme Court is not considering the strict enforceability or otherwise of what it describes generically as "nuptial agreements". It restates that the court is not bound by such agreements but has to give them weight. The issue for the court is the extent to which the circumstances detract from or enhance the weight to be given or justify departure from any agreement. This is set out, at paragraph 2 thus:

> "A court when considering the grant of ancillary relief is not obliged to give effect to nuptial agreements – whether they are ante-nuptial or post-nuptial. The parties cannot, by agreement, oust the jurisdiction of the court. The court must, however, give appropriate weight to such an agreement. This appeal raises the question of the principles to be applied by the court when considering the weight that should be attached to an ante-nuptial agreement."

It then goes on to consider the implications of the Privy Council decision in MacLeod. The opinion is critical of the distinction made in MacLeod between prenuptial (ante) and post nuptial agreements. It does not agree with that distinction (paragraph 51) and sets out its reasons for so doing.

MacLeod advanced a specific and general reason for the distinction it drew between prenuptial and postnuptial agreements.

The specific reason advance by the Board was that Sections 34 and 35 of the Matrimonial Causes Act 1973 applied to all post nuptial agreements (rather than just to separation agreements) but not to prenuptial agreements and that it would be unfair to render the latter enforceable if they could not be varied. The majority in the Supreme Court considered, however, that the original provisions in the Maintenance Agreements Act 1957 had only applied to separation agreements since, inter alia, post nuptial agreements which provided for the contingency of future separation were considered to be void. In their view, the position remained the same when Parliament incorporated the provisions of the 1957 Act into the 1973 Act. More fundamentally, they did not accept that the protection of Section 35 (permitting an application for variation) must be a precondition for holding that a nuptial agreement takes effect as a contract.

The Board's general reason was that there is a material distinction between a prenuptial and post nuptial agreement. The Supreme Court was not so persuaded. It considered there were circumstances in which it is right to distinguish between prenuptial and post nuptial agreements but that it is not right to proceed on the premise that there will always be a significant difference.

The Justices' conclusion was set out at paragraph 63 thus:

> "In summary, we consider that the Board in MacLeod was wrong to hold that post-nuptial agreements were contracts but that ante-nuptial agreements were not. That question did not arise for decision in that case any more than in this and does not matter anyway. It is a red herring. Regardless of whether one or both are contracts, the ancillary relief court should apply the same principles when considering ante-nuptial agreements as it applies to post-nuptial agreements."

The opinion then turns to examine the approach MacLeod held should be applied to post nuptial agreements. It held at paragraph 66:

> "MacLeod has done a valuable service in sweeping away the archaic notions of public policy which have tended to obfuscate the approach to nuptial agreements. But for the reasons that we have given we have not found that it assists in approaching the problem at the heart of this appeal for we have been able to accept neither its thesis that ante-nuptial agreements are fundamentally different from post-nuptial agreements nor, without reservation, its approach to post-nuptial settlements."

At paragraph 67 of the majority opinion, the issues raised on the facts by the appeal are identified thus:

(a) Were there circumstances attending the making of the agreement that detract from the weight that should be accorded to it?

(b) Were there circumstances attending the making of the agreement that enhance the weight that should be accorded to it; the foreign element?

(c) Did the circumstances prevailing when the court's order was made make it fair or just to depart from the agreement?

These matters fall to be considered because they should be to the forefront of the mind of a draftsman of a prenuptial agreement.

## Factors detracting from the weight to be accorded to the agreement

At paragraphs 68 to 73 of the majority judgment, under the above heading, there are set out various factors. These factors are founded upon the proposition that it will no longer be the case that parties who have entered into a prenuptial agreement may have been advised that it will be void. It will in future be natural to infer that parties who enter into a prenuptial agreement intend that effect should be given to it.

Accordingly the factors that detract from the weight to be given to such an agreement include:

1. Whether there was a material lack of disclosure (paragraph 69)
2. Standard vitiating factors: duress, fraud or misrepresentation (paragraph 71)
3. Unconscionable conduct such as undue pressure (falling short of duress) (paragraph 71)
4. Unworthy conduct such as exploitation of a dominant position to secure an unfair advantage (paragraph 71.)
5. Unfair terms of any agreement (paragraph 73)

## Factors enhancing the weight to be accorded to the agreement; the foreign element

At paragraph 74 the majority said:

> "When dealing with agreements concluded in the past, and the agreement in this case was concluded in 1998, foreign elements such as those in this case may bear on the important question of whether or not the parties intended their agreement to be effective. In the case of agreements made in recent times and, a fortiori, any agreement made after this judgment, the question of whether the parties intended their agreement to take effect is unlikely to be in issue, so foreign law will not need to be considered in relation to that question."

Before the majority judgment moved to address the specific facts of the appeal they recorded their observations on the questions of fairness, children, autonomy, non-matrimonial property and future circumstances at paragraphs 77 to 83.

At paragraph 75 in bold type the judgment advanced the proposition to be applied in the case of both prenuptial and post nuptial agreements, in preference to that suggested in MacLeod, namely:

> "The court should give effect to a nuptial agreement that is freely entered into by each party with a full appreciation of its implications unless in the circumstances prevailing it would not be fair to hold the parties to their agreement."

The Supreme Court recognised that this test left outstanding the difficult question of the circumstances in which it would not be fair to hold the parties to their agreement. It said this would depend upon the facts of the particular case and that it would not be desirable to lay down rules that would fetter the flexibility that the court requires to reach a fair result. However, it did go on to give some guidance directed to the situation where there were no tainting circumstances attending the conclusion of the agreement.

This guidance was under the headings referred to above as follows:

### *Children*

A prenuptial agreement cannot be allowed to prejudice the reasonable requirements of any children of the family.

### *Autonomy*

There should be respect for individual autonomy in that the court should accord this to the decision of a married couple as to the manner in which their financial affairs should be regulated. It would be paternalistic and patronising to override their agreement on the basis that the court knows best.

### *Non-matrimonial property*

There is nothing inherently unfair in an agreement that makes express provision for the disposal of existing property owned by one or other or that one or other anticipates receiving from a third party.

### *Future circumstances*

The Court considered how the changed circumstances of a couple over the length of a marriage might make it unfair to hold them to any agreement. It quoted from the judgment of Rix LJ at paragraph 73 thus:

"I have in mind (and in this respect there is no real difference between an agreement made just before or just after a marriage) that a pre-nuptial agreement is intended to look forward over the whole period of a marriage to the possibility of its ultimate failure and divorce: and thus it is potentially a longer lasting agreement than almost any other (apart from a lease, and those are becoming shorter and subject to optional break clauses). Over the potential many decades of a marriage it is impossible to cater for the myriad different circumstances which may await its parties. Thorpe LJ has mentioned the very relevant case of a second marriage between mature adults perhaps each with children of their own by their first marriages. However, equally or more typical will be the marriage of young persons, perhaps not yet adults, for whom the future is an entirely open book. If in such a case a pre-nuptial agreement should provide for no recovery by each spouse from the other in the event of divorce, and the marriage should see the formation of a fortune which each spouse had played an equal role in their different ways in creating, but the fortune was in the hands for the most part of one spouse rather than the other, would it be right to give the same weight to their early agreement as in another perhaps very different example?"

To this question the Justices said the likely answer was "No". However, where these considerations do not apply and each party is in a position to meet his or her needs, fairness may not require a departure from their agreement.

This chapter would not be complete without a short consideration of Lady Hale's dissenting judgment. She was the only family judge and woman in the court. Whilst she called for reform of nuptial agreements by parliament she considered that the proposition to be applied by the majority, as set out in paragraph 75, constituted an impermissible gloss. She said:

"166. It would be 'an inadmissible judicial gloss' to introduce a presumption or a starting point or anything which suggested that there was a burden of proof upon either party. In any event, the concept of an onus or burden of proof is inapplicable in a discretionary exercise such as this. He or she who asserts a fact must, of course, prove it. But it is for the court to carry out the exercise of discretion in the way in which Parliament requires it to do.

167. In my opinion, the test adopted by the majority (in para 75) comes close to introducing such a presumption."

She set out her own suggested test at paragraph 169:

> "The test to be applied to such an agreement, it seems to me, should be this 'Did each party freely enter into an agreement, intending it to have legal effect and with a full appreciation of its implication?' If so, in the circumstances as they now are, would it be fair to hold them to their agreement?"

Lady Hale was also concerned by what she referred to as "the gender dimension". Having commented at paragraph 137 on available precedents, in particular that set out in the first edition of this book, she observed that a court can all too easily lose sight of the fact that the "object of a prenuptial agreement is to deny the economically weaker spouse the provision to which she – it is usually although by no means invariably she – would otherwise be entitled.

She went on to say at the end of paragraph 137:

> "Would any self-respecting young woman sign up to an agreement which assumed that she would be the only one who might otherwise have a claim, thus placing no limit on the claims that might be made against her, and then limited her claim to a pre-determined sum for each year of marriage regardless of the circumstances, as if her wifely services were being bought by the year? Yet that is what these precedents do. In short, there is a gender dimension to the issue which some may think ill-suited to decision by a court consisting of eight men and one woman."

# Chapter 4

# The courts' interpretation of fairness

Whilst it remains the position that no prenuptial agreement can oust the court's jurisdiction to make orders upon an application for ancillary relief, the draftsman's task is to do his best to ensure that the terms of an agreement are such as will stand the best possible chance of being upheld by the court in the event that one party chooses to renege on the agreed terms.

As can be appreciated from the detailed analysis in Chapters 2 and 3 of the decided cases concerning prenuptial agreements and most particularly now *Radmacher*, the court "should give effect to a nuptial agreement that is freely entered into by each party with a full appreciation of its implications unless in the circumstances prevailing it would not be fair to hold the parties to their agreement".

Herein lies the inherent difficulty for the practitioner in providing advice to prospective marriage partners. The different circumstances of partners to a proposed marriage may be myriad. They may be young persons, perhaps not yet adults, for whom the future is an entirely open book. They may be mature parties who have previously been married and/or have children whose future financial interests they wish to protect. They may have existing property or property one or other anticipates receiving from a third party which one or other wishes to protect.

Their motivation for entering into a prenuptial agreement may well be precisely to avoid submitting to the court's determination of 'fairness'. As Rix LJ said in *Radmacher* in the Court of Appeal at paragraph 73:

> "if the parties to a prospective marriage have something important to agree with one another, then it is often much better, and more honest, for that agreement to be made at the outset, before the marriage, rather than left to become a source of disappointment or acrimony within marriage."

This is not to say that the terms of their proposed agreement do not accord with their own sense of fairness and it is this which must be emphasised in the preamble to any agreement.

The objective of this chapter is to examine how the court *currently* perceives 'fairness' in the context of ancillary relief awards. In doing this, one needs to look carefully both at the substance of the statutory provisions and at the most recent judicial guidance as to their interpretation.

The Matrimonial Causes Act 1973 consolidated and re-enacted the provisions of the Divorce Law Reform Act 1969 and the Matrimonial Property and Proceedings Act 1970. The 1973 Act gave the courts new and wider powers to divide the assets of divorcing spouses upon or at any time after the pronouncement of decree nisi.

Although Section 25 of the Act which contains the legislative direction as to how the court should exercise its powers and to what matters it should have regard in doing so, will be familiar, "despite the endless judicial gloss which is applied to it year in and year out at every level it is always best to start and end in that familiar section":[1]

> **25** Matters to which court is to have regard in deciding how to exercise its powers under ss 23, 24 and 24A
>
> (1) It shall be the duty of the court in deciding whether to exercise its powers under section 23, 24, 24A or 24B above and, if so, in what manner, to have regard to all the circumstances of the case, first consideration being given to the welfare while a minor of any child of the family who has not attained the age of eighteen.
>
> (2) As regards the exercise of the powers of the court under section 23(1)(*a*), (*b*) or (*c*), 24, 24A or 24B above in relation to a party to the marriage, the court shall in particular have regard to the following matters –
>
> (*a*) the income, earning capacity, property and other financial resources which each of the parties to the marriage has or is likely to have in the foreseeable future, including in the case of earning capacity any increase in that capacity which it would in the opinion of the court be reasonable to expect a party to the marriage to take steps to acquire;
>
> (*b*) the financial needs, obligations and responsibilities which each of the parties to the marriage has or is likely to have in the foreseeable future;

1 Per Coleridge J in *Charman v Charman* [2006] 1 FLR 593 at paragraph 58.

(*c*) the standard of living enjoyed by the family before the breakdown of the marriage;

(*d*) the age of each party to the marriage and the duration of the marriage;

(*e*) any physical or mental disability of either of the parties to the marriage;

(*f*) the contributions which each of the parties has made or is likely in the foreseeable future to make to the welfare of the family, including any contribution by looking after the home or caring for the family;

(*g*) the conduct of each of the parties, if that conduct is such that it would in the opinion of the court be inequitable to disregard it;

(*h*) in the case of proceedings for divorce or nullity of marriage, the value to each of the parties to the marriage of any benefit which, by reason of the dissolution or annulment of the marriage, that party will lose the chance of acquiring.

(3) As regards the exercise of the powers of the court under section 23(1)(*d*), (*e*) or (*f*), (2) or (4), 24 or 24A above in relation to a child of the family, the court shall in particular have regard to the following matters –

(*a*) the financial needs of the child;

(*b*) the income, earning capacity (if any), property and other financial resources of the child;

(*c*) any physical or mental disability of the child;

(*d*) the manner in which he was being and in which the parties to the marriage expected him to be educated or trained;

(*e*) the considerations mentioned in relation to the parties to the marriage in paragraphs (*a*), (*b*), (*c*) and (*e*) of subsection (2) above.

(4) As regards the exercise of the powers of the court under section 23(1)(*d*), (*e*) or (*f*), (2) or (4), 24 or 24A above against a party to a marriage in favour of a child of the family who is not the child of that party, the court shall also have regard –

(*a*) to whether that party assumed any responsibility for the child's maintenance, and, if so, to the extent to which, and the basis upon which, that party assumed such responsibility and to the length of time for which that party discharged such responsibility;

(*b*) to whether in assuming and discharging such responsibility that party did so knowing that the child was not his or her own;

(*c*) to the liability of any other person to maintain the child.

Prior to the enactment of the Matrimonial and Family Proceedings Act 1984 the court was required to exercise its powers to place the parties, so far as it was practicable, and, having regard to their conduct, just so to do, in the financial position in which they would have been if the marriage had not broken down and each had properly discharged his or her financial obligations and responsibilities towards the other.

This 'tailpiece', as it is commonly known,[2] was deleted by the 1984 Act and nothing was provided in its place. Whereas it might not have always been possible or desirable even, to have adhered to the directive, its existence at least provided the courts (and litigants) with some guidance as to the focus of the discretionary exercise laid out in the provisions of Section 25.

Between 1984 and 2000 the courts' approach to distribution of assets concentrated on meeting the parties' reasonable needs. In reality this meant giving the financially weaker spouse an award which met his or her 'reasonable needs' whilst the other spouse retained the surplus.

The last case of significance in which the 'reasonable requirements' approach was followed was *Dart v Dart*.[3]

Dart was a 'big money' case. The wife appealed against her award of some £9 million seeking £123 million. Her Counsel argued for half of the assets and that Section 25 implied a starting point of one half of the total assets. The Court of Appeal rejected this argument. It held that such a starting point was not even contemplated by the statute; the court was not bound by percentages but must have regard to all the relevant criteria in Section 25(2) of the 1973 Act. The award met the wife's reasonable requirements.

---

2 See for example Lord Nicholls in *White* [2000] 2 FLR 981 at 988.

3 [1996] 2 FLR 286.

Interestingly, when the House of Lords received a similar, if not identical submission four years later in *White*,[4] Lord Nicholls said:

> "It is largely for this reason [it would be an impermissible judicial gloss on the statutory provision] that I do not accept Mr Turner's [Leading Counsel for the wife] invitation to enunciate a principle that in every case the 'starting point' in relation to a division of the assets of the husband and wife should be equality."

In the light of the House of Lords' subsequent decision in *White* it is illuminating to revisit the judgment of Thorpe LJ in *Dart*, responding to what he characterised as the leading counsel for the wife's "hopeless" submission[5] that

> "challenges the entire corpus of subsequent decisions in this court on the application of the s 25 criteria to what are known as big money cases."

At the close of his judgment, on page 302 Thorpe LJ said:

> "I do wish to add one general observation on Mr Munby's [Leading Counsel for the wife] bold attack on the case-law. As he conceded, this court is not free to accept a submission which could only realistically be addressed to the House of Lords. But as I have demonstrated, the law in the field of big money cases has been settled for over a decade. That certainty has enabled practitioners to negotiate settlements in a large number of cases. Those that have the misfortune to reach the Court of Appeal are happily only a tiny minority. But manifestly even the greater number that are concluded without substantial litigation are insignificant in number and importance to those who legislate and those who form social policy. The statutory basis upon which the financial affairs of divorcing couples are decided has now been in place for a quarter of a century. It has been well tried, its operation is well understood by practitioners and it has in my estimation served society well. If a fundamental change is to be introduced it is for the legislature and not the judges to introduce it. Not only is the legislative process the democratic process but it enables the route of future change to be surveyed in advance of adoption by extensive research and consultation."

---

4 [2001] 1 AC 596at 606.

5 at page 295.

That "fundamental change" was in fact introduced by the judges in *White v White*,[6] when for the first time since its enactment the House of Lords considered substantively the issue of how the courts should exercise their discretion under Section 25.

The appellant wife was effectively seeking a one half share of the assets. The House delivered their opinions on 26 October 2000. Its decision marked a sea change in the way in which courts exercised their powers under the 1973 Act. Lord Nicholls said:[7]

> "It goes without saying that these principles [which trial judges should apply when hearing applications for financial relief] should be identified and spelled out as clearly as possible. This is important, so as to promote consistency in court decisions and in order to assist parties and their advisers and mediators in resolving disputes by agreement as quickly and inexpensively as possible."

He went on to review what he saw as the aim of the court under Section 25, as it had been amended by the Matrimonial and Family Proceedings Act 1984, thus:

> "In consequence, the legislation does not state explicitly what is to be the aim of the courts when exercising these wide powers. Implicitly, the objective must be to achieve a fair outcome. The purpose of these powers is to enable the court to make fair financial arrangements on or after divorce in the absence of agreement between the former spouses: see Thorpe LJ in *Dart v Dart* [1996] 2 FLR 286, 294. The powers must always be exercised with this objective in view, giving first consideration to the welfare of the children."

In examining how the court might be satisfied of a "fair outcome", Lord Nicholls introduced us to the concept of the "yardstick of equality". In a seminal passage of his speech at page 605 he said:

> "Sometimes, having carried out the statutory exercise, the judge's conclusion involves a more or less equal division of the available assets. More often, this is not so. More often, having looked at all the circumstances, the judge's decision means that one party will receive a bigger share than the other. Before reaching a firm

6 [2001] 1 AC 596.
7 [2001] AC 596 at 600.

> conclusion and making an order along these lines, a judge would always be well advised to check his tentative views against the yardstick of equality of division. As a general guide, equality should be departed from only if, and to the extent that, there is good reason for doing so. The need to consider and articulate reasons for departing from equality would help the parties and the court to focus on the need to ensure the absence of discrimination. This is not to introduce a presumption of equal division under another guise. Generally accepted standards of fairness in a field such as this change and develop, sometimes quite radically, over comparatively short periods of time"

With the decision in *White* appeared to die the idea that ancillary relief was concerned with the exercise of a kind of largesse towards the financially weaker spouse. No longer is an applicant's claim circumscribed according to his "reasonable requirements". The rationale behind this shift is summarised by Lord Nicholls thus:

> "But I can see nothing, either in the statutory provisions or in the underlying objective of securing fair financial arrangements, to lead me to suppose that the available assets of the respondent become immaterial once the claimant wife's financial needs are satisfied. Why ever should they? If a husband and wife by their joint efforts over many years, his directly in his business and hers indirectly at home, have built up a valuable business from scratch, why should the claimant wife be confined to the court's assessment of her reasonable requirements, and the husband left with a much larger share? Or, to put the question differently, in such a case, where the assets exceed the financial needs of both parties, why should the surplus belong solely to the husband? On the facts of a particular case there may be a good reason why the wife should be confined to her needs and the husband left with the much larger balance. But the mere absence of financial need cannot, by itself, be a sufficient reason. If it were, discrimination would be creeping in by the back door. In these cases, it should be remembered, the claimant is usually the wife. Hence the importance of the check against the yardstick of equal division."[8]

The significance of *White* is possibly that in their opinions their Lordships sought to redirect the court's attention to a broad consideration of the

8 *White* [2001] AC 596 per Lord Nicholls at 608.

Section 25 criteria[9] and away from reliance on one factor (financial needs or "reasonable requirements") or principle (equal division) as being determinative. The "yardstick of equal division" was very clearly distinguished from a starting point or presumption of equal division which would, in their Lordships' view, have still been "an impermissible judicial gloss on the statutory provision".[10]

Lord Nicholls identified in *White* that generally accepted concepts of fairness had and were continuing to change and develop. Current understanding of how the courts should achieve a fair division of assets on divorce comes from the House of Lords decision in the cases of *Miller v Miller; McFarlane v McFarlane.*[11] Lord Nicholls begins his speech by contemplating once more the elusive (one might say illusory) nature of the concept of fairness. His explanation is illuminating and indicates an appreciation that the sands are still shifting:

> "Fairness is an elusive concept. It is an instinctive response to a given set of facts. Ultimately it is grounded in social and moral values. These values, or attitudes, can be stated. But they cannot be justified, or refuted, by any objective process of logical reasoning. Moreover, they change from one generation to the next. It is not surprising, therefore, that in the present context there can be different views on the requirements of fairness in any particular case."

This passage seems to point to an implicit acceptance that there can be more than one perception of what constitutes fairness in any given situation. In their speeches Lord Nicholls and Baroness Hale, in particular, each strive to give guidance as to the best way to attain fairness within ancillary relief. In doing so they both acknowledge the influence of what they discern to be the most prevailing perceptions about fairness in this arena.[12]

There is neither scope nor need within the confines and context of this chapter to conduct the level of detailed analysis that this decision arguably requires. For present purposes three aspects need to be highlighted.

The first is that this decision is a reminder of the pointers in the Act itself which must never be overlooked. They are, first, that the court's primary

---

9 Ibid at 605 – "Self evidently, fairness requires the court to take into account all the circumstances".

10 at 606.

11 [2006] 2 AC 618.

12 See in particular Lord Nicholls at paragraph 16 and Baroness Hale at paragraphs 123, 141 and 147–148.

consideration must be given to the welfare of any minor children of the family (Section 25(1)); secondly that the court must consider the feasibility of a clean break (Section 25A(1)); and thirdly the reminder that the court will look not just at the parties' current assets but also at the position that they will be in in the foreseeable future.

No-one contemplating entering into a prenuptial agreement should overlook these three factors.

Their Lordships opinions' delineate three "elements" or "strands" of fairness which it seems must be borne in mind when looking at the division of assets in ancillary relief proceedings. These now familiar strands are needs, sharing and compensation.

Needs are to be generously interpreted and do not necessarily have to have been generated by the fact of the marriage. The courts will look backwards as well as forwards. Baroness Hale states at paragraph 138:

> "The most common source of need is the presence of children, whose welfare is always the first consideration, or of other dependent relatives, such as elderly parents. But another source of need is having had to look after children or other family members in the past. Many parents have seriously compromised their ability to attain self-sufficiency as a result of past family responsibilities. Even if they do their best to re-enter the employment market, it will often be at a lesser level than before, and they will hardly ever be able to make up what they have lost in pension entitlements. A further source of need may be the way in which the parties chose to run their life together. Even dual career families are difficult to manage with completely equal opportunity for both. Compromises often have to be made by one so that the other can get ahead. All couples throughout their lives together have to make choices about who will do what, sometimes forced upon them by circumstances such as redundancy or low pay, sometimes freely made in the interest of them both. The needs generated by such choices are a perfectly sound rationale for adjusting the parties' respective resources in compensation."

The principle of equal sharing stems, per Lord Nicholls at paragraph 16, from the "basic concept of equality permeating a marriage as understood today". This may well, in financial terms, not be a concept that is readily embraced by all prospective marriage partners but it is hard to escape the fact the courts have now accepted the idea that marriage is a partnership of equals and that at the end of that marriage, spouses are "entitled" to an equal share of the fruits of that partnership unless there is a good reason to the contrary. Lord Nicholls emphasised that the yardstick of equality should be employed as an aid rather than a rule and of course, as already observed, he specifically declined to accept leading counsel's invitation to "enunciate a principle that in every case the 'starting point' in relation to the division of the assets of the husband and wife should be equality".[13]

That there remains scope for departure from equality is borne out particularly in cases which deal with 'special' or 'stellar' contributions. Although their lordships in *White* determined that it would be improper to discriminate between financial and non-financial contributions, arguments continue to be run that some contributions are so extraordinary that they must be given recognition in the overall distribution of the assets. In *Miller*, Lord Nicholls stated firmly (at paragraph 67) that:

> "Parties should not seek to promote a case of 'special contribution' unless the contribution is so marked that to disregard it would be inequitable"

Arguments surrounding contributions were kept alive by the Court of Appeal's decision in *Charman v Charman*.[14] In spite of the fact that all the parties' assets had been built up during the course of a long marriage, in which Mrs Charman had made a full domestic contribution, she nevertheless conceded that Mr Charman's contribution, specifically to the enormous fortune the parties had accumulated, justified a departure from equality.

Further scope for departure from the principle of equal sharing lies in the nature and source of the parties' assets. Property may have been acquired during the marriage either by way of gift or inheritance. Similarly a reason for a departure from equality may lie in the fact that assets had been brought into the marriage by one party or the other.

Lord Nicholls explains the 'difference of source' as being between

> "(1) property acquired during the marriage otherwise than by inheritance or gift, sometimes called the marital acquest but more usually the matrimonial property; and
>
> (2) other property.
>
> The former is the financial product of the parties' common endeavour, the latter is not. The parties' matrimonial home, even if

13 at 606.
14 [2007] EWCA Civ 503.

> this was brought into the marriage at the outset by one of the parties usually has a central place in any marriage. So it should normally be treated as matrimonial property for this purpose"

Baroness Hale draws a distinction between 'family' assets and other assets. She stated that:

> "prime examples of family assets of a capital nature were the family home and its contents, while the parties' earning capacities were assets of a revenue nature. But also included are other assets which were obviously acquired for the use and benefit of the whole family, such as holiday homes, caravans, furniture, insurance policies and other family savings. To this list should clearly be added family businesses or joint ventures in which they both work".

In respect of 'other assets', Baroness Hale indicates that, albeit applicable in a very small number of cases, where there are

> "business or investment assets which have been generated solely or mainly by the efforts of one party"

these assets may be distinguished in the same way as premarital property, inheritance or gifts.

The principle of sharing will apply to all assets but, per Potter P in *Charman*:[15]

> "to the extent that their property is non matrimonial, there is likely to be a better reason for departure from equality".

As to property defined (per Lord Nicholls or Baroness Hale) as 'non-matrimonial' the prevailing view remains that the importance of its categorisation will diminish over time and that, as was made clear in *White* and developed in *Miller/McFarlane*, any distinction is likely to be of little significance where needs cannot be met without recourse to such property.

The third strand or element is compensation. This is likely to be of least relevance to those advising on prenuptial agreements. There is, as Coleridge J highlighted in *RP v RP*,[16] no mention of compensation in the statute and it may not add anything to the concept of "financial obligations and responsibilities which each of the parties has".

---

15 at paragraph 66.

16 [2007] 1 FLR 2105.

Need, sharing, compensation; the three elements or principles which should guide the court in making an award of ancillary relief. But is there one factor or objective which should be focused upon in order to attain fairness? Baroness Hale puts it thus at paragraph 144:

> "The ultimate objective is to give each party an equal start on the road to independent living"

The final aspect of *Miller* which provokes particular interest for those concerned with prenuptial agreements is the extent to which it explores the scope for the parties' own decisions as to how they arrange their finances during marriage to be taken account of after the breakdown of the marriage. Baroness Hale at 153 uses the example of the

> "genuine dual career family where each party has worked throughout the marriage and certain assets have been pooled for the benefit of the family but others have not".

She hints at a scenario where, after family assets have been divided equally, a court might consider it fair to leave undisturbed (i.e. *not* share) any surplus that the individual parties have acquired themselves if this was in accordance with the way the couple had chosen to run their lives.[17] Lord Mance at 170 adds support to this idea, even widening its possible applicability:

> "If one partner (and it might, with increasing likelihood I hope, be the wife) were more successful financially than the other, and questions of needs and compensation had been addressed, one might ask why a court should impose at the end of a marriage a sharing of all assets acquired during matrimony which the parties had never envisaged during matrimony. Once needs and compensation had been addressed, the misfortune of divorce would not itself, as it seems to me, be justification for the court to disturb the principles by which the parties had chosen to live their lives while married"

In *Charman*, the following observation is made:[18]

> "Lord Mance may there have foreshadowed future, albeit no doubt cautious, movement in the law towards a more frequent

17 Although note the warning bell she sounds at the same time, "what seems fair and sensible at the outset of a relationship may seem much less fair and sensible when it ends".

18 at paragraph 86.

> distribution of property upon divorce in accordance with what, by words or conduct, the parties appear previously to have agreed".

One may tentatively conclude that, whereas needs will always remain of the utmost importance, in spite of the move towards what is almost becoming a presumption of equal sharing, there may yet remain an opportunity for the parties' own decisions in relation to their finances to be afforded greater prominence.

By looking at Section 25 and considering the guidance given in some of the case law discussed above, it should be possible for a practitioner to provide reasonably accurate advice to any couple asking them how the courts would distribute their assets now. This is of course not the task that the draftsman of a prenuptial agreement is being asked to conduct; he is in fact being asked to look to an indefinite time in the future and predict then how the court might distribute a pot of future assets and liabilities, as yet unquantified.

To do so is an impossible task. Added to this it is likely that the practitioner will be asked to provide for a division of assets which would not be called fair in accordance with the principles outlined above. The role of the practitioner will therefore be to advise clearly as to what might be considered to be a fair division now, but to proceed to draft bearing in mind the objectives of the parties and sounding appropriate cautions.

# Chapter 5

# Drafting the prenuptial agreement – achieving enforceability

Practitioners are likely to find that there are a variety of reasons why individuals may seek advice regarding a prenuptial agreement. Some couples may be marrying for the first time, others may have been married before, some may intend to have children, others may have children from a previous marriage, some may be seeking to protect assets, others to reassure their partner that they will not claim against assets. Most however will be motivated by a desire for certainty from the outset as to how their assets would be divided in the event of a divorce and will be seeking, if at all possible, to avoid the unpredictability and expense of lengthy litigation. It is a difficult task to lay down any specific guidelines for such a wide group of individuals, and, like the application of Section 25 of the Matrimonial Causes Act, giving advice requires a wide degree of flexibility.

The focus of the advice given in this chapter has changed substantially since the first edition of this book in the light of the decision of the Supreme Court in *Radmacher (formerly Granatino) v Granatino* [2010] UKSC 42 (hereafter '*Radmacher*'). Where previously the concern was that an agreement would need to accord with judicially construed concepts of fairness in order to be upheld, parties will now have far greater scope for 'altering what is fair' within certain parameters.

The emphasis for the practitioner drafting a prenuptial agreement will now be upon demonstrating that the parties have entered into any agreement of their own free will and with a full understanding of its implications and setting out clearly how the parties believe their assets should fairly be divided in the event of a subsequent divorce or annulment of their marriage.

Previously practitioners, encouraged by case law and consultation papers such as *Supporting Families*, have sought to adhere to certain procedural safeguards without which a prenuptial agreement was regarded as having little prospect of being upheld. The Supreme Court clarified in *Radmacher* that there is an important distinction between giving an agreement contractual force and ensuring that it will be upheld within ancillary relief proceedings. The Court notably avoided deciding whether or not prenuptial agreements should be regarded as having contractual force and therefore whether they are enforceable *per se*. Its view was such an enquiry was a "red herring"[1] given the inability of parties to oust the jurisdiction of the court.

The Supreme Court acknowledged that where it is intended that agreements should otherwise be legally binding, there is a need for "black and white rules" in the nature of the safeguards proposed in the consultation paper. But its view was that in the law's current state such rules are not necessary, although the recommended safeguards "are likely to be highly relevant".

In its consultation paper published on 11 January 2011, the Law Commission considered the formal requirements which it suggests might be necessary to create a "qualifying nuptial agreement", that is an agreement providing for the financial consequences of separation, divorce, or the dissolution of a civil partnership which would have the effect of excluding, or greatly circumscribing, the exercise of the court's discretion on an application for ancillary relief. Its provisional proposals are summarised at the end of this chapter. Although the precedents in Chapter 6 of this book are not intended to accord strictly with these requirements, practitioners may find it helpful to bear in mind the likely developments of the law in this area.

When considering what weight should have been given to the prenuptial agreement signed by Ms Radmacher and Mr Granatino, the focus of the Supreme Court's enquiry was as to the 'circumstances' of the agreement rather than whether the agreement complied strictly with recognised safeguards.

In particular it asked itself two questions,[2] namely:

(a) Were there circumstances attending the making of the agreement that detract from the weight that should be accorded to it?

(b) Were there circumstances attending the making of the agreement that enhance the weight that should be accorded to it; the foreign element.

The ultimate conclusion of the the majority in the Supreme Court at paragraph 75 was that:

---

1 Paragraph 63.

2 Paragraph 67. The third question posed by them related to the circumstances prevailing at the time of the court's order.

> "The court should give effect to a nuptial agreement that is freely entered into by each party with a full appreciation of its implications unless in the circumstances prevailing it would not be fair to hold the parties to their agreement"

It is evident that the *terms* of a prenuptial agreement will be key in demonstrating to a court, in the event of subsequent ancillary relief proceedings:

(a) that the parties entered into the agreement of their own free will;

(b) that each party had a full appreciation of the implications of the agreement;

(c) that there were no circumstances pertaining at the time of the agreement which might detract from the weight to be afforded to it; and

(d) whether there were any circumstances which might enhance the weight to be given to an agreement.

This chapter aims to set out the essential elements for a prenuptial agreement and examine afresh the procedural safeguards that it would be advisable to employ when drafting a prenuptial agreement in the light of the Supreme Court's judgment in *Radmacher*.

## Intention

For an agreement to be upheld by the court, the parties must each intend that the agreement should be effective. It was observed by the Supreme Court that parties entering into a prenuptial agreement prior to its decision in *Radmacher* may have been advised that such agreements were void under English law and would be likely to carry little or no weight. This, it was made clear, is no longer the case and the Supreme Court has now said that:

> "In future it will be natural to infer that parties who enter into an ante-nuptial agreement to which English law is likely to be applied intend that effect should be given to it"[3]

## Laws of contract

Even if not purporting to be a contract, the agreement should seek to respect ordinary contractual principles. As a starting point the agreement

3 *Radmacher* at paragraph 70 and emphasised again at 74 where the Supreme Court concluded that the fact that the parties would have understood their prenuptial agreement to be prima facie enforceable in a foreign jurisdiction added force to the conclusion that the parties intended it to be generally effective.

should indicate that the parties intend to create legal relations with each other. The terms of the agreement should be certain; vagueness or incompleteness may render an agreement unenforceable[4]. Similarly any contingent conditions which are incorporated into the agreement (for example the birth of a child) should be clearly defined. No agreement should impose obligations on non-consenting third parties. If a third party's rights (for example a parent's interest in a matrimonial property) are to be affected they should be made parties to the agreement and should obtain their own independent legal advice.

## Understanding

### (*a*) *Legal advice*

The parties must have understood both the terms and the effect of the agreement when they entered into it. This can best be achieved by both parties obtaining legal advice,[5] which should be independently given and preferably by a lawyer specialising in matrimonial finance. It is recommended practice that this advice should be in writing[6] and adviser's certificates to this effect should be appended to the agreement. Advisers should ensure that the terms of the agreement are clear[7] and are understood by the parties.

4 Some terms may need to be defined, for example 'clean break', 'years of marriage', 'children of the family' or 'marital acquest'.

5 See the judgment of Sir Roger Ormrod in *Camm* (1983) 4 FLR 577 where at page 480 in distinguishing between bad and negligent advice he observes that " … it is not necessarily negligent advice to take a course or permit a client to take a course which a more experienced, or stronger minded legal adviser would have discouraged. … the quality of legal advice on which parties act is of some relevance to the justice of the case".

6 For guidance on nature and form of advice required to be given see the opinion of Lord Nicholls of Birkenhead in *Royal Bank of Scotland v Etridge* [2001] UKHL 44 at paragraphs 58–68.

7 It was suggested in *K v K* that a vague clause might render the whole agreement void.

***(b) Disclosure***

There should be full and certainly frank disclosure of all assets and liabilities[8]. Misrepresentation or fraud will vitiate the agreement and material non-disclosure may leave an agreement vulnerable to being discounted by a court considering its terms.

The Supreme Court however acknowledged that detailed disclosure of resources may not be necessary, providing that the parties have had the opportunity to obtain further disclosure and understand the implications of the agreement.

> "... Sound legal advice is obviously desirable, for this will ensure that a party understands the implications of the agreement, and full disclosure of any assets owned by the other party may be necessary to ensure this. But if it is clear that a party is fully aware of the implications of an ante-nuptial agreement and indifferent to the detailed particulars of the other party's assets, there is no need to accord the agreement reduced weight because he or she is unaware of those particulars. What is important is that each party should have all the information that is material to his or her decision, and that each party should intend that the agreement should govern the financial consequences of the marriage coming to an end"[9]

Disclosure may be made by way of a schedule or a Form E which should be annexed to the final agreement.

***(c) Negotiations***

It may be thought desirable, in addition to taking specialist legal advice and obtaining financial disclosure, that the parties should have the opportunity for proper negotiations as to the terms of the agreement. In *Radmacher,* however, the Supreme Court supported the Court of Appeal's conclusion that the lack of negotiations had not vitiated the agreement. Wilson LJ said:[10]

---

8 In *K v K* there was not full disclosure but the decision not to press for detailed valuation of assets came from the wife's side. Figures of up to £150 million were acknowledged by the wife's father to be in existence. The judge found that notwithstanding the absence of 'full' disclosure, the husband had not exploited his dominant position either financially or otherwise.

9 *Radmacher* at paragraph 69.

10 *Radmacher v Granatino* [2009] 2 FLR 1181 at paragraph 33.

> "The absence of negotiations seems to me of little moment. It was the husband's choice not to initiate negotiations"

What will be important is that the parties had the opportunity to enter into negotiations had they wanted to.

## Avoiding undue influence or pressure

Duress (like fraud or misrepresentation) would, if established, vitiate an agreement. However the Supreme Court also held that:

> "Unconscionable conduct such as undue pressure (falling short of duress) will also be likely to eliminate the weight to be attached to the agreement, and other unworthy conduct such as exploitation of a dominant position to secure an unfair advantage, would reduce or eliminate it"[11]

### (*a*) *Timing*

*Supporting Families*[12] suggested that no prenuptial agreement should be signed less than twenty-one days prior to the marriage in question. Others have suggested longer periods of time.[13] From a practical point of view an appreciable distance in time between the signing of the agreement and the marriage is recommended to allow for proper reflection and to reduce the risk of it being later suggested that either party was subjected to undue pressure to agree to the terms of the agreement (although it is recognised that the imminence of a wedding is by no means the only factor which might constitute 'undue pressure' for these purposes)

### (*b*) *Relevant background*

It is likely that the parties' personal circumstances will be relevant to whether either of them might have been have been under any pressure to sign an agreement or indeed whether or not they could reasonably be said to have understood the implications of the agreement. Where relevant the agreement should record the following (non exhaustive) matters:

---

11 at paragraph 72.

12 See Appendix C.

13 Per Baron J in *NA v MA* recommends agreements should provide for a "proper period of reflection being at least 28 days prior to the marriage". Resolution's report *Family Agreements: Seeking Certainty to Reduce Disputes* proposed that to be binding an agreement should have been entered into at least forty-two days prior to the marriage.

(i) the ages of the parties;

(ii) whether either party has been married or in long-term relationships before and the circumstances in which that marriage or relationship came to an end (e.g. death, divorce);

(iii) whether either party has children from a previous relationship or marriage and whether those children reside with them or not;

(iv) whether the parties are expecting a child or intend to have a child in the future;

(v) where the parties are currently domiciled/resident and where the intend to live in the future;

(vi) whether the parties have cohabited prior to marriage, and if so, for how long;

(vii) each party's intentions in relation to their current and future financial circumstances and the other's acknowledgment of such intentions; and

(viii) whether either party expects their financial circumstances to change significantly during the course of the marriage (e.g. sale of business, receipt of inheritance).

### (*c*) *Importance of the agreement*

Many signatories to prenuptial agreements are clear that they would not have married without one. If this is the case it should be recorded within the agreement, although as Baroness Hale commented this "can cut both ways, because it may or may not indicate that one has taken an unfair advantage of the other".[14]

## Fairness

Although when setting out their 'test' for giving effect to a prenuptial agreement, the Supreme Court excepted cases where "in the circumstances prevailing it would not be fair to hold the parties to their agreement", it nevertheless stated in the same paragraph that:

> "The fact of the agreement is capable of altering what is fair"[15]

It will be relevant, and important, therefore for the agreement to record the parties' understanding of fairness in the context of their financial

14 *Radmacher* at paragraph 174.

15 *Radmacher* at paragraph 75.

circumstances and expectations for the future. This is particularly so where they have been advised that a court would not necessarily make an order in the same terms were it to be exercising its discretion afresh (which fact the parties might also wish to record on the face of the agreement).

Whilst acknowledging that 'what is fair' will necessarily depend on the facts of each particular case, the Supreme Court nevertheless gave some guidance in its judgment about the parameters of 'fairness'.

### (*a*) *Children*

Despite previous expressions of caution[16], there would appear to be no reason in principle why the existence of a child of the family (even if not born or contemplated at the time of the agreement) should invalidate a prenuptial agreement. It is clear however that the requirement of Section 25(1) of the Matrimonial Causes Act 1973, that first consideration must be given to the welfare while a minor of any child of the family who is under 18, stands firm. No prenuptial agreement can be allowed to prejudice the reasonable requirements of any children of the family.[17] Irrespective of the terms of the agreement, couples should be advised that the courts (or the Child Maintenance and Enforcement Commission or equivalent) will retain jurisdiction to make orders for financial provision for children of the family albeit they are limited in their scope and duration.[18]

### (*b*) *Autonomy*

One of the most strongly articulated reasons for upholding prenuptial agreements is that there should be respect for individual autonomy. Where a couple have clear views as to the 'fair' division of assets in the event of their separation, it is important that these are incorporated within the preamble to the agreement. Their expectations will carry most weight where they address existing circumstances but may be relevant even where superseded by significant changes in their circumstances.

16 *Supporting Families* recommended that where there is a child of the family, whether or not that child was alive or a child of the family at the time the agreement was made, an agreement should not become legally binding. Baron J in *NA v MA* [2006] EWHC 2900 supported the view that a prenuptial agreement would have the best chance of being enforced where no children had been born after the marriage.

17 *Radmacher* at paragraph 77.

18 Matrimonial Causes Act 1973 ss.23(1)(d), (e) and (f) and Children Act 1989, s.15 and Schedule 1.

### (*c*) *Non-matrimonial property*

Drawing on the dicta of Lord Nicholls in *White*[19] and *Miller*[20], the Supreme Court confirmed that there would be nothing inherently unfair in an express agreement regarding the disposal of non-matrimonial property on divorce. The agreement may relate either to existing property or property which one or other party anticipates receiving in the future (e.g. by way of inheritance or through a trust).

### (*d*) *Future circumstances*

Inevitably events occurring during the marriage and the circumstances pertaining at the point of a divorce may be unforeseeable at the time of signing a prenuptial agreement. As the Supreme Court noted, the longer the marriage, the more likely this is to be the case, and the more likely a court would be to find that it would be unfair to hold parties to their agreement.

There may be little that can be done to ensure that an agreement does not subsequently become unfair but it may assist to ensure that the agreement addresses a range of foreseeable future events and/or provides for a review in the event of certain 'trigger' occurrences.

### (*e*) *Needs, compensation and sharing*

It would seem that the most likely reason for not holding parties to an agreement will be if it fails to meet their needs. (The Supreme Court considered that this might also be the case where compensation is not adequately provided for but this is likely to be a far rarer occurrence.) It does not appear that 'needs' in this context will mean 'needs generously interpreted' or even 'reasonable requirements'[21]. The clearest steer is given at paragraph 88:

> "The parties are unlikely to have intended that their prenuptial agreement should result, in the event of the marriage breaking up, in *one partner being left in a predicament of real need, while the other enjoys sufficiency or more, and such a result is likely to render it unfair to hold the parties to their agreement*"

19 *White v White* [2001] AC 596 at 608.

20 *Miller v Miller; McFarlane v McFarlane* [2006] 1 FLR 1186 at paragraphs 21–25.

21 cf reference to 'reasonable requirements' in relation to children's needs at paragraph 77.

A predicament of real need would appear to indicate a very basic level of provision, but will no doubt be interpreted relative to the circumstances of the case and in particular to the other party's 'sufficiency'.

## Substance of the agreement

The priority, from the perspective of enforceability, must be to ensure that the agreement will meet the parties' 'real' needs. This may be the starting point of the draft or check at the end but it cannot be ignored.

In so far as the children's needs are concerned (or the needs of a husband or wife as the carer of a child), although these may be addressed within the body of the agreement, the court will always retain its jurisdiction to make orders for the children's benefit. The facts of *Radmacher* itself demonstrate that an absence of specific provision for children need not undermine the force of the remainder of the agreement. It may be that the parties agree for issues relating to provision for the children's needs to be determined as a discrete issue by a court upon their divorce, or that the court, at that point, should be invited to vary the terms of the agreement only in so far as they failed to provide for the reasonable requirements[22] of any child of the marriage.

Depending upon the size of the matrimonial 'pot' which is envisaged, it is likely that the prenuptial agreement will need then to deal with the treatment of 'surplus' assets.

The most straightforward cases will be those where the parties are content to subscribe to the principle of equal sharing. So long as this provides for need (as described above) and encompasses all the parties' present and future (capital) assets,[23] such an arrangement is unlikely to present the practitioner with too many problems.

More probably, parties will wish to provide for an unequal division of their assets or will only wish to share certain categories of asset. Such an approach is unlikely to render an agreement 'unfair' *per se*. Paragraph 82 of the judgment in *Radmacher* concludes thus:

> ".. It is in relation to the third strand, sharing, that the court will be most likely to make an order in the terms of the nuptial agreement in place of the order that it would otherwise have made"

---

22 c f *Radmacher* at paragraph 77.

23 NB – Baroness Hale includes within her definition of family assets the parties' earning capacities.

It will be important in the agreement itself to begin by classifying and defining the various categories of the parties' assets. These may include for example:

- premarital property held separately by the parties in their own name;
- premarital property held separately by the parties jointly with a third party;
- premarital jointly owned property;
- property which the parties will acquire jointly in the course of the marriage;
- property which the parties will acquire separately in the course of the marriage (or jointly with a third party); or
- property which the parties acquire by way of gift or inheritance during the course of the marriage

A prenuptial agreement may record the parties' interests in the any premarital property (by reference to a schedule if appropriate). It may also be relevant to record the provenance of an asset (for example if it has been inherited, or is a business which one party established without contribution from the other). Where appropriate it may include the non-entitled party's explicit acknowledgement that they will not, upon divorce, seek for this asset to be shared. It may even go further and record that notwithstanding any contributions made directly or indirectly to that property during the course of the marriage, the parties agree that such contribution will not lead to the non-entitled party acquiring a beneficial interest in the property.

If a property is, or is to be, owned jointly by the parties they may wish either to specify that it is, or will be, held by them in equal or other specified shares or alternatively that it is, or will be, held by them in accordance with contributions made by either of them toward the purchase price.

The agreement should state the extent to which this structure of ownership is to be maintained upon separation. It may be that an agreement simply records property will continue to be held (or divided) in accordance with the parties' respective beneficial interests (providing of course that such division is sufficient to meet need) or an agreement may go further and provide for specific distribution of assets to one party.

A common approach to division of property on divorce is that only property acquired by the parties during the course of the marriage will be shared, with pre-owned assets being left out of account. This approach accords with the community of property regime[24] familiar in civil jurisdictions. In some cases the property to be shared may be referred to as the 'marital acquest' or simply as 'matrimonial property' and may include the increase in value of pre-owned assets during the currency of the marriage. If such an approach is to be adopted it is particularly important that the agreement contains a clear definition of the property which is to be shared[25] and if necessary provides for a mechanism for calculating the proportion of the increased value of pre-owned assets which are to be taken into account.

Although the decision in *Miller* made it clear that the principle of equal sharing applied as much to short marriages as it did to long marriages,[26] it remains a commonly held view amongst prospective marriage partners that the quantum of financial provision on divorce should be referable to the length of the marriage. For this reason an adviser might be asked to provide that the amount of a lump sum (or proportion of defined assets) should increase incrementally in accordance with the length of the marriage. In such a case care must be taken to ensure that the agreement is clear as to how the increments are to operate by reference, for example, to the number of years from the anniversary of the marriage.

Where specific payments (lump sums or periodical payments) are to be made to meet needs it is recommended in general that these should be linked to increases in the retail prices index.

An alternative way of ensuring that an agreement will withstand the passage of time as well as changes in the parties' circumstances is to provide for a review of the terms of the agreement to take place upon the happening of certain events. Such events may include the birth of children, a party's incapacity through disability or illness, or a party's loss of employment.

In the end the downfall for a prenuptial agreement may well be its ultimate unfairness to one party, with the concept of 'fairness' being

---

24 Systems vary but most presume joint ownership of property acquired during the marriage with the exception of property acquired by way of inheritance or gift, 'separate property'.

25 Note Charles J's cautions regarding the use of such terminology in *H v H* [2007] EWHC 459 (Fam) at paragraph 46 ff.

26 Per Lord Nicholls at paragraph 17, "This principle ['equal sharing'] is applicable as much to short marriages as to long marriages: see *Foster v Foster* [2003] EWCA Civ 565, [2003] 2 FLR 299, at 305, para [19] per Hale LJ. A short marriage is no less a partnership of equals than a long marriage. The difference is that a short marriage has been less enduring. In the nature of things this will affect the quantum of the financial fruits of the partnership."

assessed by a judge many years hence. It may be that there is little that can be done to avoid this at the time of drafting but if a draftsman is careful to ensure that where possible the recommended safeguards are respected, that the agreement sets out clearly the parties' intentions, expectations and understanding of fair outcome in the event of their divorce, and its terms do not leave either party in a predicament of real need, he should certainly be advising his client that there is a strong prospect of the agreement being upheld.

## A postscript: Summary of the Law Commission's provisional proposals in relation to the formation and enforcement of qualifying nuptial agreements

***Formation***

1. Contractual validity would be an essential prerequisite. That is:
   - There must be an intention to create legal relations.
   - It should be supported by consideration.
   - It should be enforceable in law (not contrary to public policy).
   - It should comply with Section 2 of the Law of Property (Miscellaneous Provisions) Act 19890 if creating or transferring an interest in land.
   - It may be void for a mistake about the nature of the transaction or the identity of the other party.
   - It may be voidable for material misrepresentation, duress or undue influence (although it considers that it may be necessary to reform the law relating to undue influence for qualifying prenuptial agreements only in order to ensure they could not be too readily challenged or overturned).
2. Qualifying nuptial agreements should be made in writing and signed by both parties.
3. A party, against whom it is sought to enforce a qualifying nuptial agreement, should have received at the time of making the agreement, material full and frank disclosure of the other party's financial situation. It suggests (but does not positively recommend) that it may be possible for parties to agree to waive this requirement to some degree.

4. A qualifying nuptial agreement should not be enforced against a party who did not receive legal advice at the time it was formed. It should be necessary to demonstrate that the lawyer advised that party about:

   - the effect of the agreement on that party; and
   - the advantages and disadvantages, at the time the advice was provided, to that party of making the agreement.

It is suggested (but not positively recommended) that it may be possible to take joint legal advice.

5. There would be no timing requirements imposed on qualifying nuptial agreements made before a marriage or civil partnership or in relation to post nuptial agreements.
6. It considers (but does not positively endorse):

   - A general requirement of fair process in the making of the agreement.
   - Whether there should be any control over the content of a qualifying nuptial agreement, other than what is imposed by the general law of contract.

7. Any variation of a qualifying prenuptial agreement should comply with all the prerequisites for the formation of a qualifying nuptial agreement.

***Enforcement***

8. Qualifying nuptial agreements should be able to be set aside by the court to the extent that:

   - the agreement made insufficient provision for the children of the family; and/or
   - the agreement left, or would in the foreseeable future leave, on or both parties dependent upon state benefits in circumstances where that could be avoided by the making of an order in ancillary relief.

9. It considers five possible levels of further safeguards which might be introduced to protect parties in the event of a qualifying nuptial agreement being enforced within ancillary relief proceedings. They are:

- No further safeguards beyond those relating to children and social security – the "case iron model".
- Provision for the agreement to be able to be varied or set aside by the court on the happening of specified events.
- Provision for the agreement to be varied or set aside by the court if it produced significant injustice.
- Provision for the agreement to be varied or set aside by the court to the extent that it failed to meet the parties' needs and to provide compensation for any losses caused by the relationship.
- Provision for the agreement to be varied or set aside by the court if it failed to meet the parties' needs, narrowly defined.

***Further provisions***

10. There would be rules that enable property to be identified over time, for the purpose of a marital property agreement, and that set out the consequences of investment in that property by the other party or of the mixing of that property with property of the other party.
11. It would be possible for qualifying nuptial agreements to restrict or modify the ability of either party to apply to the court for family provision under the Inheritance (Provision for Family and Dependants) Act 1975, save in so far as application is made for provision for maintenance (as that term is used in the context of the Inheritance (Provision for Family and Dependants) Act 1975).

# Chapter 6

# Precedents

This chapter gives examples of the types of clauses which may be included within a prenuptial agreement. Not all of these clauses will be relevant or appropriate in every agreement and this chapter concludes with five sample agreements (covering a variety of scenarios) designed to demonstrate how 'standard' clauses might be adapted in individual cases.

## 1 Preliminaries

The agreements in this chapter are drafted as deeds and should comply with the provisions of the Law of Property (Miscellaneous Provisions) Act 1989). The Act requires that a deed makes clear on its face that it is intended to be a deed[1] and is validly executed as a deed.[2] 'Valid execution' entails a party signing in the presence of an attesting witness and delivery as a deed.[3]

## 2 Recitals

### *2.1 Conditional upon marriage*

> *This deed is made in contemplation of and is conditional upon the celebration of the intended marriage of X and Y on DD/MM/YYYY*

### *2.2 Statement summarising the discussions which have led to the agreement and the parties' wishes and intentions as to the effect of the agreement*

> *The parties have had discussions about their financial circumstances and the financial consequences of their proposed marriage due to be celebrated DD/MM/YYYY. They have also discussed its*

1 Section 1(2)a.
2 Section 1(2)b.
3 Section 1(3).

> *possible subsequent breakdown and the manner in which their assets should be divided in this unfortunate event.*

### 2.3 *Intention to create legal relations*

> *The parties intend to create legal relations and be bound by the terms of this Deed*[4]

### 2.4 *Intention to bind heirs and successors*

> *The parties intend that this Deed shall be binding on their heirs, receivers, trustees and personal representatives*

### 2.5 *Statement of receipt of independent legal advice and identification of freely chosen legal advisers*

> *The parties have each received independent legal advice from freely chosen legal advisers as follows:*
>
> *For H:*
>
> *For W:*

It is sometimes the case that one party pays for the advice given to the other. This may be addressed as follows:

> *It is further recorded that although H/W has paid for both parties' legal advice H/W has not sought to influence W/H's legal advisers or prevent them from giving objective or independent advice*

### 2.6 *Knowledge of each other's financial circumstances and affairs as summarised and appended in schedules*

> *H and W have fully and frankly disclosed to each other their financial resources and other relevant circumstances which are set out in summary form in Annexes A and B to this Deed*

4 See *Radmacher* at paragraph 70: "in future it will be natural to infer that parties who enter into an ante-nuptial agreement to which English Law is likely to apply intend that effect should be given to it."

Where there has not been detailed disclosure but the parties are nonetheless satisfied that disclosure has been sufficient, the following clause might be appropriate:

> *H/W has made frank disclosure to W/H of the substance of his/her current assets and the same are summarised in Annex A to this Deed. W/H accepts that she/he has had the opportunity to request further particulars and/or take further advice in relation to the same but has declined do so. Accordingly H and W agree that the summary is a general but broadly accurate statement of H/W's financial affairs and that W/H considers it to be sufficient to enable her/him to decide upon the fairness of the terms of this Deed.*

### *2.7 Relevant background detail*

2.7.1 Ages of parties

2.7.2 Parties' country of domicile and residence

2.7.3 Prior marriages and children therefrom

2.7.4 Whether parties are cohabiting

2.7.5 Further explanations as to parties' capital and income positions

2.7.6 Identification of separate and/or joint property

2.7.7 Intentions regarding separate and/or joint property

2.7.8 Intentions regarding future acquired property

2.7.9 Intentions regarding future financial independence

### *2.8 Statement that parties are entering into agreement freely and voluntarily*

> *H and W are each entering into the terms of this Deed freely and voluntarily without coercion influence or pressure from any kind from the other or from circumstances or otherwise*

### *2.9 Statement that parties understand the terms of the agreement*

> *H and W each understand the nature and effect of this Deed, the rights that they are each surrendering as a result, and that the provision which it makes is not necessarily reflective of the provision which might otherwise be made for them or either of them by a court following the dissolution or annulment of their marriage*

### *2.10 Statement that the parties consider the terms of the agreement to be fair*

> *H and W agree and accept that the provisions of this agreement are regarded by them as fair just and reasonable at the date of this Deed*

### *2.11 Statement of agreement in relation to claims against estate*

> *In the event that the marriage is ended by the death of H or W it is the parties' agreement that the provision made by this Deed constitutes reasonable financial provision under the Inheritance (Provision for Family and Dependants) Act 1975*

### *2.12 If applicable, whether parties would marry without agreement*

> *Neither H nor W would wish to marry without having executed a prenuptial agreement*[5]

### *2.13 Acknowledgment that the jurisdiction of the court cannot be excluded*

> *H and W are each aware and acknowledge, having been so advised, that under the laws of England and Wales it is not possible as at the date of this agreement to exclude the jurisdiction of the courts to make orders under the Matrimonial Causes Act 1973 [and that the terms of this Deed do not necessarily reflect the manner in which a court might resolve their claims against each other in the event their marriage is dissolved or annulled]*

### *2.14 Subject to any prospective change in the law?*

> *The parties agree that the provisions of this Deed shall be subject to any prospective change in the law relating to the enforcement or recognition of prenuptial agreements*[6]

---

5 This was one of the factors to which the court had regard in *K v K (Ancillary Relief: Prenuptial Agreement)* [2003] 1 FLR 120. See also Baroness Hale in *Radmacher* at paragraph 174.

6 At the time of writing it is understood that the Law Commission will report to Parliament with its recommendations in 2012.

### *2.15 Intention to be bound wherever resident or domiciled (if applicable)*

*H and W expect and intend that this Deed be binding on them throughout the world where so ever they reside or may be domiciled [in furtherance of which they have entered into/agree to enter into mirror agreements in [country] [copies of which are annexed to this Deed]]. [However, for the avoidance of doubt, in so far as the rules of prorogation permit, they elect that the courts of England and Wales shall have exclusive jurisdiction].*

## 3 Terms of the agreement

### *3.1 Commencement/operative date*

*This Deed shall become operative upon H and W celebrating a valid ceremony of marriage on [DATE]*

### *3.2 Definitions*

For example:

- 'Years of Marriage' may be defined by reference to the time elapsed between celebration of the marriage and each anniversary thereafter.
- 'Child of the Marriage/Family' may be defined as a child born to or adopted by the parties or may be extend to include children of either party from a previous relationship.
- A 'Clean Break' may be defined as:

*A dismissal of all claims arising out of the marriage whether under the Matrimonial Causes Act 1973, the Married Women's Property Act 1882 or the Trusts of Land and Appointment of Trustees Act 1996 and such other Acts as may amend or replace this legislation as well as an agreement that neither party shall make a claim against the other under the Inheritance (Provision for Family and Dependants) Act 1975*

- 'Date of Separation' may be defined as:

*The earliest of:*

> (*a*) *the date from which the parties live in separate households (whether or not under the same roof) with the settled intention of living separately and not resuming cohabitation; or*
>
> (*b*) *the date when one party communicates to the other in writing an intention to live separate and apart and end marital cohabitation; or*
>
> (*c*) *the date of issue of any proceedings for dissolution of marriage or judicial separation.*

### *3.3 Confidentiality clause*

> *H and W acknowledge that they have given and received information which is confidential and they agree that neither of them will: -*
>
> *1.1 Reveal to any third (excluding any person to whom it is necessary to disclose relevant parts of this agreement for the purposes of implementation or professional advice or to any competent court) the terms of this Deed or any of the financial particulars disclosed during the course of its preparation*
>
> *1.2 Cause or permit publication by the press or other media of the said terms or particulars*
>
> *1.3 Take any steps as a result of which the said terms or particulars are likely to become public knowledge or are reasonably foreseeable as being likely to become public knowledge*
>
> *1.4 Fail to take any steps which either party may reasonably be expected to take to prevent the said terms or particulars from becoming public knowledge in circumstances in which they would otherwise be likely to do so*

### *3.4 Treatment of assets during marriage*

3.4.1 Separate property owned before marriage

> *Any asset held by H and W in their sole name [or in their joint name with a third party prior to the marriage] [and any income derived from it and any increase it its value] shall remain in that party's absolute beneficial ownership during the marriage [in that it shall be free from all claim charge and encumbrance of the other party]*

3.4.2 Separate property acquired during marriage

> *Any asset acquired during the marriage by either H or W [whether created by its owner or acquired by purchase, gift or inheritance or otherwise] [and any income derived from it and any increase in its value] shall remain in their respective beneficial ownership*

3.4.3 Joint property acquired during marriage

> *Any asset acquired by the parties jointly during the marriage shall be held in accordance with their formal legal ownership/ by the parties in equal shares*

### *3.5 Treatment of capital contributions during marriage – whether gift, loan or purchase of interest in asset*

> *Capital contributions by either party of more than £[SUM] shall be documented in writing as a gift or loan or as representing the purchase of an interest an asset proportionate to such contribution [or as otherwise agreed and recorded in writing]*

### *3.6 Treatment of assets upon separation*

3.6.1 Retaining/distributing different categories of assets

> *In the event of the dissolution or annulment of the marriage:*
>
> (*a*) *H and W shall retain all assets in their respective beneficial ownership free from any claim by the other*
>
> (*b*) *All jointly owned property shall be distributed between H and W equally/ in accordance with their respective financial contributions [or in such proportions as they may subsequently determine to be fair]*

3.6.2 Dependent upon duration of marriage

> *In the event of the dissolution or annulment of the marriage, H/W shall pay to W/H £[SUM] [adjusted in accordance with the Retail Price Index on the basis that the base month for calculation shall be [DATE]] in respect of each complete Year of Marriage*

3.6.3 Provision for children

> *Nothing in this Deed shall be construed as restricting the right of either party to make a claim in respect of any child of the marriage*

### *3.7 Agreement to embody terms of agreement into consent order and to present to the court for approval*

> *The parties agree that in the event of the dissolution of their marriage they shall ask the court to approve an order, incorporating, so far as the same is permitted by law, the provisions of this Deed.*
>
> *The parties further agree that they will make a joint application to the court for the approval and making of such an order immediately after the pronouncement of decree nisi.*
>
> *[Such order shall include provision that save as provided otherwise there shall be a clean break]*

### *3.8 Gifts will not affect agreement*

> *Nothing in this Deed shall be construed as preventing either party from making gifts to the other [or provision for the other by will or trust]. Such gifts [or provision] shall not be treated as varying the terms and effect of this Deed*

### *3.9 Agreement to reflect terms of agreement in wills*

> *The parties agree on or before DD/MM/YYYY to execute wills so as to reflect the distribution of their assets provided for in this Deed*

### *3.10 Provision for variation*

> *Any variation or amendment of this Deed shall only be effected if recorded in a supplemental Deed in writing executed by both parties and complying with the Law of Property (Miscellaneous Provisions) Act 1989*

### *3.11 Provision for review*

3.11.1 Upon parties having children

3.11.2 Upon illness preventing parties from maintaining themselves

3.11.3 Unemployment

3.11.4 After lapse of time

*The terms of this Deed may/shall be reviewed [with the benefit of independent legal advice] when any of the following events occur:*

(*a*) *the birth or adoption of a [further] child*

(*b*) *the ill health or disablement of either party [such that they are unable to maintain themselves]*

(*c*) *the unemployment of either party for a period in excess of X months*

(*d*) *X number of Years of Marriage*

### *3.12 Whole agreement*

*This Deed contains the whole agreement between the parties and neither of them has entered into it on the basis of any promises or representations which are not expressly included in it*

### *3.13 Severability*

*The invalidity or unenforceability of any provision of this Deed will not affect the validity or enforceability or enforceability of any other provision of this Deed and any invalid or unenforceable provision will be severable*

### *3.14 Referral to mediation*

*Any dispute arising out of this Deed shall in the first instance be referred to an accredited family mediator*

### *3.15 Costs of the agreement*

| |
|---|
| *The costs of and incidental to this agreement shall be paid by H and W equally*[7] |

### *3.16 Governed/construed in accordance with law of England and Wales*

| |
|---|
| *This Deed shall be governed by and construed in accordance with the laws of England and Wales* |

## 4 Annexures

### *4.1 Solicitor's certificate of independent advice*

*I, [name] Solicitor of [firm] of [address] certify that:*

1. *I am a solicitor of the Senior Courts of England and Wales.*
2. *Prior to [client name] executing the Deed between [name] and [name] dated DD/MM/YYYY to which this certificate is annexed I provided to [name] independent legal advice as to the following matters:*

    a. *the effect of the Deed on his/her rights*

    b. *whether at the time my advice was given it was to his/her advantage, financially or otherwise to enter into the Deed*

    c. *whether, at that time, it was prudent for him/her to enter into the Deed*

    d. *whether at that time and in the light of such circumstances as were reasonably foreseeable, the provisions of the Deed were fair and reasonable*

*Dated day of 2011*

### *4.2 Financial disclosure*

Summaries or Form Es.

7 But see paragraph 2.5 above in event of one or other party meeting all of the costs of the agreement.

# Precedent number 1 – 'The Young Couple'

Your brief:

> You are instructed by Sarah M who is engaged to be married to James D.
>
> Sarah is 28; James is 31. They both have successful careers, Sarah as a litigation solicitor, James as an accountant.
>
> They are not cohabiting but intend to purchase their first matrimonial home together shortly. They have jointly saved for a deposit and will purchase the property as joint tenants.
>
> Sarah currently lives in a small flat in Clifton, Bristol which she co-owns with her sister. The flat was purchased some years ago with money inherited from their grandmother.
>
> Other than their deposit, neither party has any other asset of significance.
>
> Sarah has confirmed that it is likely that she and James will have children in the future.
>
> Sarah wishes to retain the Clifton flat as her separate property. She has asked you to prepare a prenuptial agreement which will provide that in the event of her marriage ending in divorce, James will have no claim against the flat.

SAMPLE AGREEMENT

THIS DEED is made on the 11th day of March 2011

BETWEEN:

(1) **SARAH M** of 5 Church Road, Clifton, Bristol (hereafter referred to as "**Sarah**")

and

(2) **JAMES D** of 11D Park View, Richmond, London (hereafter referred to as "**James**")

WHEREAS:

A. This Deed is made in contemplation of and is conditional upon the celebration of the intended marriage of Sarah and James on 23 April 2011.

B. Sarah and James have had discussions about their financial circumstances and the financial consequences of their proposed marriage. They have also discussed its possible breakdown and the manner in which their assets should be divided in this unfortunate event.

C. Sarah and James wish to enter into this Deed recording their wishes and intentions regarding finances and property and each wishes their future rights and obligations arising from their intended marriage to be governed solely by this Deed.

D. Sarah and James intend to create legal relations and be bound by the terms of this Deed.

E. Sarah and James intend that this Deed shall be binding upon their heirs, receivers, trustees and personal representatives.

F. Sarah and James have each received independent legal advice from freely chosen legal advisers as follows:

   Sarah: Martin Green, Bristol Solicitors, Bristol

   James: Charles Grey, Richmond Solicitors, London

G. Sarah and James have fully and frankly disclosed to each other their financial resources and other relevant circumstances which are set out in summary form in Annexes A and B to this Deed.

H. With the exception of the monies which they have jointly saved for a deposit on a matrimonial home to be purchased in joint names following their marriage, Sarah and James have each acquired her or his property as set out in Annex A and Annex B respectively independently of and without contribution from the other.

I. Sarah and James intend that any and all assets held by each of them in their sole name or in one of their names with another person (hereinafter "separate property") shall remain that party's property and shall be free from any claim charge and encumbrance by the other during the marriage and thereafter.

J. In particular Sarah and James agree that Sarah should retain as her separate property, her legal estate and beneficial interest in 5 Church Road, Clifton, Bristol.

K. Sarah and James further accept and agree that they are both currently economically independent and self-sufficient.

L. Sarah and James are each entering into the terms of this Deed freely and voluntarily without coercion influence or pressure from any kind from the other or from circumstances or otherwise.

M. Sarah and James are each aware and acknowledge, having been so advised, that under the laws of England and Wales it is not possible as at the date of this agreement to exclude the jurisdiction of the courts to make orders under the Matrimonial Causes Act 1973.

N. Sarah and James each understand the nature and effect of this Deed, the rights that they are each surrendering as a result of this Deed and that the provision it makes is not necessarily reflective of the provision which might otherwise be made for them or either of them by a court following the dissolution or annulment of their marriage.

O. Sarah and James agree and accept that the provisions of this agreement are regarded by them as fair just and reasonable at the date of this Deed.

THIS DEED WITNESSES:

1. This Deed shall become operative upon Sarah and James celebrating a valid ceremony of marriage whether on 23 April 2011 or at any later date

2. References herein to a 'child of the marriage' shall mean any biological child of the parties or any child legally adopted by them who has not attained the age of eighteen at the date of dissolution or annulment of their marriage

3. Any asset held by Sarah and James prior to the marriage (as set out in Annexes A and B hereto) and any income derived from it and any increase in its value shall remain in that party's absolute beneficial ownership during the marriage in that it shall be free from all claim charge and encumbrance of the other party

4. It is hereby declared that James has no legal or beneficial interest in the property known as and situate at 5 Church Road, Clifton and notwithstanding any contribution which he may make directly or indirectly towards the purchase maintenance or improvement of the said property or towards the repayment of any mortgage secured thereon and regardless of whether the said property shall at any time become the parties' matrimonial home, he will acquire no beneficial interest in the property save by a further express deed in writing conforming to the Law of Property (Miscellaneous Provisions) Act 1989

5. In the event of the dissolution or annulment of the marriage:

    5.1. Sarah and James shall each retain their separate property (including 5 Church Road, Clifton) free from any claim by the other

    5.2. All jointly owned property shall be distributed between Sarah and James equally

    5.3. The provisions of this Deed shall so far as may be relevant and is permitted by law be incorporated into a consent order.

    5.4. In furtherance of this agreement the parties will make a joint application to the court for approval of such order immediately following pronouncement of decree nisi

    5.5. Nothing in this Deed shall be construed as restricting the right of either party to make a claim in respect of any child of the marriage

6. Nothing in this Deed shall be construed as preventing or precluding either Sarah or James from voluntarily making lifetime gifts to each other or from voluntarily making provision for the other by way of will, codicil trust or otherwise and such voluntary provision shall not be construed as varying the terms and effect of this Deed nor as evidence that there is or was any agreement between the parties other than is specifically contained in and provided for by this Deed

7. Sarah and James agree, on or before 23 April 2011, to execute wills so as to reflect the distribution of assets provided for in this agreement

8. The terms of this Deed shall be reviewed with the benefit of independent legal advice when any of the following events occur:

    8.1. The birth or adoption of child of the marriage

8.2. The ill health or disablement of either Sarah or James such that they are unable to maintain themselves

8.3. The unemployment of either Sarah or James for a period in excess of twelve months

8.4. Ten years

9. Any variation of amendment of this Deed shall only be effective if recorded in a supplemental deed in writing executed by both parties and complying with the provisions of the Law of Property (Miscellaneous Provisions) Act 1989
10. This Deed contains the whole agreement between Sarah and James and neither of them has entered into it on the basis of any promises or representations which are not expressly included in it
11. The invalidity or unenforceability of any provision of this Deed will not affect the validity or enforceability of any other provision of this Deed and any invalid or unenforceable provision shall be severable
12. Any dispute arising out of this Deed shall in the first instance be referred to an accredited family mediator
13. The costs of and incidental to this agreement shall be paid by Sarah and James equally
14. This Deed shall be governed by and construed in accordance with the laws of England and Wales

IN WITNESS whereof the parties hereto have executed this instrument as a Deed on the date first before written

SIGNED as a DEED by:

# Precedent number 2 – 'The Second Timers'

Your brief

> You are instructed by David W who is engaged to be married to Laura S.
>
> David is 58. He is managing director and majority shareholder in a building company, Great Builds Ltd, established by him in 1980. He has been married once before and has three children (all over 18) from his first marriage. In addition to his shareholding in Great Builds he owns a flat in London (Flat 11, 89 Peter Street) and has a one third share in a property in France (La Bergerie).
>
> He earns a good income from Great Builds but continues to maintain his former wife pursuant to a 'joint lives' periodical payments order made within ancillary relief proceedings upon the ending of that marriage.
>
> Laura is 50. She is a widow. Her late husband provided for her generously in his will. She owns a large property in Hampshire (The Grange, Overhill), which was their family home and where she has remained living with their three children (aged 21, 19 and 15). She also inherited a large portfolio of stocks and shares which provide her with a healthy income.
>
> David has recently commenced cohabitation with Laura at The Grange.
>
> David and Laura wish to enter into a prenuptial agreement. David wishes to ensure that Great Builds would be free from any claim by Laura in the event of a divorce. Laura, for her part, wishes to ensure that The Grange is retained for her children. Since Laura has a relatively secure income from her investment portfolio, she has agreed with David that she would make no claim for maintenance from him.

SAMPLE AGREEMENT

THIS DEED is made on the 20th day of April 2011

BETWEEN:

(1) **DAVID W** of The Grange, Overhill, Hampshire (hereafter referred to as "**David**")

and

(2) **LAURA S** of The Grange, Overhill, Hampshire (hereafter referred to as "**Laura**")

WHEREAS:

A. This Deed is made in contemplation of and is conditional upon the celebration of the intended marriage of David and Laura on 4 June 2011.

B. David and Laura have had discussions about their financial circumstances and the financial consequences of their proposed marriage. They have also discussed its possible breakdown and the manner in which their assets should be divided in this unfortunate event.

C. David and Laura wish to enter into this Deed recording their wishes and intentions regarding finances and property and each wishes their future rights and obligations arising from their intended marriage to be governed solely by this Deed.

D. David and Laura intend to create legal relations and be bound by the terms of this Deed.

E. David and Laura intend that this Deed shall be binding on their heirs, receivers, trustees and personal representatives.

F. David and Laura have each received independent legal advice from freely chosen legal advisers as follows:

   For David: James Brown, London Solicitors, London

   For Laura Emma White, Hampshire Solicitors, Hampshire

G. David and Laura have fully and frankly disclosed to each other their financial resources and other relevant circumstances which are set out in summary form in Annexes A and B to this Deed.

H. David (born on 15 May 1952) and Laura (born on the 29 December 1950) are both UK citizens and are habitually resident and domiciled in England and Wales

I. David was married previously to Mrs Mary W, which marriage was dissolved on 10 June 2010. He has three children from that marriage:

Louise (over 18)
Simon (over 18)
Sam (over 18)

J. Laura was married previously to the Mr Edward S, which married terminated upon Mr S's death on 11 August 2008. She has three children from that marriage:

Mark (over 18)
Susanna (over 18)
Annabel (born 1 October 1995, aged 15 at the date of this Deed)

K. It is intended that Annabel will live with David and Laura during her minority and shall be treated as a child of the family.

L. David and Laura have cohabited since 1 July 2010 at The Grange, Overhill (hereinafter "the matrimonial home").

M. David is a chartered engineer. He is the Managing Director and founder of Great Builds Limited, with a 75% shareholding. This business was established and developed over a period of thirty years prior to the commencement of his relationship with Laura.

N. David owns the following real property:

a. 'Flat 11, 86 Peter Street, London, England (in his sole name)

b. La Bergerie, Provence, France (jointly with his brother and sister in equal shares).

O. Laura does not work. She has acquired all of her financial resources, including the matrimonial home of which she is the sole proprietor, by way of inheritance or gift prior to the commencement of her relationship with David.

P. As at the date of the marriage, David and Laura do not own any asset that has been acquired by way of joint endeavour. All of the assets listed at Annexes A and B hereto and summarised at M to O above (hereinafter "separate property") have been acquired independently of and without contribution from the other party.

Q. David and Laura agree that as at the date of this Deed they are both self-supporting and can meet their needs by using their separate property. They do not anticipate this situation changing.

R. Save as expressly provided for in this Deed, David and Laura intend that their respective separate property shall remain in their respective beneficial ownership and shall be free from any claim charge or encumbrance by the other party.

S. David and Laura are each entering into the terms of this Deed freely and voluntarily without coercion influence or pressure from any kind from the other or from circumstances or otherwise.

T. David and Laura are each aware and acknowledge, having been so advised, that under the laws of England and Wales it is not possible as at the date of this agreement to exclude the jurisdiction of the courts to make orders under the Matrimonial Causes Act 1973.

U. David and Laura each understand the nature and effect of this Deed, the rights that they are each surrendering as a result of this Deed and that the provision it makes is not necessarily reflective of the provision which might otherwise be made for them or either of them by a court following the dissolution or annulment of their marriage.

V. David and Laura agree and accept that the provisions of this agreement are regarded by them as fair just and reasonable at the date of this Deed.

W. In the event that the marriage is ended by the death of H or W it is the parties' agreement that the provision made by this Deed constitutes reasonable financial provision under the Inheritance (Provision for Family and Dependants) Act 1975.

THIS DEED WITNESSES:

1. This Deed shall become operative upon David and Laura celebrating a valid ceremony of marriage whether on 4 June 2011 or at any later date

2. A 'Clean Break' shall be defined herein as 'A dismissal of all claims arising out of the marriage whether under the Matrimonial Causes Act 1973, the Married Women's Property Act 1882 or the Trusts of Land and Appointment of Trustees Act 1996 and such other Acts as may amend or replace this legislation as well as an agreement that neither party shall make a claim against the estate of the other pursuant to section 2 of the Inheritance (Provision for Family and Dependents) Act 1975'

3. David and Laura's separate property (as defined at P above) and any income derived from it and any increase in its value shall remain in

that party's absolute beneficial interest during the marriage and thereafter in that it shall be free from all claim charge and encumbrance of the other party

4. The parties hereby declare that David (and so as to bind his heirs and successors) has at the date of the marriage no legal and beneficial interest in The Grange, Overhill, Hampshire. FURTHER it is agreed that David shall not acquire any beneficial interest in the said property whether by making a contribution directly or indirectly to household repairs or to the maintenance costs of the property SAVE BY a further express deed in writing conforming to the Law of Property (Miscellaneous Provisions) Act 1989

5. Any asset acquired by either David or Laura during their marriage shall be held in accordance with their formal legal ownership

6. In the event of the dissolution or annulment of the marriage:

   6.1 Neither David nor Laura shall make any financial claim of any kind upon the other save that they agree to incorporate the terms of this Deed so far as may be relevant into a consent order of the court immediately following pronouncement of decree nisi

   6.2 In the event that either David or Laura make any application to any court of whatever jurisdiction for financial provision other than by way of a consent order to reflect the terms and provisions of this Deed in full, they agree that the court should take fully into account the terms of this Deed and that such order shall include provision that there shall be a clean break

7. Nothing in this Deed shall be construed as preventing either party from making gifts to the other or provision for the other by will or trust. Such gifts or provision shall not be treated as varying the terms and effect of this Deed

8. David and Laura will on or before 4 June 2011 execute wills so as to reflect the distribution of their assets as provided for in this Deed

9. Any variation of amendment of this Deed shall only be effective if recorded in a supplemental deed in writing executed by both parties and complying with the provisions of the Law of Property (Miscellaneous Provisions) Act 1989

10. This Deed contains the whole agreement between David and Laura and neither of them has entered into it on the basis of any promises or representations which are not expressly included in it

11. The invalidity or unenforceability of any provision of this Deed will not affect the validity or enforceability of any other provision of this Deed and any invalid or unenforceable provision shall be severable
12. Any dispute arising out of this Deed shall in the first instance be referred to an accredited family mediator
13. The costs of and incidental to this agreement shall be paid by David and Laura equally
14. This Deed shall be governed by and construed in accordance with the laws of England and Wales

IN WITNESS whereof the parties hereto have executed this instrument as a Deed on the date first before written

SIGNED as a DEED by:

# Precedent number 3 – 'The Foreign Couple'

Your brief

> You are instructed by Harry F who is engaged to be married to Ivana S.
>
> Harry is 45. He is a US citizen. He has lived and worked (as a banker) in London for 10 years. Ivana, 30, is Russian. She too is based in London, and is currently working as secretary.
>
> Neither Harry nor Ivana has been married before nor do they have any children.
>
> Harry has property and business interests in London and New York. He would estimate his net assets to be in the region of £7.5 million.
>
> He understand Ivana owns property in Russia which she states is worth no more than £100,000.
>
> Harry wishes you to draft a prenuptial agreement in advance of their wedding the following week.
>
> His instructions are that the agreement should provide for the payment of a lump sum to Ivana in the event of their divorce, the quantum of which should be determined in accordance with the duration of their marriage. He would wish the agreement to provide that in the event of their having children, and it being agreed that Ivana were to their primary carer, further provision should be made for her in the form of a settlement of property (to provide a home for her and the children during the children's minority only) and he would agree to pay child maintenance and school fees.
>
> He is keen that, so far as is possible, the agreement would be binding in England, USA and Russia.
>
> He states that he would not be prepared to marry without the benefit of a prenuptial agreement and that Ivana accepts this.

THIS DEED is made on the 1st day of March 2011

BETWEEN:

(1) **HARRY F** of 110 Eastern Wharf, London (hereafter referred to as "**Harry**")

and

(2) **IVANA S** of 20 Western Quay, London (hereafter referred to as "**Ivana**")

WHEREAS:

A. This Deed is made in contemplation of and is conditional upon the celebration of the intended marriage of Harry and Ivana on 12 March 2011.

B. Harry and Ivana have had discussions about their financial circumstances and the financial consequences of their proposed marriage. They have also discussed its possible breakdown and the manner in which their assets should be divided in this unfortunate event.

C. Harry and Ivana wish to enter into this Deed recording their wishes and intentions regarding finances and property and each wishes their future rights and obligations arising from their intended marriage to be governed solely by this Deed.

D. Harry and Ivana intend to create legal relations and be bound by the terms of this Deed.

E. Harry and Ivana intend that this Deed shall be binding on their heirs, receivers, trustees and personal representatives.

F. Harry and Ivana have each received independent legal advice from freely chosen legal advisers specialising in matrimonial law in respect of the nature and effect of the terms of this Deed.

G. Harry (born on 7 August 1965) is a US Citizen and is domiciled in the USA but resident in England and Wales.

H. Ivana (born on 10 September 1980) is a Russian citizen. She is domiciled in Russia but resident in England and Wales.

I. Neither Harry nor Ivana have been married before. They do not have any children but have discussed their desire to have children in the future.

J. Harry and Ivana intend to live in England after their marriage.

K. Harry is a banker. He has commercial and property interests in England and the United States of America. He estimates his current net capital resources to be worth approximately £7.5 million.

L. Ivana is a secretary. She owns property in Russia. She estimates her current net capital resources to be worth approximately £100,000.

M. Harry has made full disclosure to Ivana of the substance of his current assets and the same are summarised in Annex A to this Deed. Ivana accepts that the summary is a general but broadly accurate statement of his financial affairs in all material respects. Ivana confirms that both she and her advisers have reviewed Annex A and Ivana specifically acknowledges that she has not requested and does not seek:

   a. Further details of Harry's assets and income other than as set out in Annex A

   b. Further advice in respect of the terms of this Deed.

N. In the light of M above, Ivana agrees not to claim at any time that her failure to obtain additional information or seek specialist advice in all appropriate jurisdictions should be a bar to the enforcement of the terms of this Deed or any provision of it.

O. Ivana has made full disclosure to Harry of the substance of her current assets and the same are summarised in Schedule B to this Deed. Harry accepts that the summary is a general but broadly accurate statement of her financial affairs in all material respects. Harry confirms that both he and his advisers have reviewed Annex B and Harry specifically acknowledges that he has not requested and does not seek:

   a. Further details of Ivana's assets and income other than as out in Annex B

   b. Further advice in respect of the terms of this Deed.

P. In the light of O above, Harry agrees not to claim at any time that his failure to obtain additional information or seek specialist advice in all appropriate jurisdictions should be a bar to the enforcement of the terms of this Deed or any provision of it.

Q. As at the date of the marriage, Harry and Ivana do not own any asset that has been acquired by way of joint endeavour. All of the assets listed at Annexes A and B hereto (hereinafter "separate property") have been acquired independently of and without contribution from the other party.

R. Save as expressly provided for in this Deed, Harry and Ivana intend that their respective separate property shall remain in that party's separate beneficial ownership and shall be free from any claim charge or encumbrance by the other party.

S. Harry and Ivana are each entering into the terms of this Deed freely and voluntarily without coercion influence or pressure from any kind from the other or from circumstances or otherwise.

T. Harry and Ivana are each aware and acknowledge, having been so advised, that under the laws of England and Wales it is not possible as at the date of this agreement to exclude the jurisdiction of the courts to make orders under the Matrimonial Causes Act 1973.

U. Harry and Ivana each understand the nature and effect of this Deed, the rights that they are each surrendering as a result of this Deed and that the provision it makes is not necessarily reflective of the provision which might otherwise be made for them or either of them by a court following the dissolution or annulment of their marriage.

V. Harry and Ivana agree and accept that the provisions of this agreement are regarded by them as fair just and reasonable at the date of this Deed

W. In the event that the marriage is ended by the death of Harry or Ivana, the parties agree that the provision made by this Deed constitutes reasonably financial provision under the Inheritance (Provision for Family and Dependents) Act 1975.

X. Harry and Ivana agree and acknowledge that they would not be entering into this marriage without this Deed.

Y. Harry and Ivana agree and acknowledge that notwithstanding the imminence of their intended marriage next week, there has nonetheless been sufficient time for advice and reflection and that they have each given full consideration to the content and effect of this Deed and the consequences of entering into it.

Z. Harry and Ivana expect and intend this Deed to be binding on them throughout the world where so ever they reside in furtherance of which intention, Harry and Ivana hereby covenant with each other and agree that within seven days hereof with the benefit of independent legal advice they shall enter into mirror agreements reflecting the terms of this Deed in New York and Russia.

THIS DEED WITNESSES:

1. This Deed shall become operative upon Harry and Ivana celebrating a valid ceremony of marriage whether on 12 March 2011 or at any later date
2. A 'Clean Break' shall be defined herein as 'A dismissal of all claims arising out of the marriage whether under the Matrimonial Causes Act 1973, the Married Women's Property Act 1882 or the Trusts of Land and Appointment of Trustees Act 1996 and such other Acts as may amend or replace this legislation as well as an agreement that neither party shall make a claim against the estate of the other pursuant to section 2 of the Inheritance (Provision for Family and Dependents) Act 1975'
3. Harry and Ivana's separate property and any income derived from it and any increase in its value shall remain in that party's absolute beneficial interest during the marriage in that it shall be free from all claim charge and encumbrance of the other party
4. In the event of the dissolution or annulment of the marriage:

    4.1 Save as provided for in clauses 4.3 and 4.4 below, all separate property of Harry or Ivana shall respectively remain in the separate beneficial ownership of Harry or Ivana free from any claim by the other

    4.2 All jointly owned property shall be distributed between Harry and Ivana in equal shares

    4.3 In the event that there are no children of the marriage:

        4.3.1 If the dissolution or annulment is within five years of the date of the marriage Harry will pay to Ivana a lump sum of £300,000 adjusted in accordance with the Retail Price Index on the basis that the base month for calculation is March 2011

        4.3.2 If the dissolution or annulment occurs more than five years after the date of the marriage Harry will pay to Ivana the capital sum referred to at 4.3.1 above and will in addition pay to her a further lump sum of £200,000 (adjusted in accordance with the Retail Price Index as at 4.3.1 above) for every further complete year of marriage provided that the total amount payable shall not exceed £3,000,000 (adjusted in accordance with the Retail Price Index as at 4.3.1 above)

4.3.3 The lump sums provided for at 4.3.1 and/or 4.3.2 shall not become payable until decree absolute

4.4 In the event that any children are born to the parties or adopted by them during the marriage, and in the event of it being agreed that Ivana is to the be the primary carer of any or all of such children, Harry shall pay to Ivana a lump sum in accordance with 4.3 above and in addition:

4.4.1 Harry will settle on trust for Ivana during the minority of any child or children sufficient funds to purchase a property as a home for her and the said child or children

4.4.2 Harry will pay to Ivana for the benefit of the child or children during their minority periodical payments at an amount to be agreed between them at the time

4.4.3 Harry will pay, if applicable, the child or children's school fees and any reasonable extras (the choice of school(s) to be agreed between them from time to time)

4.5 Harry and Ivana agree to incorporate the terms of this Deed so far as may be relevant into a consent order of the court immediately following pronouncement of decree nisi and that such order shall include provision that there shall be a clean break

4.6 In the event that either Harry or Ivana make any application to any court of whatever jurisdiction for financial provision other than by way of a consent order to reflect the terms and provisions of this Deed in full, they agree that the court should take fully into account the terms of this Deed

5. Nothing contained within this Deed shall preclude either Harry or Ivana from voluntarily making lifetime gifts to the other from voluntarily making provision for the other by will codicil trust or otherwise. Such voluntary provision shall not be construed as a waiver of any provision of this Deed or as evidence that there is or was any agreement or understanding between and Harry and Ivana otherwise that is specifically contained within this Deed

6. Any variation of amendment of this Deed shall only be effective if recorded in a supplemental deed in writing executed by both parties and complying with the provisions of the Law of Property (Miscellaneous Provisions) Act 1989

7. This Deed contains the whole agreement between Harry and Ivana and neither of them has entered into it on the basis of any promises or representations which are not expressly included in it
8. The invalidity or unenforceability of any provision of this Deed will not affect the validity or enforceability of any other provision of this Deed and any invalid or unenforceable provision shall be severable
9. Any dispute arising out of this Deed shall in the first instance be referred to an accredited family mediator
10. This Deed shall be governed by and construed in accordance with the laws of England and Wales
11. The costs of an incidental to this agreement shall be paid by Harry and Ivana equally

IN WITNESS whereof the parties hereto have executed this instrument as a Deed on the date first before written

SIGNED as a DEED by:

# Precedent number 4 – 'The Heiress'

Your brief

> You are instructed by Eleanor F who is shortly to be married to William R.
>
> Eleanor is an only child. Upon her father's death she will inherit a relatively substantial amount of money. Whilst presently in robust health, Eleanor's father is concerned about the future. He does not approve of William, who is unemployed and seemingly dependent upon handouts from his parents, friends, and now Eleanor.
>
> Eleanor is 35. She works full time a veterinary surgeon and is a 50 per cent partner in a local practice.
>
> William is 45. He is a qualified chartered surveyor but has not worked for over ten years.
>
> Eleanor and William have already purchased a property together ("Black Barn, Hill Farm, Shropshire") which is held by them as tenants in common in proportion to their contributions to the purchase price (as to 70 per cent to Eleanor and 30 per cent to William). The mortgage and all of the outgoings are met out of Eleanor's income.
>
> Eleanor believes they may have children at some point in the future.
>
> She and her father wish, so far as is possible, for her future inheritance to be protected from any claims by William. Similarly Eleanor would wish to protect her interest in the veterinary partnership. Unless they have children, she cannot see that William would have any difficulty in accepting that his claims should be limited to realisation of his share of their joint assets.

THIS DEED is made on the 3rd day of May 2011

BETWEEN:

(1) **ELEANOR F** of Black Barn, Hill Farm, Shropshire (hereafter referred to as "**Eleanor**")

and

(2) **WILLIAM R** of Black Barn, Hill Farm, Shropshire (hereafter referred to as "**Hannah**")

WHEREAS:

A. This Deed is made in contemplation of and is conditional upon the celebration of the intended marriage of Eleanor and William on 9 July 2011.

B. Eleanor and William have had discussions about their financial circumstances and the financial consequences of their proposed marriage. They have also discussed its possible breakdown and the manner in which their assets should be divided in this unfortunate event.

C. Eleanor and William wish to enter into this Deed recording their wishes and intentions regarding finances and property and each wishes their future rights and obligations arising from their intended marriage to be governed solely by this Deed.

D. Eleanor and William intend to create legal relations and be bound by the terms of this Deed.

E. Eleanor and William intend that this Deed shall be binding on their heirs, receivers, trustees and personal representatives.

F. Eleanor and William have each received independent legal advice from freely chosen legal advisers specialising in matrimonial law in respect of the nature and effect of the terms of this Deed.

G. Eleanor (born on 1 October 1975) is a British citizen and is domiciled and resident in England and Wales.

H. William (born on 23 December 1965) is a British citizen and is domiciled and resident in England and Wales.

I. Neither Eleanor nor William has been married before although William cohabited with his previous partner for six years.

J. Eleanor and William hope that they may have children in the future.

K. Eleanor and William are currently cohabiting at Black Barn, Hill Farm, Shropshire (herein after "Black Barn"). This property is co-owned by them as tenants in common, as to 70 per cent Eleanor and 30 per cent William, which shares reflect their contribution to the purchase thereof.

L. Eleanor is a veterinary surgeon. She has a 50 per cent share in the North Street Veterinary Practice in Shrewsbury where she has worked for five years.

M. Eleanor is the sole heir of Mr Gregory F (her father) whose net estate she understands to be worth in the region of £2,000,000. The estate comprises Eleanor's family home and a small farm (Park Farm, Hay on Wye, Herefordshire, hereinafter "Park Farm") where she may one day wish to live and desires in any event to preserve for the next generation.

N. William is a qualified chartered surveyor. Although he is presently unemployed he accepts that he has an earning capacity and intends to seek a suitable position.

O. Eleanor and William have fully and frankly disclosed to each other their means and other relevant circumstances and the same are summarised respectively in Annex A and Annex B to this Deed.

P. Eleanor and William acknowledge and agree that:

   a. With the exception of Black Barn, Eleanor and William have each acquired the assets set out respectively at Annexes A and B (hereinafter "pre-marital separate property") independently of and without contribution from the other party

   b. In particular Eleanor's share in the North Street Veterinary Practice was acquired independently through her own endeavours and hard work without contribution from William

   c. Save as expressly provided for in this Deed, Eleanor and William intend that their respective separate property shall remain in that party's absolute beneficial ownership and shall be free from any claim charge or encumbrance by the other party during the marriage and thereafter.

Q. Eleanor and William further acknowledge agree and intend that:

   a. Eleanor's future inheritance and in particular Park Farm should be treated as non matrimonial and separate property in which William would have no entitlement to share in the event of the termination of their marriage whether by dissolution, annulment or Eleanor's death, and that the same principle should apply absolutely whether or not at any time Park Farm should become their matrimonial home

b. Although he is not currently working, William has an earning capacity, which the parties agree he should attempt to utilise so far as proves feasible and that there is no reason why he should not become and remain economically independent and self-sufficient

c. In the event that they have or adopt children the terms of this Deed shall be varied so that the provision which might be made under Schedule 1 Children Act 1989 applies to the claiming parent in the event that the provision anticipated hereunder fails to meet that level.

R. Eleanor and William are each entering into the terms of this Deed freely and voluntarily without coercion influence or pressure from any kind from the other or from Eleanor's family or circumstances or otherwise.

S. Eleanor and William are each aware and acknowledge, having been so advised, that under the laws of England and Wales it is not possible as at the date of this agreement to exclude the jurisdiction of the courts to make orders under the Matrimonial Causes Act 1973

T. Eleanor and William each understand the nature and effect of this Deed, the rights that they are each surrendering as a result of this Deed and that the provision it makes is not necessarily reflective of the provision which might otherwise be made for them or either of them by a court following the dissolution or annulment of their marriage.

U. Eleanor and William agree and accept that the provisions of this agreement are regarded by them as fair just and reasonable at the date of this Deed.

V. Eleanor and William agree to execute wills in contemplation of their forthcoming marriage so as to reflect the distribution of their assets provided for in this Deed.

W. In the event that the marriage is terminated by the death of either Eleanor or William, they agree the provision made by this Deed constitutes reasonable financial provision for the purposes of the Inheritance (Provision for Family Dependants) Act 1975 and any succeeding analogous legislation.

THIS DEED WITNESSES:

1. This Deed shall become operative upon Eleanor and William celebrating a valid ceremony of marriage whether on 9 July 2011 or at any later date

2. Save where specifically provided for in this Deed

   2.1 Eleanor and William's respective pre-marital separate property (as defined at O above) and any income derived from it and any increase in its value shall remain in that party's absolute beneficial interest during the marriage and thereafter in that it shall be free from all claim charge and encumbrance of the other party

   2.2 Any asset acquired during the marriage by Eleanor or William, whether created by its owner or acquired by purchase, gift or inheritance or otherwise and any income derived from it and increase in its value shall remain in the ownership of the person who created or acquired or was given or who inherited that property (hereinafter "post-marital separate property")

   2.3 Any asset owned jointly by the parties as at the date of the marriage or acquired or purchased by them jointly at a later date with an initial value in excess of £5,000 shall be held by them in accordance with their respective financial contributions and no presumption of advancement shall apply

   2.4 Any asset acquired by the parties with an initial value of less than £5,000 shall be deemed to be held in equal shares and upon the death of either shall pass to the survivor

3. In the event of the dissolution or annulment of the marriage:

   3.1 Save as provided for at 3.2 below and subject to 3.3, Eleanor and William shall each retain their pre-marital and post-marital separate property and their respective shares in any jointly owned property (in accordance with 2 above)

   3.2 All jointly owned wedding presents shall remain the property of the party whose family or friends gave the present

   3.3 In the event that at date of decree nisi any child born to or adopted by the parties has not yet attained the age of 18, the terms of this Deed shall be varied so that the provision which might be made under Schedule 1 Children Act 1989 may be made upon the claim of either party in the event that his or her other resources fell short of that level and such a claim is otherwise justified

3.4 Neither party shall make any application to a court for an order for financial provision of any kind (income or capital), save in so far as may be required to give effect the terms of this agreement

3.5 Eleanor and William agree to incorporate the terms of this Deed so far as may be relevant into a consent order of the court immediately following pronouncement of decree nisi

3.6 In the event that either Eleanor or William make any application to any court of whatever jurisdiction for financial provision other than by way of a consent order to reflect the terms and provisions of this Deed in full, they agree that the court should take fully into account the terms of this Deed

4. Nothing contained within this Deed shall preclude either Eleanor or William from voluntarily making lifetime gifts to the other from voluntarily making provision for the other by will codicil trust or otherwise. Such voluntary provision shall not be construed as a waiver of any provision of this Deed or as evidence that there is or was any agreement or understanding between and Eleanor and William otherwise that is specifically contained within this Deed

5. Any variation of amendment of this Deed shall only be effective if recorded in a supplemental deed in writing executed by both parties and complying with the provisions of the Law of Property (Miscellaneous Provisions) Act 1989

6. This Deed contains the whole agreement between Eleanor and William and neither of them has entered into it on the basis of any promises or representations which are not expressly included in it

7. The invalidity or unenforceability of any provision of this Deed will not affect the validity or enforceability of any other provision of this Deed and any invalid or unenforceable provision shall be severable

8. Any dispute arising out of this Deed shall in the first instance be referred to an accredited family mediator

9. This Deed shall be governed by and construed in accordance with the laws of England and Wales

10. Eleanor and William shall pay the costs of and incidental to this agreement equally

IN WITNESS whereof the parties hereto have executed this instrument as a Deed on the date first before written

SIGNED as a DEED by:

# Precedent number 5 – 'The Businessman'

Your brief

> You are instructed by Philip K (aged 60) who is engaged to be married to Hannah T (aged 22).
>
> Philip and Hannah have been in a relationship for c six months and have recently found out that Hannah is pregnant. They intend to marry in six weeks' time.
>
> Philip has been married three times before and has five children from these marriages all of whom he continues to support financially.
>
> Philip is a multi-millionaire with business interests in the UK, the UAE, South Africa and Chicago.
>
> He has recently purchased a substantial property in Notting Hill where it is intended that he and Hannah will live following their marriage.
>
> Hannah works part-time as a model. She has no capital resources of any significance.
>
> Philip has no desire to give detailed disclosure of his assets. He believes Hannah will accept this.
>
> His proposal is that following their marriage he will transfer the Notting Hill property into their joint names and that in the event of a divorce, this (and any other subsequently acquired joint property) would be divided equally, in addition to which he would pay Hannah a lump sum for capitalised maintenance, to be calculated in accordance with her reasonable needs.
>
> Philip wishes to include a confidentiality clause within the agreement.

THIS DEED is made on the 4th day of March 2011

BETWEEN:

(1) **PHILIP K** of 100 Holland Park Avenue, London (hereafter referred to as "**Philip**")

and

(2) **HANNAH T** of 100 Holland Park Avenue, London (hereafter referred to as "**Hannah**")

WHEREAS:

A. This Deed is made in contemplation of and is conditional upon the celebration of the intended marriage of Philip and Hannah on 16 April 2011.

B. Philip and Hannah have had discussions about their financial circumstances and the financial consequences of their proposed marriage. They have also discussed its possible breakdown and the manner in which their assets should be divided in this unfortunate event.

C. Philip and Hannah wish to enter into this Deed recording their wishes and intentions regarding finances and property and each wishes their future rights and obligations arising from their intended marriage to be governed solely by this Deed.

D. Philip and Hannah intend to create legal relations and be bound by the terms of this Deed.

E. Philip and Hannah intend that this Deed shall be binding on their heirs, receivers, trustees and personal representatives.

F. Philip and Hannah have each received independent legal advice from freely chosen legal advisers specialising in matrimonial law in respect of the nature and effect of the terms of this Deed.

G. It is recorded that although Philip has paid for both parties' legal advice he has not sought to influence Hannah's legal advisers or prevent them from giving objective of independent advice.

H. Philip (born on 1 January 1951) is a British citizen and is domiciled and resident in England and Wales.

I. Hannah (born on 10 November 1988) is a British citizen and is domiciled and resident in England and Wales.

J. Philip has been married three times before. He has five children currently under the age of 18 for whom he is committed to making ongoing financial provision during their minority. Hannah has never been married before.

K. Hannah is pregnant with Philip's child, due to be born on or around 5 September 2011.

L. Hannah has no other children.

M. Philip and Hannah intend to cohabit at 100 Holland Park Avenue following their marriage.

N. Philip is a businessman. He has extensive commercial and property interests in the United Kingdom, the United Arab Emirates, South Africa and Chicago.

O. Hannah is a part-time model. She has no significant property resources.

P. Philip and Hannah have made disclosure to each other of the substance of their current assets in broad terms and the same are summarised respectively in Annex A and Annex B to this Deed.

Q. Philip and Hannah each acknowledge and agree that that they have sufficient knowledge of each other's financial affairs so as to determine the fairness or otherwise of the proposed settlement.

R. In particular, Hannah acknowledges and accepts that

   a. Philip is committed to the ongoing support of his children from his previous relationships which support is likely to continue beyond their attaining the age of 18

   b. Philip is a man of substantial wealth all of which has been acquired by his own endeavours prior to the commencement of their relationship

   c. Although she has been advised of the 'sharing' principle usually applicable in ancillary relief proceedings, she would not consider it fair to share in Philip's separate property nor any property acquired by him after the marriage through his own endeavours or by way of inheritance or gift nor his future income, save so far as would be necessary to provide for her reasonable needs as the mother of his child (or children).

S. For his part Philip recognises and accepts

   a. That the needs of their child, and any further children born to them or adopted by them, should be provided for by him at a level commensurate with his own standard of living and that of his children from previous relationships.

b. That Hannah's needs (for capital and income) in the event of a dissolution or annulment of their marriage should be met by him at a level which recognises his financial position, at the very minimum, for so long as she remains the carer of any of their children under the age of 18.

T. Philip and Hannah each agree not to claim at any time in the future that their failure to obtain additional information or seek specialist advice in all appropriate jurisdictions shall be a bar to the enforcement of the terms of this Deed.

U. As at the date of the marriage, Philip and Hannah do not own any asset that has been acquired by way of joint endeavour. All of the assets referred to at Annexes A and B hereto (hereinafter "separate property") have been acquired independently of and without contribution from the other party.

V. Save as expressly provided for in this Deed, Philip and Hannah intend that their respective separate property shall remain in that party's absolute beneficial ownership and shall be free from any claim charge or encumbrance by the other party during the marriage and thereafter.

W. Philip and Hannah are each entering into the terms of this Deed freely and voluntarily without coercion influence or pressure from any kind from the other or from circumstances or otherwise.

X. Philip and Hannah are each aware and acknowledge, having been so advised, that under the laws of England and Wales it is not possible as at the date of this agreement to exclude the jurisdiction of the courts to make orders under the Matrimonial Causes Act 1973.

Y. Philip and Hannah each understand the nature and effect of this Deed, the rights that they are each surrendering as a result of this Deed and that the provision it makes is not necessarily reflective of the provision which might otherwise be made for them or either of them by a court following the dissolution or annulment of their marriage.

Z. Philip and Hannah agree and accept that the provisions of this agreement are regarded by them as fair just and reasonable at the date of this Deed.

AA. Philip and Hannah agree and acknowledge that they would not be entering into this marriage without this Deed.

BB. Philip and Hannah agree to execute wills in contemplation of their forthcoming marriage so as to reflect the distribution of their assets provided for in this Deed.

CC. In the event that the marriage is terminated by the death of either Philip or Hannah, they agree the provision made by this Deed constitutes reasonable financial provision for the purposes of the Inheritance (Provision for Family Dependants) Act 1975 and any succeeding analogous legislation.

DD. Philip and Hannah agree and acknowledge that this agreement is being entered into sufficient time prior to their marriage for advice and reflection and that they have each given full consideration to the content and effect of this Deed and the consequences of entering into it.

EE. Philip and Hannah expect and intend this Deed to be binding on them throughout the world where so ever they reside.

THIS DEED WITNESSES:

1. This Deed shall become operative upon Philip and Hannah celebrating a valid ceremony of marriage whether on 16 April 2011 or at any later date

2. Philip and Hannah acknowledge that they have given and received information which is confidential and they agree that that neither of them will: -

   2.1 Reveal to any third (excluding any person to whom it is necessary to disclose relevant parts of this agreement for the purposes of implementation or professional advice or to any competent Court) the terms of this Deed or any of the financial particulars disclosed during the course of its preparation

   2.2 Cause or permit publication by the press or other media of the said terms or particulars

   2.3 Take any steps as a result of which the said terms or particulars are likely to become public knowledge or are reasonably foreseeable as being likely to become public knowledge

   2.4 Fail to take any steps which either party may reasonably be expected to take to prevent the said terms or particulars from becoming public knowledge in circumstances in which they would otherwise be likely to do so

3. Save where specifically provided for in this Deed

3.1 Philip and Hannah's separate property (as defined at U above) and any income derived from it and any increase in its value shall remain in that party's absolute beneficial interest during the marriage and thereafter in that it shall be free from all claim charge and encumbrance of the other party

3.2 Any asset acquired during the marriage by Philip or Hannah, whether created by its owner or acquired by purchase, gift or inheritance or otherwise and any income derived from it and increase in its value shall remain in the ownership of the person who created or acquired or was given or who inherited that property

3.3 Any asset acquired by the parties jointly during the marriage shall be held by them in accordance their formal legal ownership (hereinafter "marital property")

4. Philip agrees to transfer the matrimonial home at 100 Holland Park Avenue in the names of himself and Hannah as joint tenants in law and in equity within 28 days of the marriage

5. In the event of the dissolution or annulment of the marriage:

5.1 Save as provided for in clauses 5.2 and 5.3 below, Philip and Hannah's separate property shall remain in their respective separate beneficial ownership free from any claim by the other

5.2 All marital property (to include the matrimonial home at 100 Holland Property or any further or alternative matrimonial home purchased by the parties on the same terms) shall be distributed between parties in accordance with formal legal ownership.

5.3 Philip will pay to Hannah a lump sum by way of capitalised maintenance, to be calculated in accordance with the 'Duxbury' tables as an amortizing fund. The quantum and term of the underlying maintenance payments shall be agreed between the parties at the time, or in default of agreement determined by the Court as a discrete issue, having regard primarily to:

5.3.1 Hannah's reasonable needs

5.3.2 Hannah's own resources and ability to become financially independent

5.3.3 Hannah's acceptance at R above that it would be unfair for her to share in any part of Philip's future income beyond what we necessary to meet her reasonable needs

5.4 Philip and Hannah agree to incorporate the terms of this Deed so far as may be relevant into a consent order of the court immediately following pronouncement of decree nisi

5.5 In the event that either Philip or Hannah make any application to any court of whatever jurisdiction for financial provision other than by way of a consent order to reflect the terms and provisions of this Deed in full, they agree that the Court should take fully into account the terms of this Deed

6. Nothing contained within this Deed shall preclude either Philip or Hannah from voluntarily making lifetime gifts to the other from voluntarily making provision for the other by will codicil trust or otherwise. Such voluntary provision shall not be construed as a waiver of any provision of this Deed or as evidence that there is or was any agreement or understanding between and Philip and Hannah otherwise that is specifically contained within this Deed

7. Any variation of amendment of this Deed shall only be effective if recorded in a supplemental deed in writing executed by both parties and complying with the provisions of the Law of Property (Miscellaneous Provisions) Act 1989

8. This Deed contains the whole agreement between Philip and Hannah and neither of them has entered into it on the basis of any promises or representations which are not expressly included in it

9. The invalidity or unenforceability of any provision of this Deed will not affect the validity or enforceability of any other provision of this Deed and any invalid or unenforceable provision shall be severable

10. Any dispute arising out of this Deed shall in the first instance be referred to an accredited family mediator

11. This Deed shall be governed by and construed in accordance with the laws of England and Wales

12. Philip shall pay the costs of and incidental to this agreement

IN WITNESS whereof the parties hereto have executed this instrument as a Deed on the date first before written

SIGNED as a DEED by:

# Appendix A

# Case Digest

This digest summarises, in chronological order, the principal authorities that deal with both pre and post nuptial agreements. In many of these cases one party has tried to enforce, and the other has sought to renege upon, agreed terms for division of their assets and financial support upon the breakdown of their marriage. In the context of these cases 'prenuptial agreement' means an agreement concluded prior to a marriage ceremony and 'post nuptial agreement' means one concluded after the parties have married.

## *Hyman v Hyman* [1929] AC 601 (House of Lords, April 1929)

### *Summary*

The wife sought an increase in the provision to which she had agreed in a post nuptial agreement. The husband opposed. The wife succeeded.

### *Digest*

The husband and wife married in 1912. They separated in 1919. They entered into an agreement under which the husband covenanted to pay the wife £20.00 per week. The wife covenanted not to take proceedings to compel the husband to allow alimony or maintenance beyond that level.

In 1927 the wife petitioned for divorce and a decree nisi was granted which was subsequently made absolute. The wife petitioned for further maintenance which application the husband resisted on the basis of the wife's covenant in the 1919 separation deed. At first instance the court held that the wife was not, by reason of her covenant, prevented from presenting the petition for increased maintenance. The husband appealed to the Court of Appeal. Three out of the five-judge Court of Appeal held that the wife was not bound by her covenant but was free to take proceedings for permanent maintenance. Two of the Court of Appeal judges considered the wife should be bound by her covenant and not entitled to seek maintenance.

The husband appealed further to the House of Lords. His appeal was unanimously dismissed. The Lord Chancellor, Lord Hailsham said, at page 608, that:

> "I am prepared to hold that the parties cannot validly make an agreement either:
>
> 1. not to invoke the jurisdiction of the Court Order, or
> 2. to control the powers of the Court when its jurisdiction is invoked."

The wife's legal team (two KCs and two juniors) were not even called upon.

## *Wright v Wright* [1970] 3 All ER 209 (Court of Appeal, March 1970)

### *Summary*

The wife sought an increase in the provision to which she had agreed as part of a compromise to defended divorce proceedings. The husband opposed. The wife failed and was held to her agreement.

### *Digest*

As part of the terms upon which a defended divorce was compromised the wife indicated that it was her

> "present intention not to apply for further maintenance, unless there is any unforeseen circumstance making it impossible for her to work at all or otherwise to maintain herself."

The wife subsequently applied for maintenance. The Court of Appeal found that, although the agreement could not deprive the court of its right to review the question of maintenance, nor should the agreement be construed so strictly as to forbid any possible award of maintenance, in the current circumstances, the wife was not entitled to apply for maintenance. It held her to her agreement, Sir Gordon Wilmer saying, at page 214:

> "that the existence of this agreement, having regard to the circumstances in which it was arrived at, at least makes it necessary for the wife, if she wants to justify an award of maintenance, to offer

> prima facie proof that there have been unforeseen circumstances, in the true sense, which make it impossible for her to work or otherwise maintain herself."

## *Brockwell v Brockwell* [1975] Court of Appeal Transcript 468

### *Summary*

The wife sought to resile from her agreement on divorce to give up all her interest in the matrimonial home. She subsequently sought provision under Section 17 of the Married Women's Property Act 1882 and under Sections 23 and 24 of the Matrimonial Causes Act 1973. Both applications were dismissed at first instance. The Court of Appeal dismissed the wife's claim under the Married Women's Property Act but allowed her appeal on her Matrimonial Causes Act claims to the extent of ordering a re-trial

### *Digest*

The Court of Appeal accepted that where there was an agreement entered into with full knowledge and with the advantage of the advice of both parties' legal advisers it was something to which considerable attention should be paid by the court. This was all the more so where, as here, one party had done all that was required by him pursuant to the agreement. Nevertheless, the court decided that the wife should have the opportunity to show that, notwithstanding the agreement, it should exercise its discretion in her favour to award a lump sum payment.

Ormrod LJ further considered that:

> "the agreement was a very important piece of conduct under Section 25 of the 1973 Act, because what the Court was required to arrive at eventually was such an order as would be just and practicable having regard, among other things to the conduct of the parties; clearly when people made an agreement like this, it was a very important factor in considering what should be the just outcome of the proceedings".

## *Dean v Dean* [1978] Fam 161

### *Summary*

The parties agreed financial terms. Negotiations started before issue of proceedings but agreement was concluded after issue. The wife sought to renege. The husband succeeded in keeping her to the agreement.

***Digest***

Following negotiations between the respective solicitors, agreement was reached on the wife's financial provision. Each party signed a copy of the draft minutes of the agreement. The agreement was headed: "Draft minutes of order to be submitted for approval by a registrar with a view to incorporation in the order made on decree nisi." The husband filed a petition for divorce on the basis of the wife's adultery. The wife sought to resile from the agreement.

Both parties accepted that whilst there had been no disclosure, the agreement was reached upon an arm's length basis, with both parties represented by solicitors and without improper pressure either way.

At paragraph 165 Bush J set out the following:

> "On the authority of Smallman v Smallman [1972] Fam. 25 the agreement is binding on the parties unless and until it is not approved by the court. Lord Denning M.R. said, at p. 31:

'It is very common for agreements to be made in divorce proceedings "subject to the approval of the court." This has been so ever since the enactment of the Matrimonial Causes Act 1963 (now section 5 of the Matrimonial Causes Act 1965) which validates a bargain which represents an honest negotiation between the parties provided it is disclosed to the court. In Nash v Nash [1965] P 266, 277, Scarman J. said that it was in these days quite proper to come to an agreement which is intended to make reasonable provision for the parties: …'

Lord Denning M.R. quoted Scarman J. in Nash v. Nash and went on:

'Since the Divorce Reform Act 1969 also it is common for agreements to be made "subject to the approval of the court" and to seek the opinion of the court under section 7 as to the reasonableness of them. In my opinion, if the parties have reached an agreement on all essential matters, then the clause "subject to the approval of the court" does not mean there is no agreement at all. There is an agreement, but the operation of it is suspended until the court approves it. It is the duty of one party or the other to bring the agreement before the court for approval. If the court approves it, it is binding on the parties. If the court does not approve, it is not binding.'

Bush J held the wife to the agreement saying that in performing its duty under Section 25, where there was an agreement between the parties it should adopt the broad rather than the particular approach; whilst it had a duty under Section 25 it also owed a duty to uphold agreements, especially where made between parties at arm's length, negotiated by legal advisers, where there had been no change of circumstances, and which were not against public policy.

Accordingly, in all the circumstances, Bush J found that reasonable provision had been made for the wife and she should be held to her bargain and at page 173.

> "Indeed, it would be unconscionable in my view not to hold her to her agreement."

## *Edgar v Edgar* [1980] 1 W.L.R. 1410 (Court of Appeal, July 1980)

### *Summary*

The wife sought lump sum in divorce proceedings following an agreement in which she agreed not to claim. The husband opposed. The wife was held to her bargain.

### *Digest*

The husband and wife executed a deed of separation in April 1976, which was negotiated by the parties with the benefit of solicitors' advice. The husband was a multi-millionaire. The wife agreed not to seek a capital payment.

She subsequently petitioned for divorce in 1980 when she claimed a capital payment. At first instance the husband was ordered to make the wife a lump sum capital payment of £670,000. The husband appealed to the Court of Appeal where he succeeded. Whilst the Court indicated this was a "wholly exceptional case on the facts" it decided that the parties should be kept to their agreement.

At the bottom of page 1416, Ormrod LJ, with whose judgment Oliver LJ agreed, referred to what he had said in *Brockwell*, namely

> "that an agreement not to claim a lump sum should be taken into account under the heading of conduct and added 'when people make an agreement like that it is a very important factor in considering what is the just outcome of the proceedings'. I see no reason to resile from that statement."

He went on to say at 1417C:

> "To decide what weight should be given in order to reach a just result, to a prior agreement not to claim a lump sum, regard must be had to the conduct of both parties, leading up to the prior agreement, and to their subsequent conduct, in consequence of it. It is not necessary in this connection to think in formal legal terms, such as misrepresentation or estoppel, all the circumstances as they affect each of two human beings must be considered, in the complex relationship of marriage. So, the circumstances surrounding the making of the agreement are relevant. Undue pressure by one side, exploitation of a dominant position to secure an unreasonable advantage, inadequate knowledge, possibly bad legal advice, an important change of circumstances, unforeseen or overlooked at the time of making the agreement, are all relevant to the question of justice between the parties. Important too is the general proposition that, formal agreements, properly and fairly arrived at with competent legal advice, should not be displaced unless there are good and substantial grounds for concluding that an injustice will be done by holding the parties to the terms of their agreement. There may well be other considerations which affect the justice of this case; the above list is not intended to be an exclusive catalogue."

Oliver LJ said, at page 1420:

> "Men and women of full age, education and understanding, acting with competent advice available to them, must be assumed to know and appreciate what they are doing and their actual respective bargaining strengths will in fact depend in every case upon a subjective evaluation of their motives for doing it."

Further on, at page 1424, he said:

> "… in a consideration of what is just to be done in the exercise of the court's powers under the Act of 1973 in the light of the conduct of the parties, the court must, I think, start from the position that a solemn and freely negotiated bargain by which a party defines her own requirements ought to be adhered to unless some clear and compelling reason, such as for instance, a drastic change of circumstances, is shown to the contrary."

En passant it is worthy of note that at the end of page 1419 Ormrod LJ said:

> "This court has not yet had occasion to consider the application of the principles of section 25 to cases involving very rich people."

## *Camm v Camm* (1983) 4 FLR 577 (Court of Appeal, December 1982)

### *Summary*

The wife applied for periodical payments having agreed, following breakdown, to forego them. The husband opposed. The wife succeeded and was awarded periodical payments

### *Digest*

The parties agreed, in July 1975, prior to divorce that the matrimonial home would be sold with a new house being purchased from the proceeds for the wife and the children. The husband agreed to make periodical payments to the children. Both parties agreed not to make any future financial claims.

The parties divorced in December 1975. In 1980 the wife applied for periodical payments for herself.

The Court of Appeal allowed the wife's appeal for an increase in the provision allowed for her by both the Registrar and the judge. All three courts held that it would be unfair and unjust to hold that the wife should be bound to the 1975 agreement. The Court of Appeal addressed the principles applicable to the situation where a party had agreed not to ask for periodical payments. Sir Roger Ormrod set out the principles which are worth quoting at length:

> "The principles of law, I think, are perfectly clearly understood and they are common ground in this court. At least since the time of *Hyman v Hyman* [1929] AC 601, it has been established that the parties to divorce proceedings cannot bind the court by any contractual arrangement which has been made between themselves and cannot, therefore, oust the jurisdiction of the court which is conferred by the relevant statute. The principle of that case has been consistently followed thereafter and it is common ground that the court here has jurisdiction to entertain the wife's claim. As it has jurisdiction it has to exercise its jurisdiction in accordance with the prevailing statutory provisions which are s. 25 of the Matrimonial Causes Act 1973. But the problem arises – and it was recognized in *Hyman v Hyman* and has been recognized in all subsequent cases – as to what weight to give in any particular case to the fact that an agreement was entered into by the parties themselves under which the wife would not seek

periodical payments for herself. It has been stressed all through those same cases that the court must attach considerable importance, the amount of importance varying from case to case, to the fact that there was an agreement, because the court, naturally, will not lightly permit parties who have made a contractual agreement between themselves, even if it is not legally enforceable, to depart from that contractual agreement unless some good reason is shown.

I suggested some time ago in the case of *Brockwell v Brockwell* (unreported) [1975] CAT 468, that the right way to approach these cases now was to regard the fact of entering into a contractual arrangement as part of the conduct which was to be taken into account in arriving at a just result under the latter part of s. 25. That seems a convenient way of approaching the problem in any event. But it is much more difficult in practice than in theory to decide what weight to give to the fact of this agreement having been entered into.

The judge, perhaps a little reluctantly, came to the conclusion that this was not a case in which the wife should be held to her agreement and, therefore, not a case in which to reject her application for periodical payments altogether. That left him with a further difficult problem of evaluating the whole history of the case and all the circumstances in order to arrive at a figure which would be just between the parties. No question of practicability arises in this case.

The judge decided in the end to make the order, as I have indicated, in the sum of £900 for the wife, and he also substantially increased the existing interim order in favour of the children, putting them up to the maximum of the tax-free level. He increased the available income to the wife quite appreciably because the order had been for about £1,000 a year for each child; so he, in effect, gave the wife about an extra £2,000.

This problem was considered by the court in some depth in the case of *Edgar v Edgar* (1981) 2 FLR 19 to which we have been referred, and I do not think any useful purpose will be served in this judgment by repeating what I and Oliver LJ said in giving judgment in that case. In view of one observation by the judge, perhaps I should say that I do not wish to resile from one phrase, on p. 25, where I set out some of the matters which the court must take into account in evaluating the importance of the 'contract'. I said there:

'Undue pressure by one side, exploitation of a dominant position to secure an unreasonable advantage, inadequate knowledge' [then the phrase] 'possibly bad legal advice, and important change of circumstances, unforeseen or overlooked at the time of making the agreement, are all relevant to the question of justice between the parties.'

And I made it clear that that was not, of course, an exclusive list. I still think it was right to refer to bad legal advice, although in that passage I was not thinking in terms of negligence by the solicitor. The unfortunate fact in this case was that the hearing below was occupied to a considerable extent in questioning the wife's solicitor, who is himself the defendant in a pending action for negligence which may or may not be proceeded with. In that passage I certainly was not thinking in terms of negligence: I was thinking in terms of exactly what I said, 'bad legal advice', and we are all familiar with cases in which parties are badly advised. That is to say, it is not necessarily negligent advice to take a course or permit a client to take a course which a more experienced, or a stronger minded legal adviser would have discouraged. It seems to me plain if one compares the facts of this case with the facts in *Edgar v Edgar* that the quality of legal advice on which parties act is of some relevance to the justice of the case. In *Edgar v Edgar* the wife was fully legally advised, and strongly advised not to enter into the deed of separation containing a particular clause which limited her capital thereafter; but nonetheless, she went ahead. In this case there was very much less clear legal advice by her solicitor and the whole matter was dealt with, obviously, on quite a different level. In *Edgar v Edgar* the whole thing was formally negotiated between solicitors for a period of months, and there could have been no possible misunderstanding or shadow of a doubt in the mind of the wife when she elected to ignore the legal advice she had been given. In this case there is no question, I think, of the wife ignoring any legal advice. It is said that she was told, somehow, that the effect of entering into this agreement might deprive her of all future maintenance but, like Mr Thorpe, I would have expected that at least she would have been required by her solicitor to sign a document which would make it absolutely clear that she knew what she was doing. I think the quality of legal advice is relevant on the issue of justice, but not in terms of

> negligence actions. That is the situation, so far as the wife is concerned, with which we now have to deal."

## *Smith v McInerney* [1994] 2 FLR 1077 (June 1994)

### *Summary*

The parties agreed separation terms before divorce. The husband sought to renege upon agreed financial terms. He succeeded at first instance but the wife succeeded on appeal.

### *Digest*

The parties were married for seventeen years. Under the terms of a separation agreement drawn up by solicitors the husband agreed to transfer his share of the matrimonial home to the wife. He was released from any further liability to the wife and children. Upon his subsequent redundancy he applied for a property adjustment and lump sum order.

At first instance he was granted a charge of 35 per cent of the former matrimonial home. This was overturned on appeal when the husband's claim was dismissed.

Thorpe J said, at page 1081, that:

> "As a matter of general policy I think it is very important that what the parties themselves agree at the time of separation should be upheld by the courts unless there are overwhelmingly strong considerations for interference."

He also said, at page 1080:

> "the decision of the Court of Appeal in *Camm v Camm* (1983) 4 FLR 577, (but that) was a truly exceptional case and is, so far as I know, the only case in the Court of Appeal post-*Edgar v Edgar* in which an applicant has been allowed more than he or she contracted for".

## F v F (Ancillary Relief: Substantial Assets) [1995] 2 FLR 45 (October 1994)

### *Summary*

This is the first reported case which mentions a prenuptial agreement. The wife agreed limited provision in a German prenuptial agreement. Following breakdown the wife sought increased provision which the husband opposed. The wife was not held to agreement.

***Digest***

The parties were of German origin. At the time of divorce the husband was 50 and the wife 36. They had been married for eleven years. The husband said he had capital assets of not less than £150 million.

Prior to the marriage prenuptial contracts were executed, the primary one in Germany regulating arrangements in accordance with German and Swiss Law and a second one in England intended to be governed by American Law. The parties had three children.

Thorpe J dealt with the position in relation to the prenuptial agreements, at page 66, as follows:

> "The other special condition which has to be considered in this case, albeit briefly, is the existence of the antenuptial contracts. It is not in dispute that contracts of this sort are common place in the society from which the parties come. They are much emphasised by the husband in his affidavits, since if strictly applied they would have the ridiculous result of confining the wife to the pension of a German judge, whatever that may be. Equally, in the affidavits the wife is urgent in protesting the circumstances in which they came to be signed. I regard the protestations of both in relation to these contracts as having an urgency that the documents themselves do not demand. In this jurisdiction they must be of very limited significance. The rights and responsibilities of those whose financial affairs are regulated by statute cannot be much influenced by contractual terms which were devised for the control and limitation of standards that are intended to be of universal application throughout our society. It is said that these contracts would be strictly enforced against the wife in Germany. I have declined to enlarge the arena to allow evidence from German experts in that field. I cannot think that even in Germany the wife would not have the right to deploy a case either that there was some inequality of bargaining power, alternatively undue influence, or that they are inconsistent with social policy in Germany. For the purposes of my determination I do not attach any significant weight to those contracts."

## N v N (Foreign Divorce: Financial Relief) [1997] 1 FLR 900 (December 1996)

### *Summary*

The parties entered into a prenuptial agreement in Sweden. The husband sought provision. The case was effectively remitted to Sweden.

### *Digest*

This was a case in which Swedish nationals had executed a prenuptial agreement prior to their marriage. The agreement was entered into in Stockholm and the parties then married at the Swedish Embassy in Paris.

They were divorced in 1993 by agreement in Stockholm. In 1996 the husband issued proceedings seeking financial provision in England, the wife having moved to London.

Cazalet J. considered that the prenuptial agreement had a bearing on the case. The husband's application for ancillary relief was in fact dismissed.

Although Cazalet J. did not need to rule on the enforceability or relevance of the prenuptial agreement he said, *per curiam*, at pages 912/913 as follows:

> "Furthermore the Swedish Court, in my view, is the appropriate court in which to decide the effect of the prenuptial agreement. It would be binding in Sweden as against being no more than a material consideration in this court under Section 25 of the Matrimonial Causes Act 1973. Indeed, by coming to this court, the husband may obtain an advantage in that the court here in considering its award can step outside the constriction of the prenuptial agreement and may grant the husband more than his entitlement under Swiss law by taking into consideration the wife's overall assets, including her inheritance from her father, a matter expressly excluded from the husband's reach by the prenuptial agreement."

## S v S (Divorce: Staying Proceedings) [1997] 2 FLR 100 (March 1997)

### *Summary*

A prenuptial agreement was concluded in New York. The wife tried to seek relief in England. She failed and her claim was effectively remitted to New York.

***Digest***

The husband and wife met in 1983. The husband had been twice married and wife once. The husband was not prepared to marry again without the protection for him and his children of a prenuptial agreement. The wife conceded as she knew he would not marry her without such an agreement.

A prenuptial agreement was executed. The parties were advised by independent New York based lawyers. Wilson J. found that the wife's evidence, that the prenuptial agreement was never fully explained to her, was "not very convincing".

Wilson J. also found that:

> "there is no doubt that the wife would undergo a period of painful adjustment in creating her future life upon assets of perhaps little more than £1m"

if she were confined to the provision under the Agreement. Whilst there was a dispute as to the value of the husband's assets his evidence was that:

> "he and trusts set up by him own shares currently worth only $84m. Additionally there are, at least, the real properties and the chattels".

The wife issued proceedings in England on 15 November 1996. The husband issued proceedings in New York on 21 November 1996 and subsequently applied for a stay of the wife's English proceedings.

After a hearing of about five days (Wilson J. said "... at times I wondered whether I was allowing it to proceed for too long") he held that the wife's English proceedings should be stayed because New York was

> "clearly more appropriate than England as a forum for the proceedings for divorce and for the determination of financial issues between the parties".

Wilson J. indicated, at page 114, that:

> "but the provisions of the prenuptial agreement, both the substantive financial provisions and in particular the provisions as to forum, have weighed heavily with me. Even if (which I doubt) this agreement were to be of limited significance in any substantive analysis by this court of the wife's financial claims pursuant to Section 25 of the 1973 Act, it in no way follows that it must be of very limited significance in the despatch of the current application. Fairness requires otherwise".

Wilson J. also indicated, at page 102, as follows:

> "I am aware of a growing belief that, in the despatch of a claim for ancillary relief in this jurisdiction, no significant weight will be afforded to a prenuptial agreement whatever the circumstances. I would like to sound a cautionary note in that respect. No-one could have more profound respect than I for the observations of Thorpe LJ. In *F v F (Ancillary Relief: Substantial Assets)* [1995] 2 FLR45, 66G he said:

'In this jurisdiction [prenuptial agreements] must be of very limited significance. The rights and responsibilities of those whose financial affairs are regulated by statute cannot be much influenced by contractual terms which were devised for the control and limitation of standards that are intended to be of universal application throughout our society.'

> There is a danger that these wide words might be taken out of context. There is no doubt that, where the English court proceeds to determine an application for ancillary relief, Section 25 of the 1973 Act precludes any choice of foreign law, however vividly circumstances of the case might protest its relevance. So the application is of English law and under Section 25(1) regard must be had to all the circumstances of the case. In *F v F* itself, the results of a strict application of the effect of the prenuptial agreements would have been, as the judge said, 'ridiculous'. In those circumstances they inevitably constituted circumstances of negligible significance. But there will come a case – were I to refuse a stay, might this be it? – where the circumstances surrounding the prenuptial agreement and the provision therein contained might, when viewed in the context of other circumstances of the case, prove influential or even crucial. Where other jurisdictions, both in the USA and in the European Union, have been persuaded that there are cases where justice can only be served by confining parties to their rights under prenuptial agreements, we should be cautious about too categorically asserting the contrary. I can find nothing in Section 25 to compel a conclusion, so much at odds with personal freedoms to make arrangements for ourselves, that escape from solemn bargains, carefully struck by informed adults, is readily available here. It all depends.
>
> The matter must be left open and on the footing that, were she to be enabled to claim ancillary relief in England, the wife *might* secure an award of substantial further provision. In what follows

my duty is to appraise the relevance of the prenuptial agreement to the determination not of the wife's potential application of ancillary relief but of the entirely different issue as to forum".

## N v N (Divorce: Ante-Nuptial Agreement) [1999] 2 FCR 582 (July 1999)

### *Summary*

The provisions in a prenuptial agreement for the husband to apply for a Get were not enforced by the court.

### *Digest*

The husband and wife were Orthodox Jews who entered into an ante-nuptial agreement. This was made three weeks before they married and contained provisions that would have effect in the event of the breakdown of their marriage. Inter alia it recorded that neither party would make any financial claims of any kind on the other. Any dispute would be determined by the Court of the Chief Rabbi, the London Beth Din, and both parties would comply with instructions of the Beth Din. The wife complained to the court that the husband did not comply with the Beth Din's instructions because he took no steps to procure the writing of a Get.

Wall J. indicated, at page 590, that three questions arose:-

1. Are ante-nuptial agreements as a class specifically enforceable?
2. If the answer to the first question is no are particular and severable clauses of an otherwise unenforceable ante-nuptial agreement specifically enforceable?
3. If the answer to 1 and 2 is no in each case, can an ante-nuptial agreement or particular clauses in an ante-nuptial agreement be enforced by other means?

In his judgment Wall J. answered each of these questions at pages 590–595 and in doing so provided a useful analysis of the law as it then stood.

In response to the first question Wall J. said at the foot of page 593

"Leading Counsel for the wife did not cite to me any case in which an ante-nuptial agreement had been specifically enforced. The reason he was unable to do so, in my judgment, is that there is no

> such case and that, as a class, ante-nuptial agreements are not specifically enforceable in English law".

As regards the second question Wall J. referred to the provision in the agreement that the invalidity or unenforceability of any provision of the deed "shall not affect the validity or unenforceability of any other provision and any invalid or unenforceable provision will be severable".

He said

> "even if one divides up the ante-nuptial agreement in this case, and looks at the individual clauses separately, one cannot, in my judgment, avoid the fundamental proposition that each is part of an agreement entered into before marriage to regulate the parties' affairs in the event of divorce. The public policy argument, therefore continues to apply".

As regards the third question Wall J. concluded that in the particular circumstances of the case the clauses could not be enforced by other means. He said

> "it follows therefore, despite the fact that I reach the conclusion with considerable reluctance, that the wife's Summons must be dismissed".

## C v C (Divorce: Stay of English Proceedings) [2001] 1 FLR 694 (May 2000)

### *Summary*

French nationals executed a prenuptial agreement in France. The wife attempted to litigate in England. The matter was effectively remitted to France.

### *Digest*

The husband and wife are both French nationals. They had entered into a prenuptial agreement under French law executed on the day of their marriage. They had also executed mutual wills in France reaffirming the prenuptial agreement.

Following marriage breakdown the wife issued divorce proceedings in England and the husband issued divorce proceedings in France. The husband applied for a stay of the wife's English divorce proceedings.

The prenuptial agreement was executed in circumstances of formality before a notary. It was the notary's duty to ensure both parties understood the significance of the document. The wife said she did not truly understand the significance of what she was signing and that the notary failed to perform his duty of ensuring that she did. Johnson J. was not asked to hear oral evidence relating to that issue but he said:

> "it seems to me to be doubtful, to say the least, that the wife's account of that is correct".

Johnson J granted the husband's application for a stay of the wife's English proceedings. He considered that under Section 5(6) of the Domicile and Matrimonial Proceedings Act 1973 the balance of fairness was in the issues between the parties being resolved in the French courts.

One of two particular factors that weighed heavily in his balancing exercise was the

> "positive and joint decision to execute the pre-marital contract in France according to French law in terms which envisaged issues, such as those presently arising being resolved according to the French Civil Code."

## *M v M* (*Pre-nuptial Agreement*) [2002] 1FLR 654 (19 July 2001)

### *Summary*

The parties executed a prenuptial agreement in Canada. The wife reneged and sought additional provision. The wife succeeded – she was awarded more but the prenuptial agreement was partially effective.

### *Digest*

The husband and wife were both Canadians who entered into a prenuptial agreement shortly before their marriage.

The judge described the characteristics of the case as unusual. At the hearing the wife was 39. She had previously been married which marriage was childless. The husband was 55. He had three children from his first marriage.

The wife fell pregnant, claiming this was accidental. The husband claimed it was deliberate. Whilst the wife considered an abortion the husband was adamantly opposed. The wife insisted on marriage because she was not prepared to contemplate bringing up a child as a single mother. The husband, still very bruised as a result of expensive and hostile litigation relating to his first marriage, was not prepared to marry the wife unless she entered into a prenuptial agreement.

The husband's lawyers produced a prenuptial agreement. The wife sought legal advice. The first two lawyers she approached refused to represent her, insisting financial disclosure from the husband was essential before they could give proper advice. The wife eventually received advice from an experienced Canadian lawyer who advised that she should not sign the agreement because he thought it was fundamentally unfair. His attempts to negotiate with the husband's lawyer produced cosmetic adjustment only. The wife insisted on signing the agreement because this was the only way she could ensure the marriage went ahead. She duly did so.

The agreement provided that after a marriage of five years the wife would be entitled to a capital payment of £275,000. The husband contended the wife should be held to the contractual bargain in the agreement. The wife contended that at most the agreement was a material circumstance, an aspect of conduct for the court to bear in mind. It should not determine the wife's application. She claimed a lump sum once and for all payment of £1.3 million.

Connell J considered the prenuptial agreement as one of the circumstances of the case. He said, at page 661:

> "Sometimes such an agreement is considered by the court as part of the conduct of each of the parties which it would be inequitable to disregard under section 25(2)(g) of the Act. In my view it matters not whether the court bears such an agreement in mind as part of the circumstances of the case (a very important factor) or as an aspect of the parties' conduct. Under either approach the court should look at any such agreement and decide in the particular circumstances what weight should, in justice, be attached to it. Given that a significant percentage of marriages these days end in divorce, it is understandable that mature adults, and in particular those who have been married before, might wish to agree what should happen in the event of a breakdown. The desire for certainty, or the wish to know where you stand, is not unusual. It is clear, of course, that the existence of such an agreement does not oust the jurisdiction of the court and leading counsel has not argued in this case that the court has no jurisdiction to entertain this claim. The public policy objection to such agreements,

> namely that they tend to diminish the importance of the marriage contract, seems to me to be of less importance now that divorce is so commonplace.".

The judge went on to refer to *F v F* and *S v S*. He then considered the terms of the agreement and said at paragraph 26:

> "On the one hand this husband would not have married the wife unless she signed the agreement. On the other hand this wife signed the agreement because she was pregnant and did not relish single parenthood either herself or for her child and because she wanted to marry the husband. In my view it would be as unjust to the husband to ignore the existence of the agreement and its terms as it would be to the wife to hold her strictly to those terms. I do bear the agreement in mind as one of the more relevant circumstances of this case, but the court's overriding duty remains to attempt to arrive at a solution which is fair in all the circumstances, applying section 25 of the Matrimonial Causes Act 1973."

The judge concluded by awarding the wife a lump sum of £875,000. She had contended for £1.3 million and the husband had contended for the £275,000 as per the prenuptial agreement.

## *X v X* (*Y and Z Intervening*) **[2002] 1 FLR 508 (9 November 2001)**

### *Summary*

An agreement was reached in context of breakdown of the marriage. The wife sought to renege but was held to the agreed terms.

### *Digest*

The parties' five-year marriage broke down. As part of an agreement whereby the husband would apply for a Get, it was agreed that the wife would pay the husband £500,000. The wife appeared without means and the court was not prepared to sanction the order requested.

The husband applied requiring the wife to show cause why an order should not be made in the terms agreed. Munby J held the wife to her agreement.

In an analysis of the case law the judge "teased out" the propositions he had to apply. These included, at paragraph 103 the following:

> The court will not lightly permit parties who have made an agreement between themselves to depart from it. The court should be slow to invade the contractual territory, for as a matter of general policy what the parties have themselves agreed should, unless on the face of it or in fact contrary to public policy or subject to some vitiating feature of the type referred to by Ormrod LJ, be upheld by the courts.
>
> - A formal agreement, properly and fairly arrived at with competent legal advice, should be upheld by the court unless there are 'good and substantial grounds' for concluding that an 'injustice' will be done by holding the parties to it (I adopt Ormrod LJ's formulation in preference to that of Thorpe J: his references to 'the most exceptional circumstances' and 'overwhelmingly strong considerations' seem to me, with respect, to put the matter perhaps a little too high).
> - The mere fact that one party might have done better by going to court is not of itself generally a ground for permitting that party to resile from what was agreed.
> - The court must none the less have regard to all the circumstances. The circumstances are to be judged in their totality and with a broad perspective rather than individually one by one.
> - In particular the court must have regard to the circumstances surrounding the making of the agreement, the extent to which the parties themselves attached importance to it and the extent to which the parties themselves have acted upon it.
> - The relevant circumstances are not limited to the purely financial aspects of the agreement: social, personal and, I would add, religious and cultural considerations, all have to be taken into account.
> - The court should bear in mind the undesirability of stirring up problems with parties who have come to an agreement.
> - On the contrary the court should if possible, and consistent with its duty under s 25, seek to bring about family peace and finality.

He held the wife to her agreement.

## K v K (Ancillary Relief: Pre-nuptial Agreement) [2003] 1 FLR 120 (5 July 2002)

### *Summary*

A prenuptial agreement executed. The wife sought to renege on its terms. The wife was held to its capital but not income provision.

### *Digest*

This was a divorce where the parties had separated after fourteen months of marriage. They had entered into a prenuptial agreement. They had each received independent advice. Their agreement provided that if the marriage was dissolved within five years the wife would receive £100,000 and the husband would make reasonable provision for any children.

The wife sought a lump sum payment for herself of £1.6 million and periodical payments for herself of £57,000. The husband proposed payment to the wife of £120,000 plus £600,000 in trust to provide a home for the wife with their child until he finished his education with reversion to the husband. He offered no periodical payments to the wife. They had agreed the husband would pay £15,000 per annum a year for the maintenance of the child.

The judge summarised the circumstances surrounding the marriage and the prenuptial agreement. The wife fell pregnant, which was a serious shock to both parties. The wife did not wish to be a single mother. She wanted to marry or she would have the pregnancy terminated. The husband did not believe in abortion and was wholly against termination but he did not feel that he and the wife were ready to marry.

They did eventually agree to marry but the husband called the engagement off. The wife's family intervened and the wife's mother told the husband that he should either agree to marry the wife or she (the wife's mother) would take her to have the pregnancy terminated.

In the course of a discussion between the husband and the wife's father the possibility of a prenuptial agreement was raised. The judge found that at no time did the husband tell the wife that he would not marry her without a prenuptial agreement.

It appears that the wife's father advanced the matter of the prenuptial agreement. The wife's father made an appointment with his solicitors and they eventually prepared a draft of the prenuptial agreement which they sent to the husband.

The prenuptial agreement was eventually settled and signed by both parties.

The judge considered its effect and set out his distillation from the various authorities. His analysis on pages 131–132 is set out in full as follows:

> "I distil from those authorities the following questions, which I ask myself in determining the issue whether as against the wife the agreement is binding or influential in any of the decisions I have to make.
>
> (1) Did she understand the agreement? Yes.
>
> (2) Was she properly advised as to its terms? Yes.
>
> (3) Did the husband put her under any pressure to sign it? No.
>
> (4) Was there full disclosure? No. There was disclosure of assets, but the decision not to press for values came from the wife's side and it was known that the husband was very wealthy; figures of up to £150 million were mentioned by the wife's father.
>
> (5) Was the wife under any other pressure? The circumstances in which she found herself put her under pressure and there was pressure from her own family but she was not under pressure to sign the agreement. The husband too was under pressure. He was being pressed by the wife's family to enter into a marriage about which he had serious misgivings. The wife says in one affidavit that she signed the agreement in a hurry the day before the marriage. But the terms of the agreement had been discussed and agreed before then and she had had plenty of time to consider it. Having heard her evidence I do not accept that she felt under any pressure at the time she signed the agreement.
>
> (6) Did she willingly sign the agreement? Yes.
>
> (7) Did the husband exploit a dominant position, either financially or otherwise? No.
>
> (8) Was the agreement entered into in the knowledge that there would be a child? Yes.
>
> (9) Has any unforeseen circumstance arisen since the agreement was made that would make it unjust to hold the parties to it? No.
>
> (10) What does the agreement mean? It is suggested on behalf of the wife that clause 4 is so vague as to render the whole

agreement bad. I consider the agreement is clear as to the capital provision to be made for the wife if the marriage broke down within 5 years. Clause 4 means that provision for the child was to be either agreed or adjudicated upon by the court bearing in mind that such provision would have to include the mother as full-time carer for the child.

(11) Does the agreement preclude an order for periodical payments for the wife? I think not. If the agreement had meant to bar any claim by the wife for periodical payments, it would surely have said so. It does not. It refers to 'property' which I interpret as capital. But if I am wrong see paragraph [16] below.

(12) Are there any grounds for concluding that an injustice would be done by holding the parties to the terms of the agreement? My answer is no; not insofar as capital for the wife is concerned. On the contrary, I think an injustice would be done to the husband if I ignored the terms

(13) Is the agreement one of the circumstances of the case to be considered under s 25? Yes.

(14) Does the entry into this agreement constitute conduct which it would be inequitable to disregard under s 25(2)(g)? Yes.

(15) Am I breaking new ground by holding the wife to the capital terms of the agreement? No. Pre-nuptial agreements have been regarded as influential by Wilson J in *S v S (Divorce: Staying Proceedings)* [1997] 1 WLR 1200, [1997] 2 FLR 100 and by Connell J in *M v M (Pre-nuptial Agreement)* [2002] 1 FLR 654.

(16) Insofar as maintenance for the wife is concerned, if I am wrong in my interpretation of the agreement as above, and if the agreement does preclude a maintenance claim, would it be unjust to hold the parties to that aspect of the agreement? My answer is yes, it would be unjust to the wife but not to the husband. The wife has a child to bring up. Although this was a short marriage with no contribution by the wife to the acquisition of the husband's wealth, I must have regard under s 25(2)(f) to the contribution that the wife has made and is now making and is likely for the next 18 years or so to be making in caring for their child. That is an enormous contribution. The wife is now 28. When the child has finished

> full-time education the wife will be approaching 50. Furthermore, any earning capacity she may have is clearly prejudiced by the time she must invest in bringing up their child. I accept that, but for the child, the wife would not have been financially prejudiced by this short marriage, but to suggest that in the circumstances as they are, she should have no maintenance, either because of the shortness of the marriage or because of the pre-nuptial agreement strikes me as wholly unjust to her. On the other hand her maintenance claim in my judgment should be in her capacity as a mother and to enable her to live as mother to a reasonable standard commensurate with the wealth of the husband/father.

In my judgment, therefore, the wife should receive a lump sum of £120,000 in accordance with the agreement and the husband's offer. She should have no further capital claims upon him for herself, apart from a canteen of cutlery, which I will come to later."

As indicated at the conclusion of the above extract the judge held the wife to the agreement as regards the lump sum of £120,000.

## J v V (Disclosure: Offshore Corporations) [2004] 1 FLR 1042 (16 December 2003)

### *Summary*

A prenuptial agreement was executed but held to be of no significance.

### *Digest*

This case mentions a prenuptial agreement. Coleridge J said, at paragraph 41:

"I should also, as a preliminary point, deal with the prenuptial agreement. I mention it only to put it to one side in this case. Nowadays, occasionally, their existence can be of some significance but not in this case. This contract was signed on the very eve of the marriage, without full legal advice, without proper disclosure and it made no allowance for the arrival of children. It must, in my judgment, therefore, in this jurisdiction fall at every fence, quite apart from the fact that the terms were obviously unfair, preventing the wife from claiming against the husband's assets."

## *NA v MA* [2007] 1 FLR 1760 (24 November 2006)

### *Summary*

The parties agreed financial provision prior to divorce proceedings. The wife sought to renege on the agreed terms. The court allowed the wife to do so upon the basis that she had been subjected to undue pressure and influence.

### *Digest*

After a seven-year marriage, during which the parties had two children, two months before the issue of proceedings they had executed a post nuptial agreement. The wife's adultery with the husband's best friend had been discovered. The husband agreed a reconciliation on the basis that the wife signed a post nuptial agreement setting out the financial division that would be effective if the marriage broke down.

The husband simply "alighted" (paragraph 73) upon the figures in the post nuptial agreement upon the basis that he considered them to be fair and generous.

The marriage did subsequently break down. The wife contended that she should not be bound by the terms of the agreement.

Baron J indicated that in assessing the wife's contention that she should not be bound by the agreement she needed to address what Ormrod LJ had referred to in *Edgar* as "undue pressure" and she equated this with the issue of whether or not the husband had exercised 'undue influence' in accordance with the principles detailed in *RBS v Etridge* (*No 2*) [2001] 2 FLR 1364.

After a comprehensive analysis of the authorities the judge concluded that the wife should not, as a matter of fact, be bound because the husband had pressurised and bullied the wife into signing the agreement. The wife's free will had been overborne. She had been placed under "intolerable, undue and unwarranted pressure" (paragraph 123). His behaviour amounted to undue pressure and undue influence and accordingly the agreement should not be given effect.

In her judgment Baron J made the following observations, *obiter*, upon prenuptial agreements at paragraphs 12 and 90 respectively:

> "12)It is an accepted fact that an agreement entered into between husband and wife does not oust the jurisdiction of this court.

For many years, agreements between spouses were considered void for public policy reasons but this is no longer the case. In fact over the years, prenuptial 'contracts' have become increasingly common place and are, I accept, much more likely to be accepted by these courts as governing what should occur between the parties when the prospective marriage comes to an end. That is, of course, subject to the discretion of the court and the application of a test of fairness/manifest unfairness. It may well be that Parliament will provide legislation but, until that occurs, current authority makes it clear that the agreements are not enforceable per se although they can be persuasive (or definitive) depending upon the precise circumstances that lead to their completion."

"90) Given the timing of Mr. Z's correspondence, nothing happened before Christmas. The letter which enclosed the first draft referred to the document as a 'pre- nuptial' agreement. Of course, it was not. It was not prepared with a marriage in mind but it was prepared with possible divorce in mind. If this had been a prenuptial agreement, it would have stood the best chance of being enforced if there was:-

(i) full disclosure,

(ii) a proper period for reflection being at least 28 days prior to the marriage,

(iii) proper independent legal advice with proper negotiations with

(iv) no children born after marriage. (See the Green Paper 'Supporting Families').

## *Ella v Ella* [2007] 2 FLR 35 (17 January 2007)

### *Summary*

The parties entered into a prenuptial agreement in Israel. The wife sought to renege by issuing proceedings in England. The case was effectively remitted to Israel.

### *Digest*

The husband and wife had dual Israel and British nationality. Prior to their marriage they had entered into a prenuptial agreement which stated that the provisions of Israeli law should apply on any question affecting property. Upon the breakdown of their marriage, the wife petitioned for divorce in England. The husband, although aware of the wife's petition, issued a competing petition in the Tel Aviv courts. Prior to final determination of the wife's application, the husband made a without notice application for a stay of the English proceedings. The stay was granted and the judge held that the rabbinical courts had exclusive jurisdiction. The wife appealed against this decision and argued that the judge had erred in considering the existence of the prenuptial agreement to be a major factor.

The Court of Appeal upheld the judge's decision and determined that she had been right to give such weight to the prenuptial agreement. It considered that the agreement would have been of "considerable effect" in Israel and was therefore a crucial factor in the proceedings.

## *Crossley v Crossley* [2008] 1FLR 1467 (Court of Appeal, 19 December 2007)

### *Summary*

The parties had entered into a prenuptial agreement before marrying in 2006. The wife issued divorce proceedings in 2007 and sought to challenge the prenuptial agreement on the grounds of the husband's alleged non-disclosure of assets. The court had a discretionary power to require a party to show cause why a prenuptial agreement should not govern the division of assets on the dissolution of the marriage.

### *Digest*

The parties executed a prenuptial agreement in November 2005, married in January 2006 and the wife filed a divorce petition in August 2007.

In the prenuptial agreement, which was made following negotiations between experienced lawyers, the husband declared assets of £44 million and the wife declared assets of just under £18 million. The husband, who was 62, had been married before and had had a long-term previous relationship and had three children. The wife, who was 50, had been married three times previously and had three children from those previous marriages.

The prenuptial agreement provided that:

> "Neither party shall apply to any court in any jurisdiction for any order for financial provision of any kind based on the marriage of Stuart and Susan …"

Notwithstanding the terms of the prenuptial agreement the wife applied for ancillary relief. The husband applied for an order that the wife show cause why her claims for ancillary relief should not be resolved in accordance with the prenuptial agreement.

Bennett J gave case management directions on 30 October 2007 on both the husband's show cause application and the wife's substantive application. These were for the parties to explain "why the prenuptial agreement is of such great importance, or from the wife's point of view why it is not and that there should be a full investigation and a full hearing".

The wife appealed against the case management directions. The Court of Appeal granted permission to appeal but dismissed the appeal. In doing so it made some general observations, in paragraph 17, as to the

> "developing view that prenuptial contracts are gaining in importance in a particularly fraught area that confronts so many parties separating and divorcing"

At paragraph 15 Thorpe LJ observed:

> All these cases are fact dependent and this is a quite exceptional case on its facts, but if ever there is to be a paradigm case in which the court will look to the prenuptial agreement as not simply one of the peripheral factors in the case but as a factor of magnetic importance, it seems to me this is just such a case."

He further observed, at paragraph 17 that:

> "It does seem to me that the role of contractual dealing, the opportunity for the autonomy of the parties, is becoming increasingly important."[1]

## MacLeod v MacLeod [2010] 1 AC 298

### *Summary*

The parties had signed a prenuptial agreement prior to their marriage in the US. Following their living for a number of years in the Isle of Man

1 On 13 February 2008 the *Times* reported that Mrs Crossley had abandoned her claim.

they entered into a deed that varied the provision in the prenuptial agreement. In subsequent divorce proceedings the wife sought ancillary relief but the court at first instance and the Privy Council, to which she appealed, kept her substantially to her bargain.

### *Digest*

Before their marriage in February 1994 the parties executed a prenuptial agreement in Florida where they had both lived. This provided for each spouse to retain the separate property they had brought into the marriage and for the ownership of after-acquired property to depend upon legal title. On divorce each party waived their right to any maintenance. Joint properties would be divided equally. The husband would pay the wife a lump sum of US$25,000 per year of marriage.

After they had been married for eight years, in 2002 the parties executed a deed that varied the provisions in their prenuptial agreement. The variation increased the sums payable to the wife in the event of divorce.

The wife claimed ancillary relief following the grant of a decree in October 2004 and the husband invited the court to keep her to her bargain in the 2002 variation of the prenuptial agreement.

The Privy Council kept the wife substantially to the 2002 variation. Baroness Hale said at paragraph 45 that "However lacking in generosity the provision made for the wife, and of course it was much less than she could have expected had there been no agreement, there was no basis for interfering with it."

## Radmacher (formerly Granatino) v Granatino [2010] UKSC 42[2]

### *Summary*

In 1998 the husband and wife, who were respectively French and German nationals, had entered into a prenuptial agreement in Germany under German law. They were divorced in England in 2008. The husband applied for ancillary relief. At first instance Baron J held that the prenuptial agreement was defective but that his award should be circumscribed

2 Having regard to the importance of this decision to the issues dealt with in this book a full copy of the judgment of the Supreme Court given on 20 October 2010 is included in Appendix D.

to a degree to reflect the terms of the prenuptial agreement. On appeal to the Court of Appeal by the wife, it held that the judge had been wrong not to give decisive weight to the prenuptial agreement. On further appeal by the husband to the Supreme Court, that decision was upheld by a majority of eight to one.

### *Digest*

Before the parties had married in 1998 they had entered into a prenuptial agreement. The wife had great riches and the prenuptial agreement provided that neither party was to benefit from the property of the other during the marriage or upon its termination.

The husband applied for ancillary relief arguing that he should not be bound by the prenuptial agreement. At first instance Baron J held that the prenuptial agreement did not bind the parties and awarded the husband something over £6 million to provide for what she identified as his needs.

The wife appealed to the Court of Appeal. It overturned the first instance decision and held that the agreement should have been given decisive weight. It directed that provision should only have been granted to the husband indirectly in his capacity as a homemaker for the two children.

The husband appealed to the Supreme Court. In an extremely full and comprehensive judgement the Supreme Court reviewed the field of nuptial (pre and post nuptial) agreements and concluded that the husband should be "held to his agreement and that it would be unfair to depart from it".

The majority advanced that the proposition to be applied in the case of both prenuptial and post nuptial agreements was thus:

> The court should give effect to a nuptial agreement that is freely entered into by each party with a full appreciation of its implications unless in the circumstances prevailing it would not be fair to hold the parties to their agreement."

# Appendix B

# Postscript to *Charman*

## POSTSCRIPT: CHANGING THE LAW[1]

106. Section 25 of the Act was not an innovation but the consolidation of section 5 of the Matrimonial Proceedings and Property Act 1970. The 1970 Act was the companion to the Divorce Reform Act 1969. As the courts came to apply the new law, the case of Wachtel was seen at the time, and is still seen to be, fundamentally important. It established, amongst other things, that the acrimonious disputes as to the causes of the breakdown of marriage, which had characterised the law of divorce prior to the 1969 Act, were not to be born again in the arena of financial disputes. However the judicial decisions that were more profound and far-reaching were the subsequent decisions of this court in O'Donnell v O'Donnell [1976] Fam 83 and Preston v Preston [1982] Fam17. They provided trial judges and practitioners with a method for the determination of those cases in which the available assets significantly exceeded the simple needs of the family. The applicant's reasonable requirements became the focus of the case, throughout its preparation and in its final determination. This method brought predictability and clarity, characteristics that were refined by a mechanism for capitalising the applicant's future spending requirement, a mechanism inferentially sanctioned by this court in its decision in Duxbury v Duxbury [1987] 1 FLR 7. The emphasis on the applicant's reasonable requirements as the yardstick of the award satisfied the anxiety of judges and others that we should not be drawn into the extravagance of some American states, particularly California, where very large awards were commonplace. This judicial preference for moderation ruled essentially for a generation from the mid 1970s to the year 2000. It suited the society of its day.

107. However the amendments introduced by the Matrimonial and Family Proceedings Act 1984 did nothing to restrict the width of the judicial discretion, whilst north of the border the Family Law (Scotland) Act 1985 introduced a statutory structure for the determination of outcome that preferred clarity and certainty over the flexibility achieved by wide judicial discretion.

1 Missing footnote

108. Dissatisfaction with the state of our law was augmented by extravagant interlocutory proceedings largely uncontrolled by the court. This led to the formation in 1992 of a group of specialist judges, practitioners and academics which, under the President's banner, proposed procedural reforms inspired by the Australian model with firm judicial control at all stages. The proposals had much in common with the civil justice reforms subsequently introduced by Lord Woolf.

109. In advancing its proposals the committee collaborated with government officials and the collaboration was sealed by the adoption of the committee by the Lord Chancellor. The committee thus adopted was available for consultation on issues in this specialist field. The introduction of the new rules was the subject of cautious piloting and evaluation by outside consultants before their general application to all ancillary relief applications.

110. Other issues brought to the committee concerned the enforcement of orders, routes of appeal and costs in ancillary relief. Thus the concentration of the committee was on practice and procedure rather than on primary law reform.

111. However in February 1998 the government announced an intention to reform section 25 of the Act as a high priority. The Lord Chancellor referred this major issue to the committee for consultation. Given its high priority the committee was asked to submit its recommendation by the end of July 1998. The committee was particularly invited to consider the possibility of adopting in this jurisdiction the Scottish model. Although the committee was united in rejecting the Scottish option there was a divergence of view as to the alternatives.

112. The report delivered by the committee undoubtedly influenced the proposals for reform that the government put out for public consultation in the White Paper, "Supporting Families", that autumn. The proposal was for a number of prioritised aims within an overarching objective. The government also proposed to give limited statutory force to written nuptial agreements.

113. Subsequently the government published responses to the consultation which, although few, did not discourage progress. However the enthusiasm for reform apparently died after a single season without explanation. Indeed thereafter the government showed a marked disinclination to discuss the issue and proponents of reform experienced only frustration. Legislative inertia is not unusual in the reform of family law:

see Dr Cretney, Same Sex Relationships O.U.P. 2006. Nevertheless he concludes that reforms are ultimately better achieved by Parliament than by the judges.

114. Was the need for reform met by the decision of the House in White? The decision deprived practitioners and judges of the old measure of reasonable requirements, offering instead the cross check of equality to ensure fairness and to banish discrimination.

115. Of course these innovations were well founded on profound social change, particularly in the recognition that marriage is a partnership of equals and that the role of man and woman within the marriage are commonly interchangeable. In the majority of cases the innovations resulting from White were timely and beneficial.

116. However a social change that was not perhaps recognised in that decision was the extent to which the origins and the volume of big money cases were shifting. Most of the big money cases pre White involved fortunes created by previous generations. The removal of exchange control restrictions in 1979, a policy that offered a favourable tax regime to very rich foreigners domiciled elsewhere, and a new financial era dominated by hedge-funds, private equity funds, derivative traders and sophisticated off-shore structures meant that very large fortunes were being made very quickly. These socio economic developments coincided with a retreat from the preference of English judges for moderation. The present case well illustrates that shift. At trial Mr Pointer achieved for his client an award of £48 million. Before us he freely conceded that he could not have justified an award of more than £20 million on the application of the reasonable requirements principle. Thus, in very big money cases, the effect of the decision in White was to raise the aspirations of the claimant hugely. In big money cases the White factor has more than doubled the levels of award and it has been said by many that London has become the divorce capital of the world for aspiring wives. Whether this is a desirable result needs to be considered not only in the context of our society but also in the context of the European Union of which we are a singular Member State, in the sense that we are a common law jurisdiction amongst largely Civilian fellows and that in the determination of issues ancillary to divorce we apply the lex fori and decline to apply the law more applicable to the parties.

117. In the case of Cowan the need for legislative review in the aftermath of the case of White was articulated: see paragraphs 32, 41 and 58.

Undoubtedly the decision in White did not resolve the problems faced by practitioners in advising clients or by clients in deciding upon what terms to compromise.

118. However this court adopted a cautious approach both in Cowan and in the later case of Lambert. In his submission Mr Singleton drew attention to an article by Joanna Miles in International Journal of Law, Policy and the Family 19 (2005) 242. He told us that he had incorporated the article in his argument for Mrs McFarlane in the House of Lords. The article criticises the earlier decision of this court in the conjoined appeals of McFarlane and Parlour [2005] Fam 171 for having declined the opportunity to identify principles underpinning the exercise of judicial discretion under the Act of 1973. The article is particularly interesting in that it demonstrates that the principles discussed in the article (needs, entitlement and compensation), were subsequently the principles identified by the House of Lords in deciding the conjoined appeals of Miller and McFarlane.

119. The discussion in the article is founded on the statutory scheme legislated in New Zealand in the Property (Relationships) Act 1976 and the Family Proceedings Act 1980, both amended in 2001. In the article's analysis of the New Zealand experience, some emphasis is placed on the difficulty of combining needs, entitlement and compensation in one scheme.

120. It remains to be seen whether the impact of the decision of Miller and McFarlane will be as great as has been the decision of White in very big money cases. There is no doubt but that specialist practitioners have not received the decision in Miller and McFarlane as one that introduces the benefit of predictability and improvement of the prospect of compromise: see the leader from Andrew Greensmith, National Chair of Resolution, at [2007] Fam Law 203. If this is so, it is highly unfortunate.

121. As Lord Hope pointed out in Miller and McFarlane, at [105], the report of the Law Commission on the Financial Consequences of Divorce (Law Com No. 112), in recommending flexibility over a structured statutory scheme, added "... that any future legislation dealing with the financial consequences of divorce should be subject to continuous monitoring and periodical reports to Parliament". Clearly that recommendation has not been heeded. The thrust of Lord Hope's speech is to identify the need for the reform of the Family Law (Scotland) Act 1985. Arguably the English statute, in its fundamental provisions fifteen years older, is in equal need of modernisation in the light of social and other changes as well as in the light of experience.

122. There is a limitation on the resources of even the judges of the House of Lords to conduct wide-ranging comparative studies as a prelude to establishing a new principle, or perhaps to abandoning an existing principle in what is essentially a social policy field. The Money and Property Sub-Committee of the Family Justice Council at its meeting on the 20 February 2007 agreed to approach the Law Commission with the request that the reform of section 25 be included in its future work programme and the request has since been articulated in a letter to the Chairman.

123. Should this request be acted upon, careful analysis will be required of the interrelationship of our ancillary relief law with the law of other jurisdictions. Globalisation particularly affects the ultra-rich. They are unlikely to inhabit only one country. With a string of properties acquired for diverse purposes they are likely to be subject to the jurisdiction of at least two courts when the marriage falls apart. London is increasingly likely to be one of the jurisdictions. Now that London is regularly described in the press as the "divorce capital of the world" it is inevitable that applicants will seek to achieve a London award. If there are no international conventions applicable to the dispute there will be a forum conveniens battle, often at quite disproportionate cost to the parties' assets or, more importantly, the means of one of the spouses. Even if international conventions apply, expensive struggles can still escalate. Recently in this court the case of Bentinck v Bentinck [2007] EWCA Civ 175 demonstrated the expenditure of £330,000 in legal costs despite the fact that the jurisdictional rules of the Lugano Convention applied. Even more recently, in the case of Moore v Moore [2007] EWCA Civ 361, approximately £1.6 million had been expended on the wife's endeavours to achieve a London award, rather than a Marbella award, despite the application of the Regulation Brussels I.

124. Any harmonisation within the European region is particularly difficult, given that the Regulation Brussels I is restricted to claims for maintenance and the Regulation Brussels II Revised expressly excludes from its application the property consequence of divorce. In the European context this makes sense because in Civilian systems the property consequences of divorce are dealt with by marital property regimes. Almost uniquely our jurisdiction does not have a marital property regime and it is scarcely appropriate to classify our jurisdiction as having a marital regime of separation of property. More correctly we have no regime, simply accepting that each spouse owns his or her own separate property during the marriage but subject to the court's wide distributive powers in prospect upon a decree of judicial separation, nullity or divorce. The difficulty

of harmonising our law concerning the property consequences of marriage and divorce and the law of the Civilian Member States is exacerbated by the fact that our law has so far given little status to pre-nuptial contracts. If, unlike the rest of Europe, the property consequences of divorce are to be regulated by the principles of needs, compensation and sharing, should not the parties to the marriage, or the projected marriage, have at the least the opportunity to order their own affairs otherwise by a nuptial contract? The White Paper, "Supporting Families", not only proposed specific reforms of section 25 but also to give statutory force to nuptial contracts. The government's subsequent abdication has not been accepted by specialist practitioners. In 2005 Resolution published a well argued report urging the government to give statutory force to nuptial contracts. The report was subsequently fully supported by the Money and Property Sub-Committee of the Family Justice Council.

125. The European Commission is also in search of progress in this difficult area. On 17 July 2006 it published its Green Paper on Conflict of Laws in Matters Concerning Matrimonial Property Regimes, including the question of jurisdiction and mutual recognition. In our jurisdiction a stakeholder group prepared a response which was subsequently considered by the North Committee but the response has been complicated by the fact that the Green Paper does not seem to fully understand our law of equitable redistribution or that we do not have a matrimonial property regime as such.

126. We would wish to lend our own weight to this call for a review of these matters by the Law Commission.

# Appendix C

# *Supporting Families* consultation paper and the response of the judges of the Family Division

In November 1998 the Home Office published a consultation document, *Supporting Families*.[1] It was the work of the Ministerial Group on the Family which was set up by the prime minister in September 1997 to develop a coherent government strategy to increase the support and help available to families.

The relevant sections in the consultation paper are as follows:

> "**4.20** Couples can already make agreements between themselves, under the ordinary laws of contract, which deal with the ownership and disposal of property during marriage. Some couples also seek to reduce the scope for conflict on divorce by making agreements which deal with the way their property would be divided if they did divorce. These are often called 'nupital' or 'pre-nuptial' agreements. There is, however, no requirement for the courts to take any account of such an agreement in deciding how to award property on divorce. This lack of certainty may well discourage couples from making such agreements.
>
> **4.21** The Government is considering whether there would be advantage in allowing couples, either before or during their marriage, to make written agreements dealing with their financial affairs which would be legally binding on divorce. This could give people more choice and allow them to take more responsibility for ordering their own lives. It could help them to build a solid foundation for their marriage by encouraging them to look at the financial issues they may face as husband and wife and reach agreement before they get married.
>
> **4.22** Providing greater security on property matters in this way could make it more likely that some people would marry, rather

1 www.national archives.gov.uk/ERO/records/ho415/1/acu/suppfam.htm

than simply live together. It might also give couples in a shaky marriage a little greater assurance about their future than they might otherwise have had. Nuptial agreements could also have the effect of protecting the children of first marriages, who can often be overlooked at the time of a second marriage – or a second divorce.

**4.23** There would be no question of written agreements being made mandatory for couples intending to marry. Also, we would protect the interests of a party to the agreement who is economically weaker and the interests of children through six safeguards. If one or more of the following circumstances was found to apply, the written agreement would not be legally binding:

- where there is a child of the family, whether or not that child was alive or a child of the family at the time the agreement was made
- where under the general law of contract the agreement is unenforceable, including if the contract attempted to lay an obligation on a third party who had not agreed in advance
- where one or both of the couple did not receive independent legal advice before entering into the agreement
- where the court considers that the enforcement of the agreement would cause significant injustice (to one or both of the couple or a child of the marriage)
- where one or both of the couple have failed to give full disclosure of assets and property before the agreement was made
- where the agreement is made fewer than 21 days prior to the marriage (this would prevent a nuptial agreement being forced on people shortly before their wedding day, when they may not feel able to resist)".

Question 15 of the consultation document asked for views upon the desirability of allowing couples to make written agreements dealing with their financial affairs on divorce and as to the safeguards which would lead to an agreement not being legally binding.

Over 1,000 responses were received and these were analysed and published in 1999. There were 157 replies to Question 15. The respondents were divided in their opinions. Eighty agreed it would be helpful to allow nuptial agreements to be binding. Seventy-seven felt that this would foster negative expectations on the part of those contemplating marriage.

The response of the judges of the Family Division [2] was of particular interest, not only on the issue of prenuptial agreements but also on the idea of 'equality'. Although the response was written in June 1998 it well worth revisiting with the benefit of the knowledge of hindsight. It is set out in full below.

The government subsequently announced that it had no present intention to bring forward any new legislation[3] and accordingly the approach taken by the courts will follow existing case law.

***Response of the Judges of the Family Division to Government Proposals (made by way of submission to the Lord Chancellor's Ancillary Relief Advisory Group)***

**Family Law**

**Fam LJ 29 (159)**

**1 March 1999**

*Nicholas Wilson*

*13 June 1998*



## GENERAL APPROACH

The law of ancillary relief merits reconsideration in the sense that every law which has been in place for 14 years (and mostly for 27 years) merits reconsideration. We approve a rolling programme of critical revisitation of the law, particularly in an area, such as this, which has a profound impact on many lives, attracts strong public interest and needs to be attuned to social change.

The level of legal costs to the parties (and, through legal aid, to the public) presently incurred in resolution of issues of ancillary relief merits full survey; but we feel provisionally that it adds force to the impetus for reconsideration. We have all seen ancillary relief

2 (1999) Family Law 159.

3 See Footnote 6 in the Introduction

cases where the level of costs is disproportionate and self-defeating, although we lack the essential facility to put such cases into the general statistical picture, still less to compare costs incurred in other jurisdictions. The proliferation of litigants in person is suddenly becoming a serious (and, for the system, expensive) problem in the Family Division and we are particularly keen to see a reduction in costs incurred under some ancillary relief legal aid certificates if that would release funds to bring some litigants in person back into legal aid. The difficult question is whether the excessive costs, whatever their overall scale, are mainly caused by the procedure set for ancillary relief or its substantive law. Our instinct is that the excessively adversarial climate has been mainly to blame; and that the effect on costs of the financial dispute resolution (FDR) scheme and of the mediation encouraged by the Family Law Act 1996, when both are fully operational, could be dramatic and must be awaited before any costs-driven reform of the substantive law could sensibly be undertaken.

All 17 of us are convinced that the Government would be unwise to introduce either of the proposed reforms addressed below, but in particular the equal division, without a much fuller pre-consideration than is currently proposed.

The unusually sensitive context of a claim for ancillary relief is that it is made between parties who have had, and may still have, intense feelings about each other and who will often need to co-operate in the future. Its result will usually have profound, inverse effects on the quality of each of their lives. This confers especially high value upon a just resolution of it, elusive though that often is. Obviously it also places a premium on a consensual resolution of the issue, provided again that the settlement reached in accordance with law is accepted as just. An unjust resolution, whether consensual or otherwise, can be particularly corrosive: for it can create or augment the bitterness which destroys future co-operation and, worse, which spills over into a party's relationship with the children.

In the law of ancillary relief the optimum tension between the predictability which flows from firm rules and the flexibility to secure justice in the individual case is notoriously difficult to achieve. A number of jurisdictions have wrestled anxiously with it. As a prelude to its enactment in 1970 and 1984 our law of ancillary relief was the subject of thorough expert appraisal, contained in particular in the reports of the Law Commission, Law Com Nos 25 (1969) and 112 (1981). The latter noted the proposals in the report of the Scottish Law Commission, No 67 (1981), which were to lead to the Family Law (Scotland) Act 1985, but recommended that they be not followed in England and Wales. Each of the two English reports was preceded by working or discussion papers and extensive attendant discussion. The Scottish report was the product of intermittent consultation over 5 years.

The law of 1970, as amended in 1984, has been developed and its proper application clarified in a wealth of case-law, mainly in the Court of Appeal. Because the impact of the law of ancillary relief is so widespread, a large band of judges and practitioners has had to become familiar with it and is in place to apply it. We and they can adjust to dramatic change; but the public costs of jettisoning an old system and of getting a new one into running order must presumably be measured and then justified.

In his speech dated 21 February 1998 the Parliamentary Secretary stated that the object of both proposed reforms would be to bring greater certainty into the law. But it is not clear to us what material justifies the conclusion that the balance struck by the present law is weighted too heavily in favour of flexibility and against certainty. We know of no general clamour, professional or public, to such effect. Our belief is that the application of the law to the facts of most cases is, within a reasonable bracket of figures, predictable. We acknowledge, however, that we are not in the best position to make this crucial judgment. It needs sophisticated departmental or other research both as to the ratio of cases contested to those settled (in comparison also with other jurisdictions) and as to whether the former were contested because the application of the law was unclear or (for example) because a litigant refused to make full disclosure or to accept advice about what to offer or accept. In any inquest into a cross-section of contested cases we would be happy to assist.

In the light of the importance of the proposals, a reference spanning 4 months to an Advisory Group, the members of which are fully occupied in other spheres and meet occasionally, unsupported by full-time staff and without research or even dedicated secretarial facilities, is wholly inappropriate and (we believe) will be widely so regarded. Furthermore, the Group is composed only of lawyers yet the proposals raise issues not only of legal principle but also of social and economic policy which cut across traditional departmental boundaries. On 18 May 1998 *The Times* reported that the principle of pre-nuptial agreements had been endorsed by the Government's Family Policy Group and approved by cabinet ministers. If this report is accurate, it calls into question the very nature of this consultation process.

## EQUAL DIVISION OF ASSETS

The idea of an equal division of assets sounds attractive as a fitting end to a partnership dependent upon different although prima facie equally important contributions. But our experience convinces us that the attraction is superficial. To leave the parties in a truly equal position is a reasonable objective in many cases; but such an outcome usually requires an unequal division of assets. For the parties exit from the marriage not just with their share of the assets but in the shadow of two other interrelated factors: their respective earning capacities and their responsibilities to others, particularly the children. There are occasionally further factors such as likely future inheritance. These factors usually bear upon the parties in very unequal proportions so a disposal governed by equality in the division of assets bequeaths enduring inequality.

The idea of an equal division of assets does not break new ground for courts in England. The principles which came into force in 1971 were sufficiently flexible to allow the idea to gain a foothold in the early years. In *Wachtel v Wachtel* [1973] Fam 72 it was suggested that, unless spousal periodical payments were to be made, an equal division of assets was a reasonable starting-point; another arithmetical starting-point (one-third of assets and of joint incomes) was suggested for when periodical payments were also to be made. But, once they saw the practical effects of such an approach, the courts were quick to backtrack on it. Led by Scarman LJ in *Calderbank v Calderbank* [1976] Fam 93 and thereafter by Ormrod LJ in *P v P* [1978] 1 WLR 483 and *Page v Page* (1981) FLR 198, the Court of Appeal pulled the law back from any arithmetical approach because it was thought to be too arbitrary. The equal division was the first to go, followed by the one-third division of assets. For periodical payments, however, the one-third division of joint incomes still lingers on, usually unexpressed, in some judicial thinking.

It is rare for us to conclude that the just result is an equal division of the assets. *Smith v Smith* [1992] Fam 69 is about the only recent reported example of such a conclusion.

In the early development of the present law there was another more limited introduction of equality into asset division. It was more limited because it related solely to the matrimonial home and because the children's need to live there required the division to be delayed. The order in *Mesher v Mesher and Hall* [1980] 1 All ER 126 (but decided in 1973) was that the wife should have exclusive occupation until the child became 17 but that there should then be a sale and equal division. After 1973 *Mesher* orders were frequently made. Later, however, the courts began to contemplate the effect of such orders in the common circumstances where the children had grown up but the wife, having forfeited her earning capacity in their interests, was not able to rehouse herself with only one half of the equity. The *Mesher* order became discredited (see, for example, *Carson v Carson* [1983] 1 WLR 285). The arithmetical division had been too arbitrary.

The best recent example of the introduction of an arithmetical formula into ancillary relief is the Child Support Act 1991. The difference in the complexity of the arithmetic required by the Act and by an equal division of assets could not be more stark. But the complexities of the 1991 Act only reflect Parliament's vain struggle to cater justly for the individual case with an arithmetical system.

No one mourns the loss in 1984 of the objective originally set by the concluding words of s 25 of the 1973 Act, namely to place the parties in the position in which they would have been had the marriage not broken down; and we do not accept that the absence of any replacement conclusion has left the discretionary exercise devoid of direction. Not only is there in s 25A(1) the exhortation to the clean break; there is the introduction into s 25(1) of the primacy of the interests of the children. The balance was well struck in giving the children's interests primacy rather than paramountcy, which would have gone too far. Our view is that the principle of primacy for the children is valuable and we question how any principle of equal asset division can be reconciled with it. Either the principle of equal division would be subordinate, in which case its effect would be severely emasculated; or the two principles would stand together, in which case their frequent clashes might not easily be resolved; or the children principle would become subordinate, which, we sense, would be as unacceptable to the public as to ourselves.

The interests of children and of wives are often identical. The effect on women of introducing the principle of equal asset division would depend on its relationship with the children principle and the width of provision for departures from equality. But our provisional feeling is that the introduction would be adverse to the interests of most women; and the male lobby would say not before time. The older woman, following a long marriage during which the man had amassed more than (say) £5m, would clearly benefit from such a change. But the average wife, currently awarded the whole of the £50k equity in order to house the children, would be, at least, more vulnerable. Some such awards are arguably unfair on husbands. But to find the right balance is acutely difficult. It would be important to survey the social consequences of the reform, in particular in relation to the demand for public housing and housing benefit.

Our knowledge of the detailed working of the Scottish system is rudimentary. But, as is already clear, we cannot subscribe to the central principle set out in s 10(1) of the 1985 Act that fair sharing of matrimonial property is equal sharing save in special circumstances. We appreciate that special circumstances are widely defined in s 10(6), particularly at (d); but we would not be happy with the slant of a law which described common circumstances as special. The Scottish system inevitably requires the identification of the pot of matrimonial property within the pot of joint assets. Although sensible, if arbitrary, rules are in place to prevent the tracing exercise from getting out of hand, we would be interested to learn whether this extra dimension of the inquiry adds to its cost and complexity; and whether the requirement that the smaller pot, once identified, should in principle be divided equally creates a need for precision in its valuation which increases costs and obstructs compromise where values are in dispute.

One cannot look at one species of ancillary relief, namely lump sum and property adjustment, without the other, namely spousal periodical payments. The Scots have linked their principle of equal division of assets to principles relating to periodical payments different from ours. It appears that in Scotland periodical payments should not generally be awarded for more than 3 years (see s 9(1)(d), but also (c) and (e)). This is a much fiercer propulsion towards the clean break than we have here, where an indefinite duration is still common. There is, we think rightly, no suggestion of adopting this half of their jurisprudence; but the transplantation of only one half of a system demands extreme caution.

Indeed, we think that prior to any reform the perspective should be broader still. These laws are catering for a reducing percentage of the population because of the decline in marriage. Discretionary provision for former cohabitants is already under active consideration at least in relation to the family home and we feel that, if any such provision for them were developed in tandem with the wider provision for former spouses, the necessary differences would be more logical.

In conclusion, we are unanimous in opposing any introduction of equality in the division of assets as a governing principle even subject to departures. So we are unanimous in not wishing to follow Scottish law. Subject to the deep concern of all of us about the danger of hurried and piecemeal reform in this area, some of us believe that it might be worthwhile to consider the reamendment of the 1973 Act so as to cast a duty on the court beyond that currently articulated in s 25A(1), namely to consider whether it would be practicable and just to exercise its powers under [the capital provisions] so as to divide the joint assets equally. Subject to the same caveat, others of us put forward the possibility of the reintroduction of concluding words into what is now s 25(2): one of various possible principles would be to require the court so to exercise its powers as to place each party, so far as it is practicable and just to do so, in a position of economic security commensurate with that of the other. Both such provisions would require alignment, not altogether easily achieved, with the primacy of the interests of the children. But a third group of us has prima facie reservations about each of them, believing that the court is already accustomed to discharge the suggested duties and that the necessary references to practicability and justice, coupled in the second case with the less crude notion of commensurate economic security, would rob the reform of the certainty which is its only suggested *raison d'être*.

## PRE-NUPTIAL AGREEMENTS

We do not perceive a necessary link between the pre-nuptial agreement and equality of asset division. We appreciate that the message of the law could in theory be 'unless you contract out of it, the equality principle will apply'. But it could equally well be 'unless you contract out of them, ordinary principles will apply'.

There are two allied but distinct questions. What effect should the law give to pre-nuptial agreements when, following divorce (or death), they give rise to results different from the product of ordinary principles? And should the law strive to encourage pre-nuptial agreements? The questions are allied in that the greater the effect, probably the greater the encouragement.

We have reservations about whether the law should strive to encourage pre-nuptial agreements. We all still believe strongly in the institution of marriage as a source of personal and social stability and wonder whether the pre-nuptial agreement conditions the couple to the failure of their marriage and so helps to precipitate it. This deserves research. Some of us also feel that the institution of marriage is devalued if, while entering it, a couple can elect to sever some of its most important, if contingent, legal effects. Others of us consider, hesitantly, that marriage is made for mankind, not vice versa, and that, subject to obvious limits, adults should be allowed to cast their relationships in their own way. We are at one that this is profoundly difficult terrain.

Although we are asked to focus on pre-nuptial agreements, the law could not logically distinguish them from post-nuptial agreements. Indeed, the latter would probably have stronger claims to legal efficacy in that, the nearer the time of the agreement to the breakdown of the marriage, the more likely would it be to cater for the then circumstances in a manner akin to the product of ordinary principles. The most likely time for entry into a post-nuptial agreement is soon after the final breakdown of the marriage but it might also crop up earlier, in particular at the time of attempted reconciliation. Thus the nuptial agreement, surveyed over all, is likely to be entered into at one of three moments of extreme emotional susceptibility, namely just prior to marriage or to post-marital reconciliation or soon after final breakdown. We are clear that, if it were to have any effect in law, the nuptial agreement would need to have been preceded by not only full financial disclosure but also separate legal advice on each side; and we presume that state-funded legal advice would in principle be available for this purpose. But it is the emotional moment when legal advice is most easily brushed aside. Hard cases would fall through this safety-net. We doubt whether any system of registration would narrow the mesh.

Apart from lack of disclosure or of separate legal advice, any ground under which a contract is void or voidable at common law would need to apply to the nuptial agreement. For example it would be important for public policy to strike down an agreement which inappropriately transferred financial responsibility for family members to the state. But there is a wider point to be collected from the law of contract. The child of the family, whether or not yet born, is not a party to the nuptial agreement and his rights cannot thereby be eroded. This is perhaps to say more than that the court's jurisdiction to make orders to or for the benefit of the child cannot be fettered. For if, as a result of the agreement, the home owned by the wife and occupied by her and the child is inferior to what she would have been awarded under ordinary principles, should the child be thus prejudiced? If, as we think, the presence of a child should deprive the nuptial agreement of much if not all of its effect, the role of the agreement in the law is much circumscribed.

Under the present law a nuptial agreement is one of the circumstances to which the court must have regard under s 25(1) of the 1973 Act. Its impact upon the result will therefore depend upon the weight to be attached to it and the other circumstances. The weight to be attached to a post-nuptial, and specifically a post-breakdown, agreement can be determinative of the result (see *Edgar v Edgar* [1980] 1 WLR 1410). Whether a pre-nuptial agreement would be given such weight is a little less clear, perhaps because no suitable case for doing so has yet arisen.

The majority of us are of the view that slightly, but only slightly, greater prominence might be given to the nuptial agreement in the law of ancillary relief. To be specific, the majority view is that an additional matter might be added into s 25(2), at (i), namely the terms of any agreement reached between the parties in contemplation of or subsequent to their marriage. There would be no need to spell out the elementary requirements (i e of disclosure, separate advice and of the common law) or the saver for the interests of the child or any general power to make different provision where justice plainly required: this would all be accommodated in the weight-giving exercise. A minority of us would go a little further. Despite our unanimous lack of enthusiasm for the pre-nuptial agreement, the provisional view of the minority is that, where there is an agreement, whether pre- or post-nuptial, which satisfies the elementary requirements, the shape of the law should be that it be enforced 'unless … '. The minority feels that the current law of ancillary relief has inherited a paternalistic strain, rather too hostile to contract (formerly collusion) and in this respect rather too jealous of its own discretion, for the protection, in effect, of the downtrodden wife, and that, while she still exists, she may no longer be apt as a governing stereotype; that even in *Edgar*, progressive though it was, the dicta too readily deprived agreements of weight, for example in their reference to bad legal advice; and that the overall balance needs gentle redress but, by means of the 'unless' clause, making enforcement subject to the interests of the child and to a residual discretion to depart in the plain case.

In either case analogous amendments would have to be made to the Inheritance (Provision for Family and Dependants) Act 1975 in respect of claims against the estate made by the deceased's ex-spouse and, where a nuptial agreement catered for death in the absence of divorce, by the surviving spouse.

The President and all the other judges of the Family Division have approved this memorandum.

# Appendix D

# Radmacher (formerly Granatino) v Granatino judgment[1]

**Radmacher (formerly Granatino) (Respondent) *v* Granatino (Appellant)**

**before**

**Lord Phillips, President**
**Lord Hope, Deputy President**
**Lord Rodger**
**Lord Walker**
**Lady Hale**
**Lord Brown**
**Lord Mance**
**Lord Collins**
**Lord Kerr**

**JUDGMENT GIVEN ON**

**20 October 2010**

**Heard on 22 and 23 March 2010**

| *Appellant* | *Respondent* |
|---|---|
| Nicholas Mostyn QC | Richard Todd QC |
| Deepak Nagpal | Geoffrey Kingscote |
| (Instructed by Payne Hicks Beach) | Jonathan Harris |
| | (Instructed by Vardags (formerly Ayesha Vardag Solicitors)) |

**LORD PHILLIPS, LORD HOPE, LORD RODGER, LORD WALKER, LORD BROWN, LORD COLLINS AND LORD KERR**

---

1 The judgment is protected by Crown copyright. This copy is reproduced under the terms of the Open Government Licence.

*Introduction*

1. When a court grants a decree of divorce, nullity of marriage or judicial separation it has the power to order ancillary relief. Ancillary relief governs the financial arrangements between the husband and the wife on the breakdown of their marriage. Sometimes the husband and wife have already made an agreement governing these matters. The agreement may have been made before the marriage ("an ante-nuptial agreement") or after the marriage ("a post-nuptial agreement"). Post-nuptial agreements may be made when the husband and wife are still together and intend to remain together, or when they are on the point of separating or have already separated. The latter type of post-nuptial agreement can be described as "a separation agreement". We shall use the generic description "nuptial agreements" to embrace both ante-nuptial and post-nuptial agreements.
2. A court when considering the grant of ancillary relief is not obliged to give effect to nuptial agreements – whether they are ante-nuptial or post-nuptial. The parties cannot, by agreement, oust the jurisdiction of the court. The court must, however, give appropriate weight to such an agreement. This appeal raises the question of the principles to be applied by the court when considering the weight that should be attached to an ante-nuptial agreement. The Privy Council recently considered this question in relation to a post-nuptial agreement in *MacLeod v MacLeod* [2008] UKPC 64, [2010] 1 AC 298 and it will be necessary to consider the implications of that decision.
3. The approach of English law to nuptial agreements differs significantly from the law of Scotland, and more significantly from the rest of Europe and most other jurisdictions. Most jurisdictions accord contractual status to such agreements and hold the parties to them, subject in some cases to specified safeguards or exceptions. Under English law it is the court that is the arbiter of the financial arrangements between the parties when it brings a marriage to an end. A prior agreement between husband and wife is only one of the matters to which the court will have regard. The uncertainty as to the weight that the court will attach to such agreements has led to calls for reform. The history of steps taken towards the reform of our law is set out in the judgment of Thorpe LJ at paras 16 to 23 of his judgment in this case in the Court of Appeal. For present purposes it suffices to note the following.
4. In 1998 the Home Office published a consultation document, "Supporting Families", which included the following statement in para 4.21:

"The Government is considering whether there would be advantage in allowing couples, either before or during their marriage, to make written agreements dealing with their financial affairs which would be legally binding on divorce."

5. In para 4.23 the Government proposed that any such agreement should be subject to six safeguards. It would not be legally binding:

"– where there is a child of the family, whether or not that child was alive or a child of the family at the time the agreement was made

- where under the general law of contract the agreement is unenforceable, including if the contract attempted to lay an obligation on a third party who had not agreed in advance
- where one or both of the couple did not receive independent legal advice before entering into the agreement
- where the court considers that the enforcement of the agreement would cause significant injustice (to one or both of the couple or a child of the marriage)
- where one or both of the couple have failed to give full disclosure of assets and property before the agreement was made
- where the agreement is made fewer than 21 days prior to the marriage (this would prevent a nuptial agreement being forced on people shortly before their wedding day, when they may not feel able to resist)."

6. There are many, including some members of the Family Bar and Bench, who would favour a reform along the lines proposed, but the Government has not taken its proposals further. The Law Commission is, however, currently considering this area of the law and is expected to report in 2012.

7. There can be no question of this Court altering the principle that it is the Court, and not any prior agreement between the parties, that will determine the appropriate ancillary relief when a marriage comes to an end, for that principle is embodied in the legislation. What the Court can do is to attempt to give some assistance in relation to the approach that a court considering ancillary relief should adopt towards an ante-nuptial agreement between the parties. Earlier this year Resolution, an organisation of over 5,700 family lawyers, published an updated paper on "Family Agreements", which proposes

legislative reform to the law of ante-nuptial and post-nuptial agreements. This quotes statistics that show that about 45% of marriages are likely to end in divorce. It comments on the strain and expense that are involved in disputes about ancillary relief, which are increased by the uncertainty of the outcome.

8. In order to address the facts of this particular case it will be necessary, in due course, to set these out in a little detail. At this stage we propose to give a summary that will provide a context for the consideration of the relevant principles that will follow.

9. The appellant ("the husband") is a French national. The respondent ("the wife") is a German national. They signed the ante-nuptial agreement in Germany on 1 August 1998. The husband was then aged 27 and the wife 29. They were married in London on 28 November 1998. They had two children, Chiara, born on 4 September 1999 and Chloe, born on 25 May 2002. In October 2006, after 8 years of marriage, they separated.

10. The wife petitioned for divorce in the Principal Registry of the Family Division that same month. The husband cross-petitioned in November. They agreed to proceed undefended on cross decrees and were divorced in July 2007.

11. Meanwhile, the wife had applied for permission to take the girls to live in Germany. In September 2007, His Honour Judge Collins granted that application but made a shared residence order providing that the children should divide their time between their parents. Under his order, they were to spend just under one third of the time with their father and two thirds with their mother. The husband made an unsuccessful application for permission to appeal that order to the Court of Appeal. The wife took the children to live in Germany in February 2008. However, in November 2008 (after the judgment of Baron J in the ancillary relief proceedings), she applied to the German court for permission to take them to live in Monaco. The husband resisted this, but permission was granted in May 2009 and that is where they now live.

12. The ante-nuptial agreement was drawn up in Germany by a notary. It contained a choice of law clause that provided that the effects of their marriage, including the laws of matrimonial property and succession, were to be subject to the law of the Federal Republic of Germany. The main part of the agreement provided first for separation of property. In clause 3 it was declared that the statutory matrimonial regime was to be excluded, and that each party was to manage

his or her assets entirely independently. By clause 4 the parties excluded the equalisation of pension rights. By clause 5 they waived claims for maintenance after the marriage was terminated. Clause 6 contained a waiver of the statutory right to a portion of the estate of the first one of them to die. The effect of the agreement was that neither party was to derive any interest in or benefit from the property of the other during the marriage or on its termination. It made no provision for what was to happen in the event of their having children.

13. The parties entered into this ante-nuptial agreement at the instigation of the wife. She came from an extremely rich family. Some of the family wealth had already been transferred to her, so that she enjoyed substantial unearned income. She expected to receive a further portion of the family wealth if, but only if, she entered into the ante-nuptial agreement to protect this. Her father insisted upon this. She herself was anxious that the husband should show, by entering into the agreement, that he was marrying her for love and not for her money.

14. The husband was working for JP Morgan & Co and, at the time of the ante-nuptial agreement, was earning about £120,000 a year and had excellent prospects. These were realised inasmuch as he earned about $475,000 dollars in 2001 and about $320,000 in 2002. He then became disenchanted with banking and embarked on research studies at Oxford with the object of obtaining a D Phil in biotechnology.

15. Despite the terms of the ante-nuptial agreement the husband brought a claim for ancillary relief, seeking an order against the wife both for periodical payments and for a lump sum. The hearing of his claim began before Baron J on 23 June 2008 and she handed down her judgment on 28 July 2008: [2008] EWHC 1532 (Fam) [2009] 1 FCR 35. The issue that lay at the heart of the proceedings was the weight that should be given to the ante-nuptial agreement. Baron J held that the circumstances surrounding the conclusion of the agreement fell foul of a number of the safeguards set out in para 4.23 of the Home Office consultation document (see para 5 above), and for that reason, the weight to be attached to it fell to be reduced. None the less, she held that his award should be circumscribed to a degree to reflect the fact that he had signed the agreement. Her award also had to make provision for the two children, whose arrival had not been anticipated in the agreement. In the event she awarded the husband a total of £5,560,000, on the basis that this would provide him with an annual income of £100,000 for life and enable him to buy a home in London,

where the two children could visit him. She awarded him periodical payments of £35,000 a year for each child until they ceased full time education. In addition she awarded a sum to enable him to buy a home in Germany (which would remain owned by the wife) where the two children could stay with him.

16. The wife appealed successfully to the Court of Appeal against Baron J's order. The Court held that Baron J had been wrong to find that the circumstances in which the ante-nuptial agreement had been reached reduced the weight to be attached to the agreement. It was not evident that the fact of the agreement had had any significant impact on her award. In the circumstances of the case she should have given the agreement decisive weight. The award should make provision for the husband's role as the father of the two children, but should not otherwise make provision for his own long term needs. The case was remitted to Baron J.

*Ancillary relief*

17. The power to grant a decree of divorce was conferred on a new Court for Divorce and Matrimonial Causes by the Matrimonial Causes Act 1857. Section 32 of that Act gave the court power to order the husband to secure maintenance for the wife's life. The Matrimonial Causes Act 1866 gave the court power to order the husband to pay unsecured maintenance to the wife. Having identified this starting point of the power to award ancillary relief we can jump to 1969.

18. The Divorce Reform Act 1969 revolutionised the English law of divorce by replacing the old grounds of divorce which were based on fault with the single ground that the marriage had irretrievably broken down. This change was accompanied by a fresh approach to the financial consequences of divorce, which was supplied initially by the Matrimonial Proceedings and Property Act 1970, the provisions of which were largely re-enacted as Part II of the Matrimonial Causes Act 1973 ("the 1973 Act"). Significant changes were made to these provisions by the Matrimonial and Family Proceedings Act 1984 and the Family Law Act 1996. The following provisions of the 1973 Act, as amended, are particularly material.

19. Section 23 gives the court the power, on granting a decree of divorce, of nullity of marriage or of judicial separation to make a wide variety of orders. These include an order that either party pay to the other, or pay for the benefit of any child of the family, periodical payments, and that either party pay to the other, or for the benefit of any child of the marriage, a lump sum. Section 24 gives the court power to direct a

party to transfer specified property to the other party or to or for the benefit of a child. No power is given to vary a property adjustment order. Section 24B gives the court power to make a pension sharing order. Section 31 gives the court power to vary a periodical payments order but not an order to pay a lump sum.

20. Section 25 provides that "it shall be the duty of the court" when deciding whether, and in what manner to exercise powers including those referred to above to have regard to:

> "all the circumstances of the case, first consideration being given to the welfare while a minor of any child of the family who has not attained the age of eighteen"

21. The section goes on to provide that as regards the exercise of its powers in relation to a party to the marriage the court shall in particular have regard to the following matters:

> "(a) the income, earning capacity, property and other financial resources which each of the parties to the marriage has or is likely to have in the foreseeable future, including in the case of earning capacity any increase in that capacity which it would in the opinion of the court be reasonable to expect a party to the marriage to take steps to acquire;
>
> (b) the financial needs, obligations and responsibilities which each of the parties to the marriage has or is likely to have in the foreseeable future;
>
> (c) the standard of living enjoyed by the family before the breakdown of the marriage;
>
> (d) the age of each party to the marriage and the duration of the marriage;
>
> (e) any physical or mental disability of either of the parties to the marriage;
>
> (f) the contributions which each of the parties has made or is likely in the foreseeable future to make to the welfare of the family, including any contribution by looking after the home or caring for the family;
>
> (g) the conduct of each of the parties, if that conduct is such that it would in the opinion of the court be inequitable to disregard it;
>
> (h) in the case of proceedings for divorce or nullity of marriage, the value to each of the parties to the marriage of any benefit …

which, by reason of the dissolution or annulment of the marriage, that party will lose the chance of acquiring."

22. The principles to be applied to the grant of ancillary relief have twice been considered by the House of Lords, in cases involving substantial assets. In *White v White* [2001] 1 AC 596 the parties had been married for 33 years, during which time they had together carried on the business of farming. Their net assets were some £4.6 million. The judge awarded the wife a lump sum of a little less than £1 million, on the basis that this would meet her reasonable needs. The Court of Appeal allowed her appeal and held that she was entitled to a lump sum of £1.5 million, reflecting her contribution both to the business and to the family. In the House of Lords, where the decision of the Court of Appeal was upheld, Lord Nicholls of Birkenhead gave the leading speech. He identified the following principles. Fairness, and indeed the 1973 Act itself, required the court to have regard to all the circumstances of the case, and there was one principle of universal application. No distinction should be drawn between the different ways in which husband and wife contributed to the welfare of the family. There should be no bias in favour of the money-earner against the home-maker and the child-carer. As a general guide equality in the division of assets should only be departed from for good reason (p 605).

23. Lord Nicholls went on to draw a distinction between property that one party brought to the marriage, or inherited during the marriage ("inherited property") and property acquired by the labours of one or both parties during the marriage ("matrimonial property"). Lord Nicholls recognised that there was a case for saying that a party should be allowed to keep inherited property, but commented:

> "Plainly, when present, this factor is one of the circumstances of the case. It represents a contribution made to the welfare of the family by one of the parties to the marriage. The judge should take it into account. He should decide how important it is in the particular case. The nature and value of the property, and the time when and circumstances in which the property was acquired, are among the relevant matters to be considered. However, in the ordinary course, this factor can be expected to carry little weight, if any, in a case where the claimant's financial needs cannot be met without recourse to this property." (p 610)

24. In *Miller v Miller; McFarlane v McFarlane* [2006] UKHL 24; [2006] 2 AC 618 two appeals were heard together, one in respect of a

marriage that had lasted less than three years. Lord Nicholls started his judgment under the heading "*The requirements of fairness*" by observing that under the 1973 Act the first consideration had to be given to the welfare of the children of the marriage. After this a number of strands could be identified. The first was financial needs. He commented at para 11:

> "The parties share the roles of money-earner, home-maker and child-carer. Mutual dependence begets mutual obligations of support. When the marriage ends fairness requires that the assets of the parties should be divided primarily so as to make provision for the parties' housing and financial needs, taking into account a wide range of matters such as the parties' ages, their future earning capacity, the family's standard of living, and any disability of either party. Most of these needs will have been generated by the marriage, but not all of them. Needs arising from age or disability are instances of the latter."

25. A second strand was compensation.

> "This is aimed at redressing any significant prospective economic disparity between the parties arising from the way they conducted their marriage. For instance, the parties may have arranged their affairs in a way which has greatly advantaged the husband in terms of his earning capacity but left the wife severely handicapped so far as her own earning capacity is concerned. Then the wife suffers a double loss: a diminution in her earning capacity and the loss of a share in her husband's enhanced income. This is often the case. Although less marked than in the past, women may still suffer a disproportionate financial loss on the breakdown of a marriage because of their traditional role as home-maker and child-carer." (para 13)

26. A third strand was sharing. Lord Nicholls postulated that marriage was a partnership. When a marriage ended each was entitled to an equal share of the assets of the partnership unless there was good reason to the contrary, albeit that the yardstick of equality was to be applied as an aid, not a rule. One good reason might be the difference between "matrimonial property" generated during the marriage and "non-matrimonial property" – property brought by one party to the marriage or inherited by or given to one party during the marriage.

27. There was general agreement among the other members of the House with these propositions, although not all agreed on the precise

definition of "matrimonial property" nor on the relevance of the length of the marriage to the principle of sharing. Lady Hale, with whom Lord Mance agreed, identified a sub-category of matrimonial property, which the parties treated as separate property and which might not be subject to the sharing principle.

28. The implications of these two decisions were considered by the Court of Appeal, Sir Mark Potter P, Thorpe and Wilson LJJ in *Charman v Charman (No 4)* [2007] EWCA Civ 503; [2007] 1 FLR 1246. The court observed that in *Miller* the House had unanimously identified three main principles which governed distribution of property in ancillary relief proceedings – "need (generously interpreted), compensation and sharing" and that each of the matters set out in sub-paragraphs (b) to (h) of section 25(2) of the 1973 Act could be assigned to one of the three (paras 68–69).

29. As to the principle of sharing, the court said this, at para 66:

> "To what property does the sharing principle apply? The answer might well have been that it applies only to matrimonial property, namely the property of the parties generated during the marriage otherwise than by external donation; and the consequence would have been that non-matrimonial property would have fallen for redistribution by reference only to one of the two other principles of need and compensation to which we refer in para 68, below. Such an answer might better have reflected the origins of the principle in the parties' contributions to the welfare of the family; and it would have been more consonant with the references of Baroness Hale of Richmond in *Miller* at paras 141 and 143 to 'sharing … the fruits of the matrimonial partnership' and to 'the approach of roughly equal sharing of partnership assets'. We consider, however, the answer to be that, subject to the exceptions identified in *Miller* to which we turn in paras 83 to 86, below, the principle applies to all the parties' property but, to the extent that their property is non-matrimonial, there is likely to be better reason for departure from equality. It is clear that both in *White* at p 605 F-G and p 989 respectively, and in *Miller*, at paras 24 and 26, Lord Nicholls of Birkenhead approached the matter in that way; and there was no express suggestion in *Miller*, even on the part of Baroness Hale of Richmond, that in *White* the House had set too widely the general application of what was then a yardstick."

30. The "exceptions identified in *Miller*" referred to the possible exception in respect of assets that the parties had treated as separate property. As to these the court commented that the discussion about these perhaps

> "foreshadowed future, albeit no doubt cautious, movement in the law towards a more frequent distribution of property upon divorce in accordance with what, by words or conduct, the parties appear previously to have agreed."

*Nuptial agreements, separation agreements and public policy*

31. It used to be contrary to public policy for a married couple who were living together, or a couple about to get married, to make an agreement that provided for the contingency that they might separate. Marriage involved a duty to live together and an agreement making provision for the possibility of separation might act as an encouragement to separate. Such agreements were void and the court would pay no regard to them: Cocksedge v Cocksedge (1844) 14 Sim 244; 13 LJ Ch 384; H v W (1857) 3 K & J 382. The same was not true of an agreement to separate or an agreement that governed a separation that had already taken place. Lord Atkin in Hyman v Hyman [1929] AC 601 at p 625–626 gave a short history of such contracts and commented on their effect:

> "We have to deal with a separation deed, a class of document which has had a chequered career at law. Not recognized by the Ecclesiastical Courts, such contracts were enforced by the common law. Equity at first frowned. Lord Eldon doubted but enforced them: cf. *St. John v. St. John* (1803) Ves. 525, 529 and *Bateman v. Countess of Ross* (1813) 1 Dow 235; and see the arguments of Sir Fitzroy Kelly and Mr Turner and of Mr Bethell in *Wilson v. Wilson* (1848) 1 H. L. C. 538, 550–553, 564, 565. Finally they were fully recognized in equity by Lord Westbury's leading judgment in *Hunt v. Hunt* (1861) 4 D. F. & J. 221, in which he followed Lord Cottenham's decision in *Wilson v. Wilson* (1846–1848) 1 HLCas 538, 550–553, 564, 565, where his argument for the respondent had prevailed. Full effect has therefore to be given in all courts to these contracts as to all other contracts. It seems not out of place to make this obvious reflection, for a perusal of some of the cases in the matrimonial courts seems to suggest that at times they are still looked at askance and enforced grudgingly. But there is no caste in contracts. Agreements for separation are formed, construed and dissolved and to be enforced on precisely

> the same principles as any respectable commercial agreement, of whose nature indeed they sometimes partake. As in other contracts stipulations will not be enforced which are illegal either as being opposed to positive law or public policy. But this is a common attribute of all contracts, though we may recognize that the subject-matter of separation agreements may bring them more than others into relation with questions of public policy."

32. In *Hyman v Hyman* the husband had left the wife for another woman. Adultery by the husband was not at the time a ground for divorce unless there were aggravating circumstances, such as incest. The parties had entered into a deed of separation under which the husband had paid two lump sums and agreed to make weekly payments of £20 for the life of the wife. The deed included a covenant by the wife that she would not institute any proceedings to make him pay more than this. When the Matrimonial Causes Act 1923 gave the wife the right to petition for divorce on the grounds of her husband's adultery alone, the wife divorced her husband and applied to the court for maintenance pursuant to section 190(1) of the Supreme Court of Judicature (Consolidation) Act 1925. This gave the court the power, on any decree for divorce, to order the husband to pay maintenance. The husband argued that the wife was precluded by her covenant from bringing this claim. The House rejected this argument. Lord Hailsham LC held at p 614 that:

    > "the power of the court to make provision for a wife on the dissolution of her marriage is a necessary incident of the power to decree such a dissolution, conferred not merely in the interests of the wife, but of the public, and that the wife cannot by her own covenant preclude herself from invoking the jurisdiction of the court or preclude the court from the exercise of that jurisdiction."

    Lord Atkin made the same point at p 629.

33. The subsequent history was set out by Lady Hale in *MacLeod v MacLeod* at paras 21 to 23. The same principle was applied to other statutory powers to award maintenance. In *Bennett v Bennett* [1952] 1 KB 249 the wife sought to enforce an agreement to pay maintenance given by her husband in consideration of her agreement not to seek a court order for maintenance. The Court of Appeal held that because that agreement was of no effect it did not constitute valid consideration for her husband's agreement and her claim failed.

34. This unfortunate situation was remedied by the Maintenance Agreements Act 1957. The preamble to this Act stated:

"An Act to make provision with respect to the validity and alteration by the court of financial arrangements in connection with agreements between the parties to a marriage, whether made during the continuance or after the dissolution or annulment of the marriage, for the purposes of those parties' living separately; and for purposes connected therewith."

35. The Act provided:

"1.—(1) This section applies to any agreement in writing made, whether before or after the commencement of this Act, between the parties to a marriage for the purposes of their living separately, being—

(a) an agreement containing financial arrangements, whether made during the continuance or after the dissolution or annulment of the marriage; or

(b) a separation agreement which contains no financial arrangements in a case where no other agreement in writing between the same parties contains such arrangements.

(2) If an agreement to which this section applies includes a provision purporting to restrict any right to apply to a court for an order containing financial arrangements, that provision shall be void but any other financial arrangements contained in the agreement shall not thereby be rendered void or unenforceable but, unless void or unenforceable for any other reason, and subject to the next following subsection, shall be binding on the parties to the agreement: …

(3) Where an agreement to which this section applies is for the time being subsisting and the parties thereto are for the time being either both domiciled or both resident in England, and on an application by either party the High Court or, subject to the next following subsection, a magistrates' court is satisfied either—

(a) that by reason of a change in the circumstances in the light of which any financial arrangements contained in the agreement were made or, as the case may be, financial arrangements were omitted therefrom, the agreement should be altered so as to make different, or, as the case may be, so as to contain, financial arrangements; or

(b) that the agreement does not contain proper financial arrangements with respect to any child of the marriage,

the court may by order make such alterations in the agreement by varying or revoking any financial arrangements contained therein or by inserting therein financial arrangements for the benefit of one of the parties to the agreement or of a child of the marriage as may appear to the court to be just having regard to all the circumstances or, as the case may be, as may appear to the court to be just in all the circumstances in order to secure that the agreement contains proper financial arrangements with respect to any child of the marriage; and the agreement shall have effect thereafter as if any alteration made by the order had been made by agreement between the parties and for valuable consideration."

36. These provisions are largely reproduced in sections 34 and 35 of the 1973 Act, albeit that the definition of a "maintenance agreement" does not state that it is an agreement made "for the purposes of their living separately". Wilson LJ at para 134 of his judgment in this case remarks that sections 34 and 35 have been dead letters for more than 30 years. It seems likely that issues as to maintenance have, since the 1973 Act came into force, been pursued in ancillary relief proceedings. As to these section 35(6) provides

"For the avoidance of doubt it is hereby declared that nothing in this section or in section 34 above affects any power of a court before which any proceedings between the parties to a maintenance agreement are brought under any other enactment (including a provision of this Act) to make an order containing financial arrangements or any right of either party to apply for such an order in such proceedings."

37. Although separation agreements do not override the powers of the Court to grant ancillary relief, they have been held to carry considerable weight in relation to the exercise of the court's discretion when granting such relief. In *Edgar v Edgar* [1980] 1 WLR 1410 the husband and wife had separated and in 1976, without any pressure from the husband but rather at the instigation of the wife, concluded a deed of separation which had been negotiated through solicitors. Under this the husband agreed to purchase a house for the wife, to confer on her capital benefits worth approximately £100,000, to pay her £16,000 a year and to make periodical payments for the children of the marriage. The wife agreed that if she obtained a divorce she would not seek a lump sum or property transfer orders.

38. The husband complied with all his obligations under the separation deed but, in 1978, the wife petitioned for divorce and applied for ancillary relief, including a lump sum payment. Ormrod LJ said this about the weight to be given to the separation agreement at p 1417:

> "To decide what weight should be given, in order to reach a just result, to a prior agreement not to claim a lump sum, regard must be had to the conduct of both parties, leading up to the prior agreement, and to their subsequent conduct, in consequence of it. It is not necessary in this connection to think in formal legal terms, such as misrepresentation or estoppel; *all* the circumstances as they affect each of two human beings must be considered in the complex relationship of marriage. So, the circumstances surrounding the making of the agreement are relevant. Undue pressure by one side, exploitation of a dominant position to secure an unreasonable advantage, inadequate knowledge, possibly bad legal advice, an important change of circumstances, unforeseen or overlooked at the time of making the agreement, are all relevant to the question of justice between the parties. Important too is the general proposition that formal agreements, properly and fairly arrived at with competent legal advice, should not be displaced unless there are good and substantial grounds for concluding that an injustice will be done by holding the parties to the terms of their agreement. There may well be other considerations which affect the justice of this case; the above list is not intended to be an exclusive catalogue.
>
> I agree with Sir Gordon Willmer in *Wright v Wright* [1970] 1WLR 1219, 1224, that the existence of an agreement,

'... at least makes it necessary for the wife, if she is to justify an award of maintenance, to offer prima facie proof that there have been unforeseen circumstances, in the true sense, which make it impossible for her to work or otherwise maintain herself.'

> Adapting that statement to the present case, it means that the wife here must offer prima facie evidence of material facts which show that justice requires that she should be relieved from the effects of her covenant in clause 8 of the deed of separation, and awarded further capital provision."

39. Oliver LJ summarised his conclusions as follows at p 1424:

> "... in a consideration of what is just to be done in the exercise of the court's powers under the Act of 1973 in the light of the conduct

of the parties, the court must, I think, start from the position that a solemn and freely negotiated bargain by which a party defines her own requirements ought to be adhered to unless some clear and compelling reason, such as, for instance, a drastic change of circumstances, is shown to the contrary."

The court held that no good reason had been shown not to hold the wife to her agreement.

40. Sitting in the Court of Appeal after his retirement, Sir Roger Ormrod in *Camm v Camm* (1982) 4 FLR 577 at p. 579, which was another case where ancillary relief was claimed in the face of the terms of a separation agreement, said:

"It has been stressed all through those same cases that the court must attach considerable importance, the amount of importance varying from case to case, to the fact that there was an agreement, because the court, naturally, will not lightly permit parties who have made a contractual agreement between themselves, even if it is not legally enforceable, to depart from that contractual agreement unless some good reason is shown."

In that case the court did not hold the wife to her agreement, which she had entered into under great pressure and which failed to make adequate provision for her needs.

41. In *Smith v McInerney* [1994] 2 FLR 1077 the husband, who had entered into a separation agreement with his wife, sought a lump sum and property adjustment order when his circumstances changed as a result of being made redundant. Thorpe J cited *Edgar v Edgar* and *Camm v Camm* and remarked at p 1081:

"As a matter of general policy I think it is very important that what the parties themselves agree at the time of separation should be upheld by the courts unless there are overwhelmingly strong considerations for interference."

The approach of the courts to separation agreements, as evidenced by the cases cited above, differed markedly from the approach to nuptial agreements that merely anticipated the possibility of separation or divorce and which were consequently considered to be void as contrary to public policy. Contrast the statement of Thorpe J in *Smith v McInerney* quoted above with what he said at about the same time in *F v F (Ancillary Relief: Substantial Assets)* [1995] 2 FLR 45. In the latter case a rich German husband relied on a marital property regime which confined the wife to the pension of a retired German judge in the event of their divorce (the wife was in the judicial civil service at the time of the marriage). Thorpe J accepted that such agreements were commonplace in the society from which the parties came, but he did "not attach any significant weight" to the ante-nuptial agreement, and said (at p 66):

> "The rights and responsibilities of those whose financial affairs are regulated by statute cannot be much influenced by contractual terms which were devised for the control and limitation of standards that are intended to be of universal application throughout our society."

43. Judges sitting in the Family Division were prepared to give some weight to ante-nuptial agreements, but certainly not to the extent of holding that they should govern the terms of ancillary relief unless there were strong reasons for departing from them. In *S v S (Matrimonial Proceedings: Appropriate Forum)* [1997] 1 WLR 1200, Wilson J suggested at pp 1203–1204 that there might come a case

> "where the circumstances surrounding the prenuptial agreement and the provision therein contained might, when viewed in the context of the other circumstances of the case, prove influential or even crucial. Where other jurisdictions, both in the United States and in the European Community, have been persuaded that there are cases where justice can only be served by confining parties to their rights under prenuptial agreements, we should be cautious about too categorically asserting the contrary. I can find nothing in section 25 to compel a conclusion, so much at odds with personal freedoms to make arrangements for ourselves, that escape from solemn bargains, carefully struck by informed adults, is readily available here."

44. In *N v N (Jurisdiction: Pre-nuptial agreement)* [1999] 2 FLR 745, 752, Wall J recognised that although they were unenforceable, ante-nuptial agreements might have evidential weight in subsequent proceedings for divorce. Some weight was given to an ante-nuptial agreement in *C v C (Divorce: Stay of English Proceedings)* [2001] 1 FLR 624 (Johnson J) (where a French ante-nuptial agreement was a significant factor in staying English proceedings); *M v M (Prenuptial Agreement)* [2002] 1 FLR 654, para 44 ("tending to guide the court to a more modest award than might have been made without it," per Connell J); and *G v G (Financial Provision: Separation Agreement)* [2004] 1 FLR 1011 (CA) (where parties had been married before).

But contrast *Haneef v Haneef* [1999] EWCA Civ 803 (a decision on leave to appeal); *J v V (Disclosure: Offshore Corporations)* [2003] EWHC 3110 (Fam), [2004] 1 FLR 1042 (Coleridge J) (agreement signed on the eve of marriage without advice or disclosure and without allowance for arrival of children). See also *X v X (Y and Z Intervening)* [2002] 1 FLR 508, paras 78–103 (Munby J), and *K v K (Ancillary Relief: Prenuptial Agreement)* [2003] 1 FLR 120, 131–132 (R Hayward Smith QC sitting as Deputy High Court Judge) for a review of the authorities.

45. Some judges cited dicta in *Edgar v Edgar* in the context of ante-nuptial agreements without observing that those dicta were made in the very different context of a separation agreement – see *N v N* at p 753; *M v M* at para 21, *K v K* at p 131.

46. A change of attitude on the part of Thorpe LJ was apparent from his decision in *Crossley v Crossley* [2007] EWCA Civ 1491, [2008] 1 FLR 1467, 1472, at para 15 Thorpe LJ described the ante-nuptial agreement there as "a factor of magnetic importance." The marriage was a short marriage between two wealthy individuals who entered into an ante-nuptial agreement after having taken legal advice. Mrs Crossley asserted that her husband's disclosure had been inadequate and therefore the agreement should be avoided. The issue before the court concerned disclosure. Thorpe LJ drew attention to these facts: the marriage was a childless marriage of very short duration, for a substantial portion of which the parties were living apart; the marriage was between mature adults, both of whom had been previously married and divorced; both parties had very substantial independent wealth; the ante-nuptial agreement provided for the retention by each of the parties of their separate properties and division of joint property (of which there was in fact none). He accepted that the combination of these factors gave rise to a very strong case that a possible result of the section 25 exercise would be that the wife receives no further financial award, and concluded (at para 15):

> "All these cases are fact dependent and this is a quite exceptional case on its facts, but if ever there is to be a paradigm case in which the court will look to the prenuptial agreement as not simply one of the peripheral factors in the case but as a factor of magnetic importance, it seems to me that this is just such a case ..."

47. Cases of post-nuptial settlements other than separation agreements are rare. One such was *NA v MA* [2006] EWHC 2900 (Fam); [2007]

1 FLR 1760. That case is of interest because, on one view, it anticipated the approach of the Privy Council in *MacLeod.* The very wealthy husband had discovered that his wife had committed adultery with one of his friends. He pressurised her into signing an agreement that provided that she would receive a specified lump sum and annual payments if their marriage ended in divorce. The wife signed it because the husband insisted that she should do so if the marriage was to continue. Despite this, Baron J held at para 67 that "as the idea of an agreement evolved it hardened into a legal, post-nuptial agreement". It was on this basis, as we understand it, that the husband sought to have the agreement converted into an order of the court. When dealing with the law the judge did not distinguish clearly between ante-nuptial, post-nuptial and separation agreements. She said at para 12:

> "It is an accepted fact that an agreement entered into between husband and wife does not oust the jurisdiction of this court. For many years, agreements between spouses were considered void for public policy reasons but this is no longer the case. In fact, over the years, pre-nuptial 'contracts' have become increasingly common place and are, I accept, much more likely to be accepted by these courts as governing what should occur between the parties when the prospective marriage comes to an end. That is, of course, subject to the discretion of the court and the application of a test of fairness/manifest unfairness. It may well be that Parliament will provide legislation but, until that occurs, current authority makes it clear that the agreements are not enforceable per se, although they can be persuasive (or definitive) depending upon the precise circumstances that lead to their completion."

48. The judge went on to apply the law of undue influence, holding at paras 20 and 21

> "I am clear that, to overturn the agreement, I have to be satisfied that this wife's will was overborne by her husband exercising undue pressure or influence over her. I am also clear that if I do not overturn the agreement per se, I still have to consider whether it is fair and should be approved so as to become a court order."

She overturned the agreement on the ground of undue influence.

*MacLeod v MacLeod*

49. This was an appeal to the Privy Council from the High Court of Justice of the Isle of Man. It involved a claim for ancillary relief

under the Manx Matrimonial Proceedings Act 2003, which contained provisions identical to sections 23 to 25 and 34 to 36 of the 1973 Act. The husband and wife had married in Florida in 1994, after signing an ante-nuptial agreement. A year later they moved to the Isle of Man. Six years and five children later the marriage ran into difficulties and the parties executed a deed which made substantial variations to the ante-nuptial agreement. By August 2003 the marriage had totally broken down and in October 2004 a provisional decree of divorce was made. The wife sought ancillary relief, arguing that the deed of variation should be disregarded. The husband contended that it should be upheld, subject to one variation in favour of the wife.

50. The Board, in an advice delivered by Lady Hale, summarised the law in relation to nuptial agreements that we have set out above and pointed out the distinction between separation agreements and agreements providing for the consequences of a possible future separation. At para 31 the Board referred to the position of ante-nuptial agreements:

> "The Board takes the view that it is not open to them to reverse the long standing rule that ante-nuptial agreements are contrary to public policy and thus not valid or binding in the contractual sense. The Board has been referred to the position in other parts of the common law world. It is clear that they all adopted the rule established in the 19th century cases. It is also clear that most of them have changed that rule, and provided for ante-nuptial agreements to be valid in certain circumstances. But with the exception of certain of the United States of America, including Florida, this has been done by legislation rather than judicial decision."

51. The Board went on to draw a distinction between ante-nuptial and post-nuptial agreements, holding that the latter did constitute contracts. We do not agree with this distinction and, in order to explain where we part company with the reasoning of the Board, we must set this out in detail.

> "35 In the Board's view the difficult issue of the validity and effect of ante-nuptial agreements is more appropriate to legislative rather than judicial development. It is worth noting, for example, that in the Florida case of *Posner v Posner* (1970) 233 So 2d 381, where such agreements were recognised, attention was drawn to the statutory powers of the courts to vary such agreements. The Board is inclined to share the view expressed by Baron J in *NG v*

*KR* (Pre-nuptial Contract) [2009] 1 FCR 35, para 130, that the variation power in section 50 of the 2003 Act (section 35 of the 1973 Act) does not apply to agreements made between people who are not yet parties to a marriage. Yet it would clearly be unfair to render such agreements enforceable if, unlike post-nuptial agreements, they could not be varied.

36 Post-nuptial agreements, however, are very different from pre-nuptial agreements. The couple are now married. They have undertaken towards one another the obligations and responsibilities of the married state. A pre-nuptial agreement is no longer the price which one party may extract for his or her willingness to marry. There is nothing to stop a couple entering into contractual financial arrangements governing their life together, as this couple did as part of their 2002 agreement. There is a presumption that the parties do not intend to create legal relations: see *Balfour v Balfour* [1919] 2 KB 571. There may also be occasional problems in identifying consideration for the financial promises made (now is not the time to enter into debate about whether domestic services constitute good consideration for such promises). But both of these are readily soluble by executing a deed, as was done here.

37 There is also nothing to stop a married couple from entering into a separation agreement, which will then be governed by sections 49 to 51 of the 2003 Act (sections 34 to 36 of the 1973 Act). As already noted, section 49 applies to 'any agreement in writing made at any time between the parties to a marriage'. There is nothing to limit this to people who are already separated or on the point of separating. It is limited to agreements containing 'financial arrangements' or to separation agreements which contain no financial arrangements. And 'financial arrangements' are limited to those governing their rights and liabilities towards one another when living separately. But section 49(1)(b) provides that such financial arrangements shall be binding 'unless they are void or unenforceable for any other reason'.

38 Leaving aside the usual contractual reasons, such as misrepresentation or undue influence, the only other such reason might be the old rule that agreements providing for a future separation are contrary to public policy. But the reasons given for that rule were founded on the enforceable duty of husband and wife to live together. This meant that there should be no inducement to either

of them to live apart: see, for example, *H v W* (1857) 3 K & J 382, 386. There is no longer an enforceable duty upon husband and wife to live together. The husband's right to use self-help to keep his wife at home has gone. He can now be guilty of the offences of kidnapping and false imprisonment if he tries to do so: see *R v Reid* [1973] QB 299. The decree of restitution of conjugal rights, disobedience to which did for a while involve penal sanctions, has not since the abolition of those sanctions been used to force the couple to live together: see *Nanda v Nanda* [1968] P 351. It was abolished by the Matrimonial Proceedings and Property Act 1970, at the same time as the Law Reform (Miscellaneous Provisions) Act 1970 abolished all the common law actions against third parties who interfered between husband and wife.

39 Hence the reasoning which led to the rule has now disappeared. It is now time for the rule itself to disappear. It has long been of uncertain scope, as some provisions which contemplate future marital separation have been upheld: see, for example, *Lily, Duchess of Marlborough v Duke of Marlborough* [1901] 1 Ch 165. This means that sections 49 to 51 of the 2003 Act (sections 34 to 36 of the 1973 Act) can apply to such agreements in just the same way as they do to any other. In particular, they can be varied in either of the circumstances provided for in section 50(2). The first is that there has been a change in the circumstances in the light of which any financial arrangements were made or omitted; following the amendment proposed by the Law Commission in 1969, this now includes a change which the parties had actually foreseen when making the agreement. The second is that the agreement does not contain proper financial arrangements with respect to any child of the family.

40 In the Board's view, therefore, the 2002 agreement was a valid and enforceable agreement, not only with respect to the arrangements made for the time when the parties were together, but also with respect to the arrangements made for them to live separately. However, the latter arrangements were subject to the court's powers of variation and the provisions which purported to oust the jurisdiction of the court, whether on divorce or during the marriage, were void. The existence of such powers does not deprive such agreements of their utility. Countless wives and mothers benefited from such agreements at a time when it was difficult for them to take their husbands to court to ask for maintenance.

Enforcing an existing agreement still has many attractions over going to court for discretionary relief.

41 The question remains of the weight to be given to such an agreement if an application is made to the court for ancillary relief. In *Edgar v Edgar* [1980] 1 WLR 1410, the solution might have been more obvious if mention had been made of the statutory provisions relating to the validity and variation of maintenance agreements. One would expect these to be the starting point. Parliament had laid down the circumstances in which a valid and binding agreement relating to arrangements for the couple's property and finances, not only while the marriage still existed but also after it had been dissolved or annulled, could be varied by the court. At the same time, Parliament had preserved the parties' rights to go to court for an order containing financial arrangements. It would be odd if Parliament had intended the approach to such agreements in an ancillary relief claim to be different from, and less generous than, the approach to a variation application. The same principles should be the starting point in both. In other words, the court is looking for a change in the circumstances in the light of which the financial arrangements were made, the sort of change which would make those arrangements manifestly unjust, or for a failure to make proper provision for any child of the family. On top of that, of course, even if there is no change in the circumstances, it is contrary to public policy to cast onto the public purse an obligation which ought properly to be shouldered within the family.

42 The Board would also agree that the circumstances in which the agreement was made may be relevant in an ancillary relief claim. They would, with respect, endorse the oft-cited passage from the judgment of Ormrod LJ in *Edgar v Edgar* [1980] 1 WLR 1410, 1417, in preference to the passages from the judgment of Oliver LJ, both quoted above, at para 25. In particular the Board endorses the observation that "It is not necessary in this connection to think in formal legal terms, such as mispresentation [sic] or estoppel". Family relationships are not like straightforward commercial relationships. They are often characterised by inequality of bargaining power, but the inequalities may be different in relation to different issues. The husband may be in the stronger position financially but the wife may be in the stronger position in relation to the children and to the home in which they live. One

may care more about getting or preserving as much money as possible, while the other may care more about the living arrangements for the children. One may want to get out of the relationship as quickly as possible, while the other may be in no hurry to separate or divorce. All of these may shift over time. We must assume that each party to a properly negotiated agreement is a grown up and able to look after him- or herself. At the same time we must be alive to the risk of unfair exploitation of superior strength. But the mere fact that the agreement is not what a court would have done cannot be enough to have it set aside."

52. We wholeheartedly endorse the conclusion of the Board in paras 38 and 39 that the old rule that agreements providing for future separation are contrary to public policy is obsolete and should be swept away, for the reasons given by the Board. But for reasons that we shall explain, this should not be restricted to post-nuptial agreements. If parties who have made such an agreement, whether ante-nuptial or post-nuptial, then decide to live apart, we can see no reason why they should not be entitled to enforce their agreement. This right will, however, prove nugatory if one or other objects to the terms of the agreement, for this is likely to result in the party who objects initiating proceedings for divorce or judicial separation and, arguing in ancillary relief proceedings that he or she should not be held to the terms of the agreement.

53. We now turn to explain why we would not draw the distinction drawn by the Board between ante- and post-nuptial agreements. The Board advances two reasons for this, one specific the other general. The specific reason is that section 35 of the 1973 Act applies to post-nuptial but not to ante-nuptial settlements and it would be unfair to render the latter enforceable if they could not be varied (para 35). The general reason is that post-nuptial agreements are very different from ante-nuptial agreements. We shall deal with each in turn.

*The specific reason*

54. Our first reservation in relation to this reason is that we question whether the Board was right to hold that sections 34 and 35 apply to all post-nuptial agreements rather than just to separation agreements. We consider that the original provisions in the Maintenance Agreements Act 1957 applied only to separation agreements. The preamble to the Act and the statement in section 1(1) that the section applies to any agreement between the parties to a marriage *for the purpose of*

*their living separately* so indicate. Furthermore post-nuptial agreements of couples living together that provided for the contingency of future separation were void, so Parliament cannot have intended the Act to apply to them.

55. When the provisions of the 1957 Act were incorporated into the 1973 Act, they did not include the preamble or the words that we have emphasised above. But it remained the case that post-nuptial agreements that made provision for the contingency of separation were considered to be contrary to public policy. For this reason we find it hard to accept that Parliament intended to extend the ambit of the relevant provisions.

56. More fundamentally, we do not accept that the protection of section 35 must be a precondition to holding that a nuptial agreement takes effect as a contract. If Wilson LJ is right to say that section 35 is a dead letter, the theoretical scope of its protection cannot be critical to the question of whether nuptial agreements have contractual effect.

*The general reason*

57. Is there a material distinction between ante-nuptial and post-nuptial agreements? Wilson LJ was not persuaded that there is (paras 125–126) and nor are we. The question should be tested by comparing an agreement concluded the day before the wedding with one concluded the day after it. Nuptial agreements made just after the wedding are not unknown and likely to become more common if the law distinguishes them from ante-nuptial agreements.

58. In *MacLeod* the Board made the following comments about the differences between ante- and post-nuptial agreements:

> "There is an enormous difference in principle and in practice between an agreement providing for a present state of affairs which has developed between a married couple and an agreement made before the parties have committed themselves to the rights and responsibilities of the married state purporting to govern what may happen in an uncertain and unhoped for future." (para 31)

59. This is true, but does not apply fully to a post-nuptial agreement entered into at the start of married life, for that also purports to govern what may happen in an uncertain and unhoped for future.

> "Post-nuptial agreements, however, are very different from pre-nuptial agreements. The couple are now married. They have

undertaken towards one another the obligations and responsibilities of the married state. A pre-nuptial agreement is no longer the price which one party may extract for his or her willingness to marry." (para 36)

60. As to the last sentence, this focuses on one possible type of duress. But duress can be applied both before and after the marriage. The same principle applies in either case. In either case the duress will lead to the agreement carrying no, or less, weight. As to the first two sentences, we do not see why different principles must apply to an agreement concluded in anticipation of the married state and one concluded after entry into the married state.

61. This is not to say that there are no circumstances where it is right to distinguish between an ante-nuptial and a post-nuptial agreement. The circumstances surrounding the agreement may be very different dependent on the stage of the couple's life together at which it is concluded, but it is not right to proceed on the premise that there will always be a significant difference between an ante- and a post-nuptial agreement. Some couples do not get married until they have lived together and had children.

*Does contractual status matter?*

62. Is it important whether or not post-nuptial or ante-nuptial agreements have contractual status? The value of a contract is that the court will enforce it. But in ancillary relief proceedings the court is not bound to give effect to nuptial agreements, and is bound to have regard to them, whether or not they are contracts. Should they be given greater weight because in some other context they would be enforceable? Or is the question of whether or not they are contracts an irrelevance? This can be tested in this way. Did the identification of the fact that there were no public policy reasons not to treat post-nuptial agreements as contracts alter the weight that the Board attached to them in *MacLeod*? The Board did not say that they had to be given more weight as a result of sweeping away the public policy objections to them. Those objections had long ceased to be relevant and had not inhibited courts from giving some and, in some circumstances, decisive weight to ante-nuptial agreements. The circumstances surrounding the conclusion of a contract will either result in the contract being of full effect, or of no effect at all. The courts have always adopted a more nuanced approach to ante- and post-nuptial agreements. We cannot see why it mattered whether or not the agreement in *MacLeod* was a contract.

63. In summary, we consider that the Board in *MacLeod* was wrong to hold that post-nuptial agreements were contracts but that ante-nuptial agreements were not. That question did not arise for decision in that case any more than in this and does not matter anyway. It is a red herring. Regardless of whether one or both are contracts, the ancillary relief court should apply the same principles when considering ante-nuptial agreements as it applies to post-nuptial agreements.

*The Board's approach to post-nuptial agreements*

64. What was the approach that the Board held in *MacLeod* should be applied to post-nuptial agreements? The Board held that the court should adopt the same approach as that laid down by Parliament for varying maintenance agreements in section 35 of the 1973 Act, "looking for a change in the circumstances in the light of which the financial arrangements were made, the sort of change which would make those arrangements manifestly unjust" (para 41). The Board also endorsed the "oft-cited passage" from the judgment of Ormrod LJ in *Edgar,* which we have cited at para 38 above.

65. These tests are appropriate for a separation agreement. They are not necessarily appropriate for all post-nuptial agreements. A separation agreement is designed to take effect immediately and to address the circumstances prevailing at the time that it is made, as well, of course, as those contemplated in the future. It will have regard to any children of the family, to the assets of husband and wife, to their incomes and to their pension rights. Thus it makes sense to look for a significant change of circumstances as the criterion justifying a departure from the agreement. The same will be true to a lesser extent where a post-nuptial agreement is made well on in a marriage, as in *NA v MA* and *MacLeod* itself, or at the start of a marriage if one or both parties bring significant property to it. But where a young couple enter into an agreement just after embarking on married life, owning no property of value, there will be no relevant circumstances prevailing at the time of their agreement. In that event change of circumstances will not be such a useful test. The circumstances will almost inevitably have changed by the time the marriage founders and the effect to be given to the post-nuptial agreement will depend on wider considerations.

66. *MacLeod* has done a valuable service in sweeping away the archaic notions of public policy which have tended to obfuscate the approach to nuptial agreements. But for the reasons that we have given we have

not found that it assists in approaching the problem at the heart of this appeal for we have been able to accept neither its thesis that ante-nuptial agreements are fundamentally different from post-nuptial agreements nor, without reservation, its approach to post-nuptial settlements.

*The issues raised*

67. The issues raised on the facts of this case can be placed under three heads:

    a. Were there circumstances attending the making of the agreement that detract from the weight that should be accorded to it?

    b. Were there circumstances attending the making of the agreement that enhance the weight that should be accorded to it; the foreign element?

    c. Did the circumstances prevailing when the court's order was made make it fair or just to depart from the agreement?

    We shall have to consider these questions in the context of the facts of this case, but at this stage we propose to address the issues of principle that they raise.

*Factors detracting from the weight to be accorded to the agreement*

68. If an ante-nuptial agreement, or indeed a post-nuptial agreement, is to carry full weight, both the husband and wife must enter into it of their own free will, without undue influence or pressure, and informed of its implications. The third and fifth of the six safeguards proposed in the consultation document (see para 5 above) were designed to ensure this. Baron J applied these safeguards, found that they were not satisfied, and accorded the agreement reduced weight for this reason. The Court of Appeal did not consider that the circumstances in which the agreement was reached diminished the weight to be attached to it. In so far as the safeguards were not strictly satisfied, this was not material on the particular facts of this case.

69. The safeguards in the consultation document are designed to apply regardless of the circumstances of the particular case, in order to ensure, inter alia, that in all cases ante-nuptial contracts will not be binding unless they are freely concluded and properly informed. It is necessary to have black and white rules of this kind if agreements are otherwise to be binding. There is no need for them, however, in the current state of the law. The safeguards in the consultation document are likely to be highly relevant, but we consider that the Court of

Appeal was correct in principle to ask whether there was any material lack of disclosure, information or advice. Sound legal advice is obviously desirable, for this will ensure that a party understands the implications of the agreement, and full disclosure of any assets owned by the other party may be necessary to ensure this. But if it is clear that a party is fully aware of the implications of an ante-nuptial agreement and indifferent to detailed particulars of the other party's assets, there is no need to accord the agreement reduced weight because he or she is unaware of those particulars. What is important is that each party should have all the information that is material to his or her decision, and that each party should intend that the agreement should govern the financial consequences of the marriage coming to an end.

70. It is, of course, important that each party should intend that the agreement should be effective. In the past it may not have been right to infer from the fact of the conclusion of the agreement that the parties intended it to take effect, for they may have been advised that such agreements were void under English law and likely to carry little or no weight. That will no longer be the case. As we have shown the courts have recently been according weight, sometimes even decisive weight, to ante-nuptial agreements and this judgment will confirm that they are right to do so. Thus in future it will be natural to infer that parties who enter into an ante-nuptial agreement to which English law is likely to be applied intend that effect should be given to it.

71. In relation to the circumstances attending the making of the nuptial agreement, this comment of Ormrod LJ in Edgar v Edgar at p 1417, although made about a separation agreement, is pertinent:

> "It is not necessary in this connection to think in formal legal terms, such as misrepresentation or estoppel; *all* the circumstances as they affect each of two human beings must be considered in the complex relationship of marriage."

The first question will be whether any of the standard vitiating factors: duress, fraud or misrepresentation, is present. Even if the agreement does not have contractual force, those factors will negate any effect the agreement might otherwise have. But unconscionable conduct such as undue pressure (falling short of duress) will also be likely to eliminate the weight to be attached to the agreement, and other unworthy conduct, such as exploitation of a dominant position to secure an unfair advantage, would reduce or eliminate it.

72. The court may take into account a party's emotional state, and what pressures he or she was under to agree. But that again cannot be considered in isolation from what would have happened had he or she not been under those pressures. The circumstances of the parties at the time of the agreement will be relevant. Those will include such matters as their age and maturity, whether either or both had been married or been in long-term relationships before. For such couples their experience of previous relationships may explain the terms of the agreement, and may also show what they foresaw when they entered into the agreement. What may not be easily foreseeable for less mature couples may well be in contemplation of more mature couples. Another important factor may be whether the marriage would have gone ahead without an agreement, or without the terms which had been agreed. This may cut either way.

73. If the terms of the agreement are unfair from the start, this will reduce its weight, although this question will be subsumed in practice in the question of whether the agreement operates unfairly having regard to the circumstances prevailing at the time of the breakdown of the marriage.

*Factors enhancing the weight to be accorded to the agreement; the foreign element*

74 The issue raised under this heading is whether the foreign elements of a case can enhance the weight to be given to an ante-nuptial agreement. In this case the husband was French and the wife German and the agreement had a German law clause. We have already explained why we do not consider it material in English ancillary relief proceedings whether the nuptial agreement under consideration is or is not a contract. The court can overrule the agreement of the parties, whether contractual or not, and applies the same criteria when considering whether to do so. When dealing with agreements concluded in the past, and the agreement in this case was concluded in 1998, foreign elements such as those in this case may bear on the important question of whether or not the parties intended their agreement to be effective. In the case of agreements made in recent times and, *a fortiori,* any agreement made after this judgment, the question of whether the parties intended their agreement to take effect is unlikely to be in issue, so foreign law will not need to be considered in relation to that question.

*Fairness*

75. *White v White* and *Miller v Miller* establish that the overriding criterion to be applied in ancillary relief proceedings is that of

fairness and identify the three strands of need, compensation and sharing that are relevant to the question of what is fair. If an ante-nuptial agreement deals with those matters in a way that the court might adopt absent such an agreement, there is no problem about giving effect to the agreement. The problem arises where the agreement makes provisions that conflict with what the court would otherwise consider to be the requirements of fairness. The fact of the agreement is capable of altering what is fair. It is an important factor to be weighed in the balance. We would advance the following proposition, to be applied in the case of both ante- and post-nuptial agreements, in preference to that suggested by the Board in *MacLeod:*

**"The court should give effect to a nuptial agreement that is freely entered into by each party with a full appreciation of its implications unless in the circumstances prevailing it would not be fair to hold the parties to their agreement."**

76. That leaves outstanding the difficult question of the circumstances in which it will not be fair to hold the parties to their agreement. This will necessarily depend upon the facts of the particular case, and it would not be desirable to lay down rules that would fetter the flexibility that the court requires to reach a fair result. There is, however, some guidance that we believe that it is safe to give directed to the situation where there are no tainting circumstances attending the conclusion of the agreement.

*Children of the family*

77. Section 25 of the 1973 Act provides that first consideration must be given to the welfare while a minor of any child of the family who is under 18. A nuptial agreement cannot be allowed to prejudice the reasonable requirements of any children of the family.

*Autonomy*

78. The reason why the court should give weight to a nuptial agreement is that there should be respect for individual autonomy. The court should accord respect to the decision of a married couple as to the manner in which their financial affairs should be regulated. It would be paternalistic and patronising to override their agreement simply on the basis that the court knows best. This is particularly true where the parties' agreement addresses existing circumstances and not merely the contingencies of an uncertain future.

*Non-matrimonial property*

79. Often parties to a marriage will be motivated in concluding a nuptial agreement by a wish to make provision for existing property owned by one or other, or property that one or other anticipates receiving from a third party. The House of Lords in *White v White* and *Miller v Miller* drew a distinction between such property and matrimonial property accumulated in the course of the marriage. That distinction is particularly significant where the parties make express agreement as to the disposal of such property in the event of the termination of the marriage. There is nothing inherently unfair in such an agreement and there may be good objective justification for it, such as obligations towards existing family members. As Rix LJ put it at para 73

> "… if the parties to a prospective marriage have something important to agree with one another, then it is often much better, and more honest, for that agreement to be made at the outset, before the marriage, rather than left to become a source of disappointment or acrimony within marriage."

*Future circumstances*

80. Where the ante-nuptial agreement attempts to address the contingencies, unknown and often unforeseen, of the couple's future relationship there is more scope for what happens to them over the years to make it unfair to hold them to their agreement. The circumstances of the parties often change over time in ways or to an extent which either cannot be or simply was not envisaged. The longer the marriage has lasted, the more likely it is that this will be the case. Once again we quote from the judgment of Rix LJ at para 73.

> "I have in mind (and in this respect there is no real difference between an agreement made just before or just after a marriage) that a pre-nuptial agreement is intended to look forward over the whole period of a marriage to the possibility of its ultimate failure and divorce: and thus it is potentially a longer lasting agreement than almost any other (apart from a lease, and those are becoming shorter and subject to optional break clauses). Over the potential many decades of a marriage it is impossible to cater for the myriad different circumstances which may await its parties. Thorpe LJ has mentioned the very relevant case of a second marriage between mature adults perhaps each with children of their own by their first marriages. However, equally or more typical will be the marriage of young persons, perhaps not yet adults, for whom the future is an entirely open book. If in such a case a pre-nuptial agreement should provide for no recovery by each spouse from

the other in the event of divorce, and the marriage should see the formation of a fortune which each spouse had played an equal role in their different ways in creating, but the fortune was in the hands for the most part of one spouse rather than the other, would it be right to give the same weight to their early agreement as in another perhaps very different example?"

The answer to this question is, in the individual case, likely to be 'no'.

81. Of the three strands identified in *White v White* and *Miller v Miller,* it is the first two, needs and compensation, which can most readily render it unfair to hold the parties to an ante-nuptial agreement. The parties are unlikely to have intended that their ante-nuptial agreement should result, in the event of the marriage breaking up, in one partner being left in a predicament of real need, while the other enjoys a sufficiency or more, and such a result is likely to render it unfair to hold the parties to their agreement. Equally if the devotion of one partner to looking after the family and the home has left the other free to accumulate wealth, it is likely to be unfair to hold the parties to an agreement that entitles the latter to retain all that he or she has earned.

82. Where, however, these considerations do not apply and each party is in a position to meet his or her needs, fairness may well not require a departure from their agreement as to the regulation of their financial affairs in the circumstances that have come to pass. Thus it is in relation to the third strand, sharing, that the court will be most likely to make an order in the terms of the nuptial agreement in place of the order that it would otherwise have made.

83. So far as concerns the general approach of the court to ante-nuptial agreements, Wilson LJ at para 130 endorsed the following comments of Baron J at first instance

"111. I am certain that English courts are now much more ready to attribute the appropriate (and, in the right case, decisive) weight to an agreement as part of 'all the circumstances of case' [within the meaning of section 25(1) of the Act of 1973] …

119. Upon divorce, when a party is seeking *quantification* of a claim for financial relief, it is the court that determines the result after applying the Act. The court grants the award and formulates the order with the parties' agreement being but one factor in the process and perhaps, in the right case, it being the most compelling factor …"

We also would endorse these comments.

84. We now turn to apply these principles to the facts of this case.

*The background to the signing of the agreement*

85. At the time the parties met in November 1997 they were both living in London. The wife comes from a very rich German family, whose wealth is derived primarily from two very successful businesses in chromatography, filtration and the processing/refinement of paper, and the manufacture of paper. The husband comes from a family which is well-off, his father having been a senior executive with IBM, at one time in charge of its European operations. He now resides in London for tax reasons, but retains property in Antibes. When the couple met the husband had been working in London for about 2 years with JP Morgan & Co, and was earning about £50,000, which was a substantial sum at that date, particularly given his age, and which had increased to about £120,000 by the time the ante-nuptial agreement was executed. They became engaged in June 1998 and were married in November 1998. They made London their home.

86. It was the wife who suggested that the parties should enter into an ante-nuptial agreement. Although the judge was sure that the wife wanted her husband to love her for herself, the wife emphasised her father's insistence, because she felt it made her seem less insensitive to her future spouse, given that the terms excluded all his potential rights (even in times of crisis). The wife did not make it obvious that she personally demanded it as a precondition of marriage. The judge found that the husband was eager to comply because he did not want the wife to be disinherited, he wanted to marry her, and he could not perceive of circumstances where he would wish to make a claim.

87. The wife's family decided that this agreement would be drawn up in Germany by a notary, Dr N Magis, who had undertaken other work for the family. The instructions to Dr Magis came originally from the wife's mother on 6 July, 1998, who told him that the marriage was to be in London in the autumn and that neither of the parties wished to make any claim on the other in the event of divorce. Dr Magis pointed out that such a deal might leave a young mother with children in difficulty but he was informed that the daughter's income was some DM500,000 a year plus other monies managed by their father and so despite the future son-in-law's excellent income "even in the worse case scenario there would be no risk to their daughter". On the same day, 6 July, 1998, Dr Magis spoke by telephone to the wife. She confirmed the facts given by her mother. It was agreed that the draft

was to be prepared as quickly as possible in order to give the husband "an opportunity to prepare for the conclusion of the contract" which was to be signed on the first weekend of August. Dr Magis was insistent that the husband had sufficient time so that he could take advice if he wished and fully understand the implications of what he was signing.

88. On 17 July, 1998 Dr Magis sent by fax to the wife a draft of the agreement, under cover of a letter in which he wrote: "You wanted to discuss the content of the agreement with your future spouse and have it translated into a language convenient for him". In the draft, which was in German, there was a clause for the parties to insert the approximate value of their respective assets; but the wife telephoned Dr Magis that day and said that the clause should be deleted and that she and the husband would separately notify each other of the value of their assets.

89. A second draft was produced by 20 July, 1998 and it was sent to the wife's father. On 23 July, 1998 the wife telephoned Dr Magis and told him that she had discussed the draft with her father and he wanted additions in relation to company shares – specifically that the husband should not be able to inherit them directly or "circuitously via their children". It was agreed that this would be dealt with by the wife's drawing up a will. A final draft version was made available to the wife in London at about this date.

90. The judge found that it was highly unlikely that the wife showed the husband the first draft, or that she informed him about her mother's or father's involvement in the drawing up the terms of the agreement. But the judge rejected the husband's evidence that he did not see the draft at all. The judge found that the wife showed him the final draft which was available on about 24 July, 1998, about one week before the signing ceremony. The basic terms were made clear to the husband, but the husband was not made aware that Dr Magis wanted him to have a translation to give him a proper opportunity to consider the precise terms and see a lawyer.

91. On 1 August, 1998 the parties attended at the office of Dr Magis near Düsseldorf. Their meeting with him lasted for between two and three hours. The husband told Dr Magis that he had seen the draft agreement but that he did not have a translation of it. Dr Magis was angry when he learned of the absence of a translation, which he considered to be important for the purpose of ensuring that the husband had had a proper opportunity to consider its terms. Dr Magis indicated that he

was minded to postpone its execution but, when told that the parties were unlikely again to be in Germany prior to the marriage, he was persuaded to continue. Dr Magis, speaking English, then took the parties through the terms of the agreement in detail and explained them clearly; but he did not offer a verbatim translation of every line. The parties executed the agreement (which bears the date of 4 August, 1998) in his presence.

92. Not only did the husband not take advantage of Dr Magis' wish to postpone execution so that he could take independent legal advice, but in the 4 months or so following the execution of the agreement at the beginning of August 1998 until the marriage in London on 28 November, 1998, the husband did not take the opportunity to seek independent advice.

*Events leading up to the breakdown of the marriage*

93. The parties lived together in London for more than a year after the marriage. In April 2000 the husband was posted to New York by his employers, J P Morgan. The family moved there, but the wife did not find life in America congenial. So she returned to London in May 2001. The husband was transferred back to London in October of that year. Their older daughter (now 11) was born here in September 1999 before they left and their younger daughter (now 8) in May 2002 after their return. In July 2003 he left his employers and embarked on his research studies at Oxford. Both parties "accepted that [he] was miserable and discontented [and] a change of tack was inevitable". He embarked upon research for a doctorate in biotechnology at Oxford University, thinking that a "combination of scientific knowledge and his banking experience would put him in a good position to capitalise upon and exploit his financial expertise in future years" (Baron J, paras 50 and 51). During the first five years of the marriage, while he was working for J P Morgan, the husband generated a very substantial amount of income. He had amassed about $500,000 of capital out of his earnings, but during the next two years he expended it for the benefit of the family. Meantime the wife's father had transferred to her a substantial amount of capital, which raised her shareholding in the two groups of companies to their present level. He also paid her a substantial sum in return for her surrender of any entitlement under German law to a portion of his estate on her death.

94. The husband's work at Oxford led him to spend many nights away from home. By this time the marriage was already in difficulties. By August 2006 separation had become inevitable and the wife moved

with the children from the matrimonial home, a rented flat in Knightsbridge where the husband still lives into another rented flat in Knightsbridge. From then on there was no way back, and proceedings for divorce followed soon afterwards. Wilson LJ's assessment was that throughout the marriage the family's standard of living had been extremely comfortable, albeit tempered by the wife's aversion to profligacy: para 117.

95. It was originally the husband's intention to return to the financial sector once he had obtained his doctorate, but he no longer wishes to do so and Baron J held that this course would not be open to him in any event.

*The foreign element and the agreement*

96. The wife was German, and the husband was French. The agreement was drafted by a German lawyer under German law. They were then living in London and London was plainly intended to be their first matrimonial home.

97. The agreement stated (in recital 2) that (a) the husband was a French citizen and, according to his own statement, did not have a good command of German, although he did, according to his own statement and in the opinion of the officiating notary (Dr Magis), have an adequate command of English; (b) the document was therefore read out by the notary in German and then translated by him into English; (c) the parties to the agreement declared that they wished to waive the use of an interpreter or a second notary as well as a written translation; and (d) a draft of the text of the agreement had been submitted to the parties two weeks before the execution of the document.

98. Clause 1 stated the intention of the parties to get married in London and to establish their first matrimonial residence there. By clause 2 the parties agreed that the effects of their marriage in general, as well as in terms of matrimonial property and the law of succession, would be governed by German law. Clause 3 provided for separation of property, and the parties stated: "Despite advice from the notary, we waive the possibility of having a schedule of our respective current assets appended to this deed."

99. Clause 5 provided for the mutual waiver of claims for maintenance of any kind whatsoever following divorce:

> "The waiver shall apply to the fullest extent permitted by law even should one of us – whether or not for reasons attributable to fault on that person's part – be in serious difficulties.

The notary has given us detailed advice about the right to maintenance between divorced spouses and the consequences of the reciprocal waiver agreed above.

Each of us is aware that there may be significant adverse consequences as a result of the above waiver.

Despite reference by the notary to the existing case law in respect of the total or partial invalidity of broadly worded maintenance waivers in certain cases, particularly insofar as such waivers have detrimental effects for the raising of children and/or the public treasury, we ask that the waiver be recorded in the above form …

Each of us declares that he or she is able, based on his or her current standpoint, to provide for his or her own maintenance on a permanent basis, but is however aware that changes may occur."

100. Clause 7(2) recorded that Dr Magis had pointed out to the parties that, despite the choice of German law, foreign law might, from the standpoint of foreign legal systems, apply to the legal relationships between the parties, in particular in accordance with the local law of the matrimonial residence, the law of the place and/or nationality of the husband, with nationality and the place where assets were located being especially relevant to inheritance. The agreement said: "The notary has pointed out that he has not provided any binding information about the content of foreign law, but has recommended that we obtain advice from a lawyer or notary practising in the respective legal system." By letter to the parties dated 3 August, 1998 Dr Magis again stressed that, before taking up permanent residence abroad, they should take the advice of a local lawyer in relation to the effect of the agreement there.

101. The unchallenged evidence before the judge was that: (a) the agreement was valid under German law; (b) the choice of German law was valid; (c) there was no duty of disclosure under German law; (d) the agreement would be recognised as valid under French conflict of laws rules.

102. The terms of the agreement recite that the parties intend to establish their first matrimonial residence in London and it confirms by clause 7(2) that the law of their matrimonial residence may come to apply to their legal relationship as spouses. It was therefore inherent in the agreement that another system of law might apply its terms and so it could never be regarded as foolproof.

*Applicable law*

103. In England, when the court exercises its jurisdiction to make an order for financial relief under the Matrimonial Causes Act 1973, it will normally apply English law, irrespective of the domicile of the parties, or any foreign connection: *Dicey, Morris and Collins, Conflict of Laws*, vol 2, 14th ed 2006, Rule 91(7), and e.g. *C v C (Ancillary Relief: Nuptial Settlement*) [2004] EWCA Civ 1030, [2005] Fam 250, at para 31.

104. The United Kingdom has made a policy decision not to participate in the results of the work done by the European Community and the Hague Conference on Private International Law to apply uniform rules of private international law in relation to maintenance obligations. Although the United Kingdom Government has opted in to Council Regulation (EC) No 4/2009 of 18 December, 2008 on jurisdiction, applicable law and enforcement of decisions and cooperation in matters relating to maintenance obligations, the rules relating to applicable law will not apply in the United Kingdom. That is because the effect of Article 15 of the Council Regulation is that the law applicable to maintenance obligations is to be determined in accordance with the 2007 Hague Protocol on the law applicable to maintenance obligations, but only in the Member States bound by the Hague Protocol.

105. The United Kingdom will not be bound by the Hague Protocol, because it agreed to participate in the Council Regulation only on the basis that it would not be obliged to join in accession to the Hague Protocol by the EU. The United Kingdom Government's position was that there was very little application of foreign law in family matters within the United Kingdom, and in maintenance cases in particular the expense of proving the content of that law would be disproportionate to the low value of the vast majority of maintenance claims.

106. For the purposes of the present appeal it is worth noting that the Hague Protocol allows the parties to designate the law applicable to a maintenance obligation, but also provides that, unless at the time of the designation the parties were fully informed and aware of the consequences of their designation, the law designated by the parties shall not apply where the application of that law would lead to manifestly unfair or unreasonable consequences for any of the parties (Article 8(1), (5)).

107. The ante-nuptial agreement had provision for separation of property and exclusion of community of property of accrued gains (clause 3),

in relation to which the chosen law would have governed: *Dicey, Morris and Collins*, vol 2, para 28–020. But although the economic effect of *Miller/Macfarlane* may have much in common with community of property, it is clear that the exercise under the 1973 Act does not relate to a matrimonial property regime: *cf* Case C-220/95 *Van den Boogaard v Laumen* (Case C-220/95) [1997] ECR I-1147, [1997] QB 759; *Agbaje v Agbaje* [2010] UKSC 13, [2010] 2 WLR 709, para 57.

108. In summary, the issues in this case are governed exclusively by English law. The relevance of German law and the German choice of law clause is that they clearly demonstrate the intention of the parties that the ante-nuptial agreement should, if possible, be binding on them (see para 74 above).

*The decision of the trial judge*

109. Baron J held that the ante-nuptial agreement was not a valid contract under English law: paras 129, 132. Nevertheless she said that in assessing the husband's needs she would take account of all the circumstances of the case and that his award should be circumscribed to a degree to reflect the fact that at the outset he agreed to sign the agreement. As she explained in para 139:

> "… he understood the underlying premise that he was not entitled to anything if the parties divorced. In essence, he accepted that he was expected to be self-sufficient. As a man of the world that was abundantly clear. His decision to enter into the agreement must therefore affect the award."

110. Baron J found that the ante-nuptial agreement fell foul of a number of the safeguards set out in para 4.23 of the Home Office consultation document and was, prima facie, unfair: para 38. She said that its preparation was very one-sided and therefore was demonstrably not neutral: para 76(d). She held that it was defective under English law because the husband received no independent advice; that it deprived him of all claims to the furthest permissible legal extent even in a situation of want, which was manifestly unfair; that there was no disclosure by the wife; that there were no negotiations; and that two children had been born of the marriage: para 137. It was with these factors in mind that she conducted her assessment.

111. In the result the judge awarded the husband £700,000 to put towards his then debts of £800,000 and £25,000 to buy a car; £2.5m to buy a home of his own in London; €630,000 to buy a home in Germany (to

remain owned by the wife or an entity set up by her) for the purpose of caring for his children in accordance with a shared residence order during his periods of residence with them (for 15 years); and £2.335m as a capitalised revenue *Duxbury* fund to provide the husband with a total annual income for life of £100,000, taking into account an annual gross taxable earning capacity of £30,000 until retirement at age 65. Thus the husband's award amounted in total to £5.560m (excluding the award of €630,000 for housing in Germany). She also awarded him periodical payments of £35,000 for each child until they ceased full time education. No indication is given in the judgment of the extent of the discount, if any, that she made to take account of the terms of the ante-nuptial agreement.

*The decision of the Court of Appeal*

112. The wife sought and was granted permission to appeal against this order to the Court of Appeal. On 2 July 2009 the Court of Appeal (Thorpe, Rix and Wilson LJJ) set aside the order of Baron J: [2009] EWCA Civ 649. Thorpe LJ said that, despite the appearance of the ante-nuptial contract as a factor, the impression given by the judge's award was of a negligible resulting discount: para 43. He held that, in order to give proper weight to the ante-nuptial contract, the sum of £2.5m for housing should not be the husband's absolutely but should be held by him only for the years of parenting. The income fund should be capitalised at a rate to cover his needs only until the younger child's 22nd birthday. Thus, while he would not interfere with the awards for the car, for the payment of the husband's debts, for housing in Germany and the periodical payments for the children, the major funds should be provided for his role as a father rather than as a former husband: para 50. Wilson LJ, who delivered the leading judgment on the facts, said that the judge's application of the law to the facts was plainly wrong. She erred in the exercise which she conducted under section 25 of the Matrimonial Causes Act 1973 in not giving decisive weight to the ante-nuptial contract. The result was that relief should have been granted to the husband only indirectly, in his capacity as a home-maker for the girls: paras 135, 149. Rix LJ, agreeing with both judgments, also said that the ante-nuptial contract should be given decisive weight in the section 25 exercise: para 81.

113. The husband cross-appealed on the sum awarded for housing in Germany based on fresh evidence. His appeal on that matter was allowed and it was remitted to the judge to determine the appropriate figure in the fresh circumstances. Wilson LJ noted that the wife had conceded that, notwithstanding her success in the appeal and thus of

her submission that the husband's claim should be limited to that of a home-maker for the girls, it was appropriate for her to be ordered to meet the costs of the financial proceedings up to July 2008 when Baron J delivered her judgment and to clear the husband's other debts: para 152. Nevertheless the costs of the appeal were awarded to the wife. She was ordered to pay the costs of the cross-appeal.

*Discussion*

*The circumstances in which the ante-nuptial agreement was made*

114. The Court of Appeal differed from the finding of the trial judge that the ante-nuptial agreement was tainted by the circumstances in which it was made. Wilson LJ, with whom the other two members of the court agree, dealt with these matters in detail. The judge had found that the husband had lacked independent legal advice. Wilson LJ held that he had well understood the effect of the agreement, had had the opportunity to take independent advice, but had failed to do so. In these circumstances he could not pray in aid the fact that he had not taken independent legal advice.

115. The judge held that the wife had failed to disclose the approximate value of her assets. Wilson LJ observed that the husband knew that the wife had substantial wealth and had shown no interest in ascertaining its approximate extent. More significantly, he had made no suggestion that this would have had any effect on his readiness to enter into the agreement.

116. The judge held that the absence of negotiations was a third vitiating factor. Wilson LJ observed that the judge had given no explanation as to why this was a vitiating factor, and that the absence of negotiations merely reflected the fact that the background of the parties rendered the entry into such an agreement commonplace.

117. We agree with the Court of Appeal that the judge was wrong to find that the ante-nuptial agreement had been tainted in these ways. We also agree that it is not apparent that the judge made any significant reduction in her award to reflect the fact of the agreement. In these circumstances, the Court of Appeal was entitled to replace her award with its own assessment, and the issue for this court is whether the Court of Appeal erred in principle.

*Need*

118. Baron J had held that the ante-nuptial agreement was "manifestly unfair" in that it made no provision for the possibility that the husband might be reduced to circumstances of real need. Wilson LJ

at para 144 appears to have thought that there was nothing unfair about this and, inferentially, that had the husband been in a situation of real need the agreement would none the less have been good reason for the court to decline to alleviate this by an order of ancillary relief. We would not go so far as this.

119. We stated at para 73 above that the question of the fairness of the agreement can often be subsumed in the question of whether it would operate unfairly in the circumstances prevailing at the breakdown of the marriage, and this is such a case. Had the husband been incapacitated in the course of the marriage, so that he was incapable of earning his living, this might well have justified, in the interests of fairness, not holding him to the full rigours of the ante-nuptial agreement. But this was far from the case. On the evidence he is extremely able, and has added to his qualifications by pursuing a D Phil in biotechnology. Furthermore the generous relief given to cater for the needs of the two daughters will indirectly provide in large measure for the needs of the husband, until the younger daughter reaches the age of 22. Finally the Court of Appeal did not upset the judge's order that the wife should fund the discharge of debts of £700,000 owed by the husband, only a small part of which she had challenged.

120. In these circumstances we consider that the Court of Appeal was correct to conclude that the needs of the husband were not a factor that rendered it unfair to hold him to the terms of the ante-nuptial agreement, subject to making provision for the needs of the children of the family.

*Compensation*

121. There is no compensation factor in this case. The husband's decision to abandon his lucrative career in the city for the fields of academia was not motivated by the demands of his family, but reflected his own preference.

*Sharing*

122. This dispute raises the question of whether, as a result of his marriage, the husband should be entitled to a portion of the wealth that his wife has received from her family, in part before the marriage and in part during, but quite independently of it. When he married her he agreed that he should have no such entitlement.

123. Our conclusion is that in the circumstances of this case it is fair that he should be held to that agreement and that it would be unfair to

depart from it. We detect no error of principle on the part of the Court of Appeal. For these reasons we would dismiss this appeal.

**LORD MANCE**

124. I concur with the conclusion reached by the majority and with most of the majority's reasoning. I address only three specific areas: (i) whether ante- and post-nuptial agreements have contractual force; (ii) the starting point when considering the weight such agreements bear; and (iii) the Court of Appeal's exercise of its discretion.

125. *(i) Do ante- and post-nuptial agreements have contractual force?* In the old cases, the public policy objections, seen as existing to both ante- and post-nuptial agreements, were based on "the policy of the law, founded upon the relation which exists between the husband and wife, and the importance to society of maintaining that relation between them": *Cartwright v Cartwright* (1853) de G, M & G 982 p.990; and see *H v W* (1857) 3 K & J 382, where a provision in an ante-nuptial settlement, whereby income would be paid to the husband instead of the wife if the wife lived separately from him "through any fault of her own" was held void, because it might induce the husband to consent to her living apart and to "refuse to take steps to enforce the restitution of conjugal rights": p.386. The reasoning in these cases is, as Lady Hale observed in *MacLeod v MacLeod* [2010] 1 AC 298, in legal terms obsolete.

126. The objections thus swept away are not however the only objections which would exist to any regime which made ante- or post-nuptial agreements binding *tout court*. Parties who make such agreements are not necessarily on an equal standing, above all emotionally. They may not have a full appreciation of such an agreement's significance and likely impact. Above all, they may well not foresee, or cater adequately for, the way in which not only their relationship but their whole lives and individual circumstances may change, especially over time and very often as a direct or indirect result of their marriage.

127. In a context, like the present, where the English courts have jurisdiction and grant a decree of divorce or nullity, the further objections identified in the preceding paragraph are catered for by Part II of the Matrimonial Causes Act 1973. Hence, the majority's description in para 63 of the legal effect of any ante- or post-nuptial agreement as a "red herring" in this case. The principle established in *Hyman v Hyman* [1929] AC 601, precluding the ousting of the court's statutory jurisdiction after such a decree, must in my view apply to any such agreement.

128. Like Lady Hale, para 138 (1) and (2) and para 156, I go no further and express no view on the binding or other nature of an ante-nuptial agreement. It is not difficult to envisage circumstances in which, if such an agreement were to be regarded as having contractual force, its enforcement could be sought before a court, particularly an overseas court, lacking the jurisdiction under Part II of the 1973 Act which applies only when the forum is an English divorce court. I also agree in this respect with what Lady Hale says in para 159.

129. *(ii) The starting point*: The majority (para 75) and Lady Hale (para 169) both accept the overriding criterion or guiding principle for exercise of the statutory discretion as being one of fairness. But they suggest differently worded tests for approaching this exercise where there has been an ante-nuptial agreement. I cannot think the difference in wording likely to be important in practice. It appears to relate primarily to the starting point or onus, when feeding into the discretionary exercise the circumstances as they currently appear compared with those that existed or were contemplated at the date of the ante-nuptial agreement. The words "intending it to have legal effect" in Lady Hale's first sentence must, in relation to any future ante-nuptial agreement, be implicit in the majority's formulation "freely entered into by each party with a full appreciation of its implications". If Lady Hale's second sentence had used the word "unfair", rather than "fair", its effect would, as I see it, match precisely that of the second part of the majority's formulation ("unless in the circumstances, etc …"). My own inclination, in agreement with the majority, is that this is how the application of the overriding criterion should be approached. Given an ante-nuptial agreement, made freely and with full appreciation of the circumstances, it is natural in the first instance to ask whether there is anything in the circumstances as they now appear to make it unfair to give effect to the agreement. But the ultimate question remains on any view what is fair, and the starting point or onus is, as I have said, unlikely to matter once all the facts are before the court.

130. *(iii) The Court of Appeal's exercise of discretion*: I agree with the majority that there is no reason to set aside the Court of Appeal's re-exercise of the statutory discretion, undertaken after concluding that Baron J had erred in principle. Baron J held the husband to be entitled to a house of his own (para 140(a)). The Court of Appeal limited this aspect of the award – confining his entitlement to the period, generously assessed, during which he could be expected to provide a home for the children, and concluding that he had no

further needs requiring him to retain such a house outright or for a longer period. Viewing the position overall, I do not see that we would be justified in concluding that the husband has or is likely after that period to have needs generated as a result of parenthood which will not be covered by the Court of Appeal's order or his own resources. It follows that I agree with Rix LJ's conclusion (para 81) that: "The provision of a home for the husband and for his needs as a father, carer and home-maker for the children will, in the circumstances, more than adequately provide him with the means to support his own needs. There is no case for making that home and financial support his to command for the whole of his life-time."

**LADY HALE**

131. The issue in this case is simple: what weight should the court hearing a claim for ancillary relief under the Matrimonial Causes Act 1973 give to an agreement entered into between the parties before they got married which purported to determine the result? I propose to call these "ante-nuptial agreements" because our legislation already uses the term "ante-nuptial" to refer to things done before a marriage. I should also point out that, although our judgments talk only of marriage and married couples, our conclusions must also apply to couples who have entered into a civil partnership.

132. The issue may be simple, but underlying it are some profound questions about the nature of marriage in the modern law and the role of the courts in determining it. Marriage is, of course, a contract, in the sense that each party must agree to enter into it and once entered both are bound by its legal consequences. But it is also a status. This means two things. First, the parties are not entirely free to determine all its legal consequences for themselves. They contract into the package which the law of the land lays down. Secondly, their marriage also has legal consequences for other people and for the state. Nowadays there is considerable freedom and flexibility within the marital package but there is an irreducible minimum. This includes a couple's mutual duty to support one another and their children. We have now arrived at a position where the differing roles which either may adopt within the relationship are entitled to equal esteem. The question for us is how far individual couples should be free to re-write that essential feature of the marital relationship as they choose.

133. A further question is how far this question can and should be determined by this Court and how far it should be left to Parliament,

preferably with the advice and assistance of the Law Commission. There is not much doubt that the law of marital agreements is in a mess. It is ripe for systematic review and reform. The Commission has a current project to examine the status and enforceability of agreements made between spouses and civil partners (or those contemplating marriage or civil partnership) concerning their property and finances and a consultation paper will be published shortly (see Law Commission, *Annual Report 2009–10*, 2010, Law Com No 323, paras 2.68 to 2.75).

134. This is just the sort of task for which the Law Commission was established by the Law Commissions Act 1965 and in which it has had such success, particularly in the field of family law. The Commission can research and review the law over the whole area, not just the narrow section which is presented by the facts of an individual case. It can consider such research as there is into the use and abuse of marital agreements of all kinds. It can commission research into the experience and attitudes of practitioners and the public. It can identify and discuss the full range of policy arguments, including a detailed examination of the experience of legislative reform in other common law countries (see, for example, I M Ellman, *Marital Agreements and Private Autonomy in the United States*, where initial enthusiasm has been tempered by experience in practice). It can examine critically their economic impact, and in particular whether they can be expected to increase certainty and decrease cost, or whether in fact the reverse may happen, and in any event whether the suggested benefits will outweigh the suggested costs (see, for example, R H George, P G Harris and J Herring, "Pre-Nuptial Agreements: For Better or Worse?" [2009] Fam Law 934). It can develop options for reform across the whole field, upon which it can consult widely. In the light of all this, it can make detailed proposals for legislative reform, which can be put before Parliament.

135. In short, that is the democratic way of achieving comprehensive and principled reform. There is some enthusiasm for reform within the judiciary and the profession, and in the media, and one can well understand why. But that does not mean that it is right. This is a complicated subject upon which there is a large literature and knowledgeable and thoughtful people may legitimately hold differing views. Some may regard freedom of contract as the prevailing principle in all circumstances; others may regard that as a 19th century concept which has since been severely modified, particularly

in the case of continuing relationships typically (though not invariably) characterised by imbalance of bargaining power (such as landlord and tenant, employer and employee). Some may regard people who are about to marry as in all respects fully autonomous beings; others may wonder whether people who are typically (although not invariably) in love can be expected to make rational choices in the same way that businessmen can. Some may regard the recognition of these factual differences as patronising or paternalistic; others may regard them as sensible and realistic. Some may think that to accord a greater legal status to these agreements will produce greater certainty and lesser costs should the couple divorce; others may question whether this will in fact be achieved, save at the price of inflexibility and injustice. Some may believe that giving greater force to marital agreements will encourage more people to marry; others may wonder whether they will encourage more people to divorce. Perhaps above all, some may think it permissible to contract out of the guiding principles of equality and non-discrimination within marriage; others may think this a retrograde step likely only to benefit the strong at the expense of the weak.

136. These difficult issues cannot be resolved in an individual case, in particular a case with such very unusual features as this one. Different people will naturally react to this particular human story in different ways, depending upon their values and experience of life. There may be some, for example, who are astonished that an intelligent young man, who was apparently happy to sign away all claims upon his bride-to-be's considerable fortune, should now be seeking to make any claims upon her at all. There may be others who are astonished that a fabulously wealthy young woman should begrudge what is a very small proportion of her estate to ensure that the father of her children can live in reasonable comfort for the rest of his days.

137. Above all, perhaps, the court hearing a particular case can all too easily lose sight of the fact that, unlike a separation agreement, the object of an ante-nuptial agreement is to deny the economically weaker spouse the provision to which she – it is usually although by no means invariably she – would otherwise be entitled (see, for example, G F Brod, "Premarital Agreements and Gender Justice" (1994) 6 Yale Journal of Law and Feminism 229). This is amply borne out by the precedents available in recent text-books (see, for example, I Harris and R Spicer, *Prenuptial Agreements: A Practical Guide* (2008, Appendix D), or H Wood, D Lush, D Bishop, and A Murray, *Cohabitation: Law, Practice and Precedents* (2009, 4th ed,

pp 583 – 592)). Would any self-respecting young woman sign up to an agreement which assumed that she would be the only one who might otherwise have a claim, thus placing no limit on the claims that might be made against her, and then limited her claim to a pre-determined sum for each year of marriage regardless of the circumstances, as if her wifely services were being bought by the year? Yet that is what these precedents do. In short, there is a gender dimension to the issue which some may think ill-suited to decision by a court consisting of eight men and one woman.

138. It is for that reason that I have chosen to write a separate judgment, for although there is much within the majority judgment with which I agree, there are some points upon which I disagree. Specifically:

(1) I disagree with the view, mercifully *obiter* to the decision in this case, that ante-nuptial agreements are legally enforceable contracts.

(2) I disagree with the view, also mercifully *obiter* to the decision in this case, that it is open to this court to hold that they are.

(3) I disagree with the view that, in policy terms, there are no relevant differences between agreements made before and agreements made after a marriage.

(4) I disagree with the way in which the majority have formulated the test to be applied by a court hearing an application for financial relief, which I believe to be an impermissible gloss upon the courts' statutory duties. However, I agree that the court must consider the agreement in the light of the circumstances as they now exist and that the way the matter was put by the Privy Council in *MacLeod v MacLeod* [2008] UKPC 64, [2010] 1 AC 298, was too rigid, and in some cases, too strong; and I broadly agree with the majority upon the relevant considerations which the court should take into account.

(5) I disagree with the approach of the Court of Appeal to the actual outcome of this case, which the majority uphold. In my view it is inconsistent with the continued importance attached to the status of marriage in English law. This is independent of the weight to be attached to the agreement in this case.

(6) I consider that the reform of the law on ante- and post-nuptial agreements should be considered comprehensively, not limited to agreements catering for future separation or divorce.

I understand that Lord Mance shares my misgivings on points (1) and (2) above. He also takes the view that the difference between our formulations of the test, referred to in point (4) above, is unlikely to be important in practice. As the ultimate question is what is fair, the starting point is unlikely to matter once all the facts are before the court. I hope that he is right.

*The story so far: the different types of agreement between husband and wife*

139. It may be helpful to give a brief account of how the law has got into its current mess (for which I must take some of the blame). The common law regarded husband and wife as one person, and that person was the husband. He acquired ownership or control over all his wife's property and income, along with liability for her pre-marriage debts. She had no contractual capacity of her own and so of course they could not make contracts with one another. If the wife's family had property, it became common to make a marriage settlement which would preserve property for the wife's separate use. This was for the purposes of avoiding the property getting into her husband's hands, providing some security for the wife, and preserving it for their children or to revert to the wife's family if the couple were childless.

140. Legislation in the 19th century progressively extended the concept of the wife's separate property, so that after the Married Women's Property Act 1882 everything which a woman owned on marriage or acquired thereafter remained or became her separate property. The system of separate property thus established remains the only matrimonial property regime applicable in the law of England and Wales. It also meant that the wife eventually acquired full contractual capacity and so a husband and wife could now make contracts with one another as well as with third parties.

141. Agreements between a husband and a wife fall into three broad categories: (a) those made during their cohabitation, (b) those made upon or during their separation, and (c) those made in connection with current matrimonial proceedings. Of these, separation (type (b)) agreements have the longest history. Unlike modern ante-nuptial agreements, their original purpose was usually to make some sort of provision for the wife rather than to deprive her of it. At common law, the husband did have an obligation to support his wife, but until statute intervened she could only enforce this by pledging his credit for "necessaries". There is no need here to trace the evolution of the statutory remedies but two points are worth noting: first, the obligation to maintain while living apart generally depended upon the

husband either having committed a matrimonial offence or having agreed to maintain his wife in a separate household; and secondly, the obligations of husband and wife only became fully mutual with the major reforms which came into force in 1971 and are now largely contained in the Matrimonial Causes Act 1973. Moreover, until then there were many more people who lived apart for a long time without ever taking divorce or other matrimonial proceedings. An enforceable contractual obligation was therefore usually a great advantage for the wife.

142. There is nothing to stop a husband and wife from making legally binding arrangements, whether by contract or settlement, to regulate their property and affairs while they are still together (type (a) agreements). These days, the commonest example of this is an agreement to share the ownership or tenancy of the matrimonial home, bank accounts, savings or other assets. Agreements for housekeeping or personal allowances, on the other hand, might run into difficulties. In *Balfour v Balfour* [1919] 2 KB 571, a husband agreed to pay his wife £30 per month when he returned to his work in Ceylon while she remained in England for medical reasons. Duke LJ doubted whether the wife had given consideration for the husband's promise. Atkin LJ would have had no difficulty in finding that her promise to spend the money for its intended purposes was consideration, but held that the couple had never intended that the arrangement should have contractual force: "… the small courts of this country would have to be multiplied one hundredfold if these arrangements were held to result in legal obligations" (p 579). But any problems posed by the doctrine of consideration or the need to express contractual intent could be solved by making the agreement by deed.

143. However, agreements between husband and wife were also subject to two quite separate rules, each of which has a basis in public policy. The first rule ("public policy rule 1") was that agreements between husband and wife (or indeed between third parties and husband and/or wife) which provided for what was to happen in the event of their *future* separation or divorce were contrary to public policy and therefore void. This rule was developed in the context of agreements or settlements which made some or better financial provision for the wife if she were to live separately from her husband (for a comparatively recent example, see *Re Johnson's Will Trusts* [1967] Ch 387). Such an agreement could be seen as encouraging them to live apart – for example, by encouraging her to leave him, if it was sufficiently generous or more than she would get if she stayed with him, or

encouraging him to leave her, or to agree to her going, if it were not so generous. Such encouragement was seen as inconsistent with the fundamental, life-long and enforceable obligation of husband and wife to live with one another.

144. The second rule ("public policy rule 2") was developed in the context of separation agreements (type (b) agreements). Agreements for an immediate or existing separation between the spouses were not caught by public policy rule 1. Their purpose was usually two fold. They relieved the couple of the duty to live together: this meant that neither was guilty of the matrimonial offence of desertion and neither could petition for or enforce a decree of restitution of conjugal rights. They might also make provision for the wife and any children. In return she might agree not to go to court for a maintenance order. However, in the leading case of *Hyman v Hyman* [1929] AC 601 it was firmly established that such agreements could not oust the statutory powers of the courts to award financial provision should the couple divorce.

145. As recounted in *MacLeod v MacLeod* [2008] UKPC 64, [2010] 1 AC 298, at paras 20 to 24, that rule was later held to apply to other statutory powers to award maintenance. But in *Bennett v Bennett* [1952] 1 KB 249, it was held that, at least if the wife's promise not to go to court was the main consideration for the husband's promise to pay and could not be severed, the whole agreement (although made by deed) was contrary to public policy and therefore the husband's promise to pay was unenforceable. Following consideration by the *Royal Commission on Marriage and Divorce 1951–1955* (see *Report*, (1956) (Cmd) 9678, pp 192 – 195), that problem was resolved, and the rule in *Hyman v Hyman* confirmed, by the Maintenance Agreements Act 1957. The promise not to go to court was void but this did not render void or unenforceable the other financial arrangements in the agreement. Recognising that this might cause hardship to the payer as well as the payee, the *quid pro quo* was a power to vary or revoke those arrangements, if there was a change in the circumstances in the light of which they were made or the agreement did not contain proper financial arrangements for a child of the family. The provisions in the 1957 Act were later amended in two significant respects by the Matrimonial Proceedings and Property Act 1970 and are now consolidated in the Matrimonial Causes Act 1973, ss 34 to 36. First, while the 1957 Act applied only to agreements made between husband and wife "for the purposes of their living separately", sections 34 to 36 of the 1973 Act apply to

"any agreement in writing made [at any time] between the parties to a marriage". Secondly, the agreement may be varied even if the change in circumstances is one which the parties had foreseen when making the agreement. Subject to this, agreements for a present or immediate separation were and remain valid and enforceable like any other contract.

146. The Court of Appeal in this case suggested (at para 134) that the power to vary such agreements has become a "dead letter". It is easy to see why this might be so. Matrimonial practice has changed out of all recognition since the days of the 1957 Act. In those days, many couples separated without ever obtaining a divorce. A divorce could only be obtained if one of the parties had been guilty of a matrimonial offence (or had been incurably of unsound mind for at least five years). The theory was that the innocent spouse was punishing the guilty one by divorcing him or her. There could be no question of divorce by consent. Until 1963, collusion was an absolute bar to obtaining the relief which, often enough, both parties desperately wanted. So the parties had to be very cautious about anything which made it look as if they had agreed terms for their divorce. And the powers of the divorce court to award financial provision were much more limited than they are now. The parties might well agree terms in a separation agreement which were quite different from, and perhaps more generous than, anything which the court might order.

147. All of that has now changed. One of the first priorities of the Law Commission was the reform of family law, and their efforts led to the radical changes brought about by the Divorce Reform Act 1969, the Matrimonial Proceedings and Property Act 1970, and the Law Reform (Miscellaneous Provisions) Act 1970. All of these came into force on 1 January 1971. The first two were consolidated in the Matrimonial Causes Act 1973. The sole ground for divorce is now that the marriage has irretrievably broken down; separation and consent to a divorce is one of the ways of proving this. The theory of the innocent party punishing the guilty has gone. Divorce has become a great deal simpler and easier to obtain. It is fair to assume that there are now far fewer married couples living apart for long periods without divorcing than there were in the 1950s.

148. The court also has comprehensive powers to award financial provision, to transfer and settle property, and to share out pension rights. So the court can now do most things that the couple might want to agree. Divorcing spouses are actively encouraged to agree between themselves what the consequences of their divorce should be.

Indeed, despite the impression given in the high profile cases which reach the press, that is what the great majority of people do (see, for example, J Eekelaar, M Maclean and S Beinart, *Family Lawyers: The Divorce Work of Solicitors* (2000); M Maclean and J Eekelaar, *Family Law Advocacy* (2009)). If they do reach agreement, it is standard practice to embody its terms in a consent order. This is, on the one hand, because public policy rule 2 means that they cannot oust the jurisdiction of the court in any event and, on the other hand, because a properly drafted court order can finally dispose of the parties' claims against one another (see, for example, *Dinch v Dinch* [1987] 1 WLR 252).

149. So another type of marital agreement (a type (c) agreement) has come on the scene, an agreement to compromise the parties' mutual financial and property claims on divorce. Unlike orders made by consent in ordinary civil proceedings, however, the matrimonial order derives its authority from the court and not from the parties' agreement, even if embodied in a deed (see, for example, *de Lasala v de Lasala* [1980] AC 546). The court has an independent duty to check the agreed arrangements and to approve them (see *Xydhias v Xydhias* [1999] 2 All ER 386, at p 394). As Butler-Sloss LJ put it in *Kelley v Corston* [1998] QB 686, at p 714,

> "The court has the power to refuse to make the order although the parties have agreed to it. The fact of the agreement will, of course, be likely to be an important consideration but would not necessarily be determinative. The court is not a rubber stamp."

In fact, as *Xydhias* itself showed, this too can cut both ways. The fact that the order derives its authority from the court rather than the parties' agreement also means that the court can treat them as having agreed upon the essentials of their arrangements, even if their agreement would not be contractually binding because they have not agreed upon all the details. The court may therefore decide to give effect to these, even though it is not a legally binding contract.

150. Thus it is not surprising if practitioners have forgotten about the power to vary marital agreements. Most couples can be persuaded to get a divorce instead. The focus has therefore changed, away from the technical question of whether or not the agreement between the spouses is enforceable as an ordinary contract, in favour of the broader question which is before us now: what is the weight to be given to an agreement between a husband and a wife as to the

financial consequences of their separation or divorce by a court which is invited to make orders about it?

151. But before turning to that question, it is necessary to consider the fate of the public policy rule 1 (see para 143 above) and the decision of the Judicial Committee of the Privy Council in *MacLeod v MacLeod* [2008] UKPC 64, [2010] 1 AC 298. *MacLeod* was concerned with an agreement made by deed between a married couple while they were still living together. It provided partly for what was to happen while they were still together and partly for what was to happen in the (by then not unlikely) event of their divorcing in the future. Its terms were similar, but not identical, to the terms of an ante-nuptial agreement entered into before the couple married in the State of Florida, where such agreements are legally binding.

152. The Board held that the rationale for the first rule of public policy no longer held good. Since the abolition of the decree of restitution of conjugal rights by the Matrimonial Proceedings and Property Act 1970, s 20, the spouses no longer have a legally enforceable obligation to live together. Providing for what is to happen in the event of a future separation or divorce no longer conflicts with the legally enforceable obligations of marriage. Hence the Board held that a post-nuptial agreement providing for future separation was valid and enforceable in the same way as any other contract between spouses. The Board would not, however, have felt able to take that step had there not been a power to vary such a contract in the light of changes in the circumstances since it was made or for the sake of the children for whom they were responsible. The injustice of enforcing maintenance agreements without any power of variation had been recognised by Parliament when it enacted the 1957 Act and confirmed in what is now section 35 of the 1973 Act.

153. Secondly, the Board held that these powers of alteration applied, not only to agreements for a current or immediate separation, but also to agreements for a future separation. Although the "financial arrangements" contained in the agreement must relate to a period when the couple are living separately, section 34(2) defines a "maintenance agreement" as "any agreement in writing made ... between the parties to a marriage". It was no longer limited to agreements made for the purpose of their living separately. The Board did express the view, *obiter*, that sections 34 to 36 did not apply to agreements made between people who were not yet husband and wife and offered some observations, again *obiter*, about why the matter should be left to Parliament.

154. To sum up the position relating to agreements between husband and wife:

(1) There is nothing to stop husbands and wives from making legally enforceable agreements about their property and finances which are to operate while they are living together, subject to the normal contractual requirements.

(2) There is nothing to stop husbands and wives who are on the point of separating, or who are already separated, from making legally enforceable agreements about their financial rights and obligations while they are living apart.

(3) Following *MacLeod v MacLeod*, there is also nothing to stop husbands and wives who are not yet separated from making legally enforceable agreements about their financial rights and obligations while they are living apart.

(4) However, the court has power to vary the financial arrangements for their separation, made in agreements between husbands and wives, under sections 35 and 36 of the 1973 Act.

(5) None of these agreements can oust the jurisdiction of the court to make financial orders should the parties separate or divorce.

(6) Even if the parties have agreed what the court's order should be, the order derives its authority from the court and not from the parties' agreement.

(7) The court therefore has its own independent duty to check the arrangements agreed between the parties and to evaluate them in the light of its statutory duties under section 25 of the 1973 Act.

*Ante-nuptial agreements*

155. So where does this leave ante-nuptial agreements, made, not between husband and wife, but in contemplation of the couple's impending marriage, and providing, perhaps among other things, for the possibility of their eventual separation or divorce? If the rationale for public policy rule 1 no longer applies to post-nuptial agreements, following MacLeod, it is hard to see how it can still apply to ante-nuptial agreements. So why should these not also be regarded as valid and enforceable in the same way as separation agreements and, if MacLeod is right, other post-nuptial agreements?

156. It was not necessary for the Board to decide that question in MacLeod and it is not necessary for this Court to decide it now. The

Court of Appeal in this case accepted that the law could only be changed by legislation and neither party has suggested otherwise to this Court. Without legislation, it is not self-evident what the right answer should be. There are many different permutations. (i) It could be that MacLeod was right to hold that sections 34 to 36 of the 1973 Act apply to post-nuptial agreements providing for a future separation and also right to express the view, obiter, that they do not apply to such agreements made before marriage. (ii) It could be that MacLeod was wrong to hold that sections 34 to 36 apply to any post-nuptial agreement, other than an agreement for a present or immediate separation. (iii) It could be that the Board was wrong to consider that the words "made between the parties to a marriage" in section 34(2) apply only to agreements made while the parties are in fact married. (iv) It could be that the existence of a power of variation is not as important as the Board thought that it was, in assessing whether there are still public policy objections to holding such agreements contractually binding.

157. It will come as little surprise that I adhere to the views expressed by the Board in MacLeod. They accord with the wording of the Act. This was not a particularly adventurous piece of statutory construction, once it is realised that the change in the definition of the agreements covered by sections 34 to 36 was made in the same Act of Parliament, the Matrimonial Proceedings and Property Act 1970, which also swept away the basis of public policy rule 1, the enforceability of the duty to live together. Indeed, that change of wording may be said to strengthen the Board's construction. Making such agreements enforceable, subject to a power of variation, would be entirely logical and consistent. It would, however, have been considerably more adventurous to interpret the words "made between the parties to a marriage", in section 34(2) of the 1973 Act, to include a couple who were not yet husband and wife when the agreement was made. After all, another feature of the reforms which came into force on 1 January 1971 was the abolition of the action for breach of promise of marriage.

158. Furthermore, without a power of variation, there remain serious policy objections, albeit different from the original ones, to recognising ante-nuptial agreements as valid and enforceable in the contractual sense. Is it to be assumed that, although section 34(1) does not apply, public policy rule 2 (the rule in Hyman v Hyman) does? If it does, what is the answer to the Bennett v Bennett problem if the beneficiary spouse wishes to sue upon the agreement? If it does not,

can it be right that the intending spouses can oust the jurisdiction of the courts before their marriage but are unable to do so afterwards? If, on the other hand, either of the spouses wishes to enforce the agreement without going to the family court, can it be right that they should be able to do so without any power of variation no matter what the circumstances?

159. It is no answer to these questions, it seems to me, that these days most people do go to the divorce courts. They should not be obliged to do so. The existence of a power of variation means that they are likely to agree a variation for themselves without going to court. There are still people with conscientious objections to divorce. There are still people who are reluctant to accept that their marriage is over even though there may be temporary difficulties. There are other people who will not be able to go to the divorce courts here because they have been pipped to the post by the "first to file" jurisdictional rules in the Brussels II Revised Regulation (Council Regulation (EC) No 2201/2003). But in any event, this Court should not be developing the common law in such a way as to produce an injustice and thus to encourage people to seek a divorce when they would not otherwise wish to do so. Even if the old rationale for public policy rule 1 has gone, I still believe that it is the public policy of this country to support marriage and to encourage married people to stay married rather than to encourage them to get divorced.

160. A better answer, it may be, is that MacLeod did not need to decide whether post-nuptial contracts providing for a future separation were legally binding either. It too was a case about the weight to be given to such an agreement when the couple came to divorce. Some may think that the question whether an agreement is contractually binding has little if any relevance to the weight which it should be given by the court. Others, however, may think differently, especially if the agreement contains provisions to be implemented during cohabitation which have in fact been honoured. At all events, as the author of (but not the only contributor to) the Board's unanimous advice in MacLeod, I must accept some of the blame for the mess in which we now find ourselves.

161. All of this is to emphasise that this Court is not deciding whether ante-nuptial agreements are contractually binding. Nor is it overruling MacLeod on the question of post-nuptial agreements. The matter is obviously one for the Law Commission to sort out. My only plea is for a comprehensive and rational approach. Should public policy rule 2 (the rule in Hyman v Hyman) apply to all marital agreements,

before or after marriage, before or after separation, and to all its terms, whether operating during cohabitation or after the couple have separated? Or if that rule is to be disapplied to any or all of them, to what extent and in what circumstances? Should there be a power to vary all marital agreements and all their terms, and if so in what circumstances and on what grounds? Should all, some or none of their terms be legally enforceable? By what rules of private international law should such agreements be governed? This last is a particularly complicated question, particularly in a case such as this, where the agreement included both a choice of matrimonial property regime and also a choice of applicable law. It would be a great help if we could clarify our choice of law rules relating to matrimonial property regimes. All of these questions require careful consideration.

162. Once again, I adhere to the view expressed in MacLeod, that there may be important policy considerations justifying a different approach as between agreements made before and after a marriage. This is recognised in those jurisdictions which have legislated to make ante-nuptial agreements enforceable. It is, for example, common for them to contain safeguards which do not apply to agreements made after the marriage. Most important is whether, and if so in what circumstances, couples should be allowed to contract out of the fundamental obligations of the married state which they are about to enter. yman d

*Taking the agreement into account*

163. It follows from the well-established principles outlined in paragraph 149 above that, as the court always has to exercise its own discretion, if there is to be a starting point for the exercise of that discretion it has to be the statutory duty under section 25 of the 1973 Act. This applies to all applications for orders for financial provision, property adjustment and pension provision ancillary to divorce, judicial separation and nullity decrees. It is in mandatory terms (see paras 20 and 21 above). Furthermore, the same rules and considerations apply to (now almost unheard of) applications to the divorce court under section 27 of the 1973 Act for financial provision in cases of neglect to maintain (see section 27(3)) and to applications for financial provision in magistrates' courts under the Domestic Proceedings and Magistrates Courts Act 1978 (see section 3(1) and (2) of that Act, which mirror section 25(1) and (2)(a) to (g) of the 1973 Act). Corresponding provisions also apply between civil partners (see Civil Partnership Act 2004, s 72(1) and (2) and Scheds 5 and 6).

164. Until 1984, as is well known, section 25 contained a "tailpiece" which directed the court as to the overall objective of its discretion. This was so to exercise its powers:

> "… as to place the parties, so far as it is practicable … to do so, in the financial position in which they would have been if the marriage had not broken down and each had properly discharged his or her financial obligations and responsibilities towards the other".

This was deleted from section 25 by the Matrimonial and Family Proceedings Act 1984. Implicitly, as Lord Nicholls of Birkenhead said in *White v White* [2001] 1 AC 596, at p 604, "the objective must be to achieve a fair outcome". But in deciding what was fair, the courts had, perforce, to work out some principled reasons for making any order at all, in the context of a separate property regime. The House of Lords eventually did so in the trio of cases, *White v White* (above) and *Miller v Miller, McFarlane v McFarlane* [2006] UKHL 24, [2006] 2 AC 618. Put simply, the House discerned three possible rationales for making an order: the sharing of matrimonial assets, meeting needs arising from or during the marriage, and compensating for sacrifices made because of the marriage. I do not understand the majority judgment in this Court to be casting any doubt, either on the overall objective of a fair outcome, or upon the three possible reasons for the redistribution.

165. *White* is important for another reason. The leading opinion, with which Lord Hoffmann, Lord Hope of Craighead and Lord Hutton agreed, was delivered by Lord Nicholls. He emphasised that there should be no discrimination between the different contributions of the spouses to the welfare of the family which should be seen as equally valuable. But he also emphasised at pp 605–606:

> "This is not to introduce a presumption of equal division under another guise … a presumption of equal division would go beyond the permissible bounds of interpretation of section 25. In this regard section 25 differs from the applicable law in Scotland … *A presumption of equal division would be an inpermissible judicial gloss on the statutory provision.* That would be so even though the presumption would be rebuttable … It is largely for this reason that I do not accept [counsel's] invitation to enunciate a principle that in every case the 'starting point' in relation to a division of the assets of the husband and wife should

be equality. He sought to draw a distinction between a presumption and a starting point. But a starting point principle of general application would carry a risk that in practice it would be treated as a legal presumption, with formal consequences regarding the burden of proof." [My emphasis]

166. These observations are, in my opinion, equally applicable to the consideration of any nuptial or ante-nuptial agreement in the mandatory exercise under section 25. It would be "an inadmissible judicial gloss" to introduce a presumption or a starting point or anything which suggested that there was a burden of proof upon either party. In any event, the concept of an onus or burden of proof is inapplicable in a discretionary exercise such as this. He or she who asserts a fact must, of course, prove it. But it is for the court to carry out the exercise of discretion in the way in which Parliament requires it to do.

167. In my opinion, the test adopted by the majority (in para 75) comes close to introducing such a presumption. For this once again I must accept some responsibility. In *MacLeod v MacLeod* , at para 41, the Board said this:

"It would be odd if Parliament had intended the approach to such agreements in an ancillary relief claim to be different from, and less generous than, the approach to a variation application. The same principles should be the starting point in both. In other words, the court is looking for a change in the circumstances in the light of which the financial arrangements were made, *the sort of change which would make those arrangements manifestly unjust*, or for a failure to make proper provision for any child of the family. On top of that, of course, even if there is no change in the circumstances, it is contrary to public policy to cast onto the public purse an obligation which ought properly to be shouldered within the family." (emphasis supplied)

This may have come as a surprise to those former practitioners, such as Wilson LJ, who (for the reasons explained earlier) had never had occasion to look at section 35. But it would of course have been odd for Parliament to adopt one test when looking at the variation of a legally enforceable contract and another test when looking at the weight which should be given to such a contract in proceedings for ancillary relief.

168. With the benefit of hindsight, I would qualify that statement heavily in two ways. First, and most important, there seems no warrant for

the inclusion of the word "manifestly" before "unjust". That is nowhere to be found in the legislation. Secondly, in so far as it may be derived from cases on separation agreements, such as *Edgar v Edgar* [1980] 1 WLR 1410, it fails to acknowledge the manifold factual differences which there may be between the different types of marital agreement. It is, as the majority point out, one thing to look for a very significant change of circumstances in a case such as *Edgar*, which concerned a deed of separation made when the parties were already separated and quite shortly before the divorce proceedings were begun, or indeed in *MacLeod*, where the marriage was already in serious trouble and the parties had the possibility of early separation and divorce very much in mind. It is another to adopt the same approach when the agreement was made many years ago, before there was any question of the couple separating, and there are bound to have been many changes in the circumstances in which it was made. In this respect, therefore, I agree with the majority that the *MacLeod* test was too strict.

169. It seems to me clear that the guiding principle in *White, Miller and McFarlane* is indeed fairness: but it is fairness in the light of the actual and foreseeable circumstances at the time when the court comes to make its order. Those circumstances include any marital agreement made between the parties, the circumstances in which that agreement was made, and the events which have happened since then. The test to be applied to such an agreement, it seems to me, should be this:

**"Did each party freely enter into an agreement, intending it to have legal effect and with a full appreciation of its implications? If so, in the circumstances as they now are, would it be fair to hold them to their agreement?"**

That is very similar to the test proposed by the majority, but it seeks to avoid the "impermissible judicial gloss" of a presumption or starting point, while mitigating the rigours of the *MacLeod* test in an appropriate case. It allows the court to give full weight to the agreement if it is fair to do so and I adhere to the view expressed in *MacLeod* that it can be entirely fair to hold the parties to their agreement even if the outcome is very different from what a court would order if they had not made it. It may well be that Lord Mance is correct in his view that the difference between my formulation and that of the majority is unlikely to be important in practice. I would prefer not to take that risk.

170. As Lord Nicholls emphasised in *Miller*, at paras 26 to 29, there can be no inflexible rule about how a judge should approach the task. It may be that a judge, if called upon to decide matters, will find it convenient to conduct the usual section 25 exercise before deciding what weight to give to the agreement. He or she will then have a view of how the usual principles would apply to the particular facts of the case. It may be, on the other hand, that the case is so clear cut, as in *Crossley v Crossley* [2007] EWCA Civ 1491, [2008] 1 FLR 1467, that it is more convenient to begin with the agreement. If, for example, all the agreement seeks to do is to preserve property acquired before the marriage for the benefit of the spouse to whom it belongs, the court would be most unlikely to interfere unless the outcome would put a spouse or children in real need. It is not for this Court to be prescriptive about how a trial judge should conduct the statutory exercise.

171. In principle, though, I agree that the test should be the same, whether the agreement is a compromise of the proceedings, a separation agreement, a post-nuptial agreement made while the couple are together, or an ante-nuptial agreement. But the way in which it works out may be very different, depending upon the facts of the case. I therefore also agree that it is difficult to be prescriptive about the factors to be taken into account, and the weight to be given to them, because this would be to "fetter the flexibility that the court requires to reach a just result" (para 76, above). It may be, however, that the court will generally attach more weight to a separation agreement, made to cater for the existing and future separation of the parties, than to a post-nuptial agreement, made while the parties are still together but also to cater for the possibility of a future separation, and more weight to such an agreement than to an ante-nuptial agreement, catering for a marriage which has not yet taken place and for a separation which the parties neither want nor expect to happen.

*The circumstances in which the agreement was made*

172. The court will be looking first for a clear indication that the parties intended a divorce court to give effect to their agreement. The textbook and other precedents which I have seen certainly do their best to make this clear. The court should also take into account the parties' understanding as to the legal effect of their agreement. This is bound to change as a result of *MacLeod* and this case. People who entered into separation agreements should always have been advised that they were legally binding as contracts unless and until varied and although not binding upon the divorce court would often be

respected on the *Edgar* principles. People who entered into post-nuptial agreements in England and Wales will have been given rather different legal advice until *MacLeod* and people who enter into ante-nuptial agreements will have been given rather different advice until this case. People who have entered into such agreements in other countries will also have been given different advice. The parties' expectations and understandings as to the effect of their agreement should they later divorce will therefore be an important factor in deciding what is fair.

173. If the parties did expect the court to give effect to their agreement, the court will then ask whether there were any vitiating factors, such as fraud, duress or misrepresentation, which would make a contract voidable in English law. If there were, the agreement should in principle be ignored. But that is not all. It would be wrong to take a more legalistic view of such factors in the case of ante- and post-nuptial agreements than has long been taken in the case of separation agreements. Hence the wise words of Ormrod LJ in Edgar v Edgar [1980] 1 WLR 1410, 1417 (quoted in para 38 above) that "it is not necessary in this connection to think in formal legal terms, such as misrepresentation or estoppel". There may be something in the circumstances in which the agreement was made which, while falling short of a vitiating factor in the usual contractual sense, indicates that one party has taken an unfair advantage over the other.

174. Relevant to whether one party has taken advantage of the other will be whether there were the safeguards which have generally been regarded as essential in those countries in the common law world which have legislated to give validity to such agreements. These normally include mutual disclosure of assets, independent legal advice, and a degree of distance in time between the agreement and the wedding. These were also included in the safeguards proposed in the Home Office Consultation Paper referred to in the majority judgment at para [5]. These factors should be taken into account in deciding how much weight should be given to the agreement whether or not they are sufficient to "vitiate" it in the *Edgar* sense. On the other hand, in the case of an ante-nuptial agreement, the court cannot avoid also asking itself whether the marriage would have taken place at all without it, difficult though it may be to discern an accurate answer to that question in the light of later events. This too can cut both ways, because it may or may not indicate that one has taken an unfair advantage of the other.

*Later events*

175. The focus both of my test and that of the majority is upon whether it is now fair to give effect to the agreement. The longer it is since the agreement was made, the more likely it is that later events will have overtaken it. Marriage is not only different from a commercial relationship in law, it is also different in fact. It is capable of influencing and changing every aspect of a couple's lives: where they live, how they live, who goes to work outside the home and what work they do, who works inside the home and how, their social lives and leisure pursuits, and how they manage their property and finances. A couple may think that their futures are all mapped out ahead of them when they get married but many things may happen to push them off course – misfortunes such as redundancy, bankruptcy, illness, disability, obligations to other family members and especially to children, but also unexpected opportunities and unexplored avenues. The couple are bound together in more than a business relationship, so of course they modify their plans and often compromise their individual best interests to accommodate these new events. They may have no choice if their marriage is to survive. And these are events which take place while it is still hoped that the marriage will survive. There may be people who enter marriage in the belief that it will not endure, but for most people the hope and the belief is that it will. There is also a public interest in the stability of marriage. Marriage and relationship breakdown can have many damaging effects for the parties, their children and other members of their families, and also for society as a whole. So there is also a public interest in encouraging the parties to make adjustments to their roles and life-styles for the sake of their relationship and the welfare of their families.

176. All of this means that it is difficult, if not impossible, to predict at the outset what the circumstances will be when a marriage ends. It is even more difficult to predict what the fair outcome of the couple's financial relationship will be. A couple who always thought that one would be the breadwinner and one would be the homemaker may be astonished to find that the homemaker has become a successful businesswoman who is supporting her homemaker husband rather than the other way about. A couple who assumed that each would run their own independent professional life and keep their finances entirely separate may find this quite impossible when they have children, especially if they have more than one or one of them has special needs. An older couple who marry a second time round may think it fair at the time to preserve their assets for the sake of the

children of their first marriages, but may find that one has to become a carer for the other and will be left homeless and in reduced circumstances if the grown-up children take priority even though they are now well-established in life and have no pressing need of their inheritance.

177. All of these are changes which would entitle the court to vary a separation (or post-nuptial) agreement which turned out to be unfair, even if the parties had foreseen them, and should now be taken into account in deciding whether it is fair to uphold their agreement. On the other hand, if things have indeed turned out much as the parties expected and intended, it could well be fair to give effect to their agreement. Some of the precedents I have seen are of comparatively wealthy couples making a prediction of comparatively generous sums which ought to provide for the "reasonable requirements" of the recipient spouse in a way which might well have attracted the "millionaire's defence" in the days before *White v White*. In effect, therefore, they are contracting out of sharing but not out of compensation and support.

178. Provided that the provision made is adequate, why should they not be able to do so? On the one hand, the sharing principle reflects the egalitarian and non-discriminatory view of marriage, expressly adopted in Scottish law (in section 9(1)(a) of the Family Law (Scotland) Act 1985 and adopted in English law at least since *White v White*. On the other hand, respecting their individual autonomy reflects a different kind of equality. In the present state of the law, there can be no hard and fast rules, save to say that it may be fairer to accept the modification of the sharing principle than of the needs and compensation principles.

*The relevance of conduct?*

179. It must also be borne in mind that these are often complicated agreements, providing not only for what is to happen on divorce or death, but also for what is to happen during the marriage. The parties' subsequent conduct in relation to the agreement must be among the relevant circumstances when considering what weight should be given to it. Both parties may have conducted, and continued to conduct, their lives on the basis that their affairs are and will be governed by their agreement. In *MacLeod*, for example, the agreement made provision for the wife while they were still together and the husband had put this into effect. In this case, the wife acquired further assets from her father, which would not have happened had

the agreement not been in place. Such factors obviously increase the weight which should be given to the agreement.

180. Conduct in relation to the agreement itself is one thing. But what about conduct in the relationship generally? In the section 25 exercise, the courts do not take conduct into account unless there is a substantial imbalance between the parties, such that it would be inequitable to disregard it. Such cases are very rare. But what if the agreement were to provide for different outcomes, depending upon how the parties have behaved during the marriage? What, for example, if the precedent referred to earlier, providing for the wife to have a predetermined sum for each year of marriage, were also to provide that she should only have this if she has been a good housewife? These are deep waters indeed, but in my view the court would be just as reluctant to enter into such an inquiry in relation to a nuptial agreement as it is now in relation to the section 25 exercise and correspondingly reluctant to hold the couple to their agreement. All the examples that I have seen, both in textbooks and in real cases, are scrupulous in making no reference to marital conduct.

*The foreign element*

181. In strict legal terms the so-called "foreign element" is irrelevant. If the proceedings take place in England and Wales, the applicable law is that of England and Wales, irrespective of where the parties come from, how long they have been here, or how close their connection is with this jurisdiction. The United Kingdom has made a deliberate choice not to adopt the Hague Protocol on the law applicable to maintenance obligations and has only agreed to participate in the Council Regulation (EC) No 4/2009 on the basis that it would not be required to do so. English family lawyers seem to have a horror of having to apply foreign law which must appear strange to European lawyers who are quite used to doing so. Anyone who chooses to divorce here must be advised that the court will apply English law and not the law of the country which the parties have chosen or with which the marriage has the closest connection.

182. In another sense, however, the foreign element cannot be totally irrelevant. It may affect the relevant considerations in a number of ways. It may be a crystal clear indication that the parties intended their agreement to be legally binding, not only upon themselves, but also on the court. On the other hand, a foreign couple may have been warned, as this couple were warned, that their agreement might not have the same effect in other countries as it did in the country where it

was made. But it means that their expectations may have been very different. The agreement may also have affected their later behaviour to a greater extent than it would have done had they not regarded it as legally binding.

183. None of this is to suggest that evidence of foreign law will be necessary in a foreign case. The relevance is not as to the effect of a foreign agreement in English law because, by the time the case gets to the divorce court, it has none. The relevance is as to the parties' intentions and expectations at the time when they entered into it.

*This case*

184. The agreement with which we are concerned was ante-nuptial, in the sense that it was made before the marriage. However, it did more than provide for what was to happen should the couple separate or divorce. It purported to choose German law as the law applicable to all aspects of the marriage; it determined the matrimonial property regime which would govern the marriage, in this case separation of property rather than the deferred community of property which is the default position in German law; it excluded the statutory equalisation of their German pension rights; each party waived the right to a compulsory portion of the estate of the first to die which they would otherwise have under German law; and each party waived any claim to maintenance of any kind whatsoever in the event of their divorce. Most of this is already English law. The matrimonial property regime of England and Wales has to all intents and purposes been a separate property regime since 1882. English law does not provide for the compulsory equalisation of pension rights or for the survivor automatically to inherit a compulsory portion of the estate of a deceased spouse. The difficulty lies with the exclusion of all claims to maintenance on divorce, because in English law this cannot be done (nor, it appears, is it entirely effective in German law).

185. No-one has argued that this agreement should be ignored. That might have been a tenable view while public policy rule 1 survived (and even while it was still thought to have survived, the courts were increasingly inclined to take these agreements into account) but that view is no longer tenable now that the rule has gone. Equally no-one has argued in this Court that the agreement should be "presumptively dispositive". As we have seen, that would be inconsistent with the statutory regime governing financial relief.

186. As may often be the case with these agreements, if the judge had first asked herself what would have been the fair outcome without the

agreement and then asked herself what difference the agreement should make, she might well have come closer to the solution adopted by the Court of Appeal. She would have asked herself whether any of the three principles identified by the House of Lords in *White, Miller*, and *McFarlane* would justify an award to the husband. She would have concluded that there was no scope for the sharing of matrimonial assets, because in effect there were none. Unusually, this couple had acquired no matrimonial home or other property together. The wife was already independently wealthy before they married and was given even greater wealth during the marriage. But this was undoubtedly intended for her alone. It would not have come to her had her family not been confident that it would remain her separate property. The judge might well also have concluded that there was no scope for compensating the husband for sacrifices made for the sake of the marriage and the family, although I have some reservations about this. The husband had (perhaps) sacrificed a career in investment banking for a much less lucrative career in scientific research. But it could be said that that was for his own sake rather than for the sake of the family. In the circumstances, he was probably right to concede that the basis of any award should be "needs" rather than "sharing" or "compensation".

187. However, "needs" is a convenient shorthand for a rather more complicated concept, which is the (now) mutual commitment which each spouse makes to support the other. Under the former "tailpiece" or statutory objective, this was a life-long commitment, surviving divorce although ending on the receiving party's remarriage. Under the present law, it is no longer life-long. Each party has a responsibility to try to adjust to living without such support. But they may still be entitled to support for requirements which arose as a result of or during the marriage. Usually, of course, this is because of the demands of child-rearing and the (often life-long) financial disadvantage which results. But among the statutory factors is disability. If this arises during the marriage, it may be entirely proper to expect the normal support commitment to continue after the marriage ends.

188. In some cases, the support requirement generated by the marriage might go further than this. Most spouses want their partners to be happy – partly, of course, because they love them and partly because it is not much fun living with a miserable person. So, choices are often made for the sake of the overall happiness of the family. The couple may move from the city to the country; they may move to another country; they may adopt a completely different life-style;

one of them may give up a well-paid job that she hates for the sake of a less lucrative job that she loves; one may give up a dead-end job to embark upon a new course of study. These sorts of things happen all the time in a relationship. The couple will support one another while they are together. And it may generate a continued need for support once they are apart. Whether this is seen as needs or compensation may not matter very much. It can only be for this reason that the husband in this case had any real claim upon his wife apart from his claims as the father of her children.

189. In those circumstances, is it fair to give effect to their agreement? First, did the parties intend it to have legal effect? There can be no doubt that they did. Second, were there any contractually vitiating circumstances? There is nothing to suggest that there were. Thirdly, is there anything in the circumstances in which it was made to suggest that the wife-to-be was taking an unfair advantage of her husband-to-be? I think not. He did not have an English translation and he did not have independent legal advice. He was presented with a "take it or leave it" agreement. This must have been what the judge meant when she referred to the lack of negotiations, and it could be an indication that an unfair advantage has been taken. But in this case the husband did know the essence of what he was agreeing to and there is nothing at all to suggest that he wanted to negotiate for something different. He was not a naïve young person in a vulnerable position. He was a financially sophisticated and highly educated young man. He was marrying for love and not for money. In common with the Court of Appeal, therefore, I see nothing in the circumstances in which the agreement was made to make it unfair to hold the parties to it (although I worry that this very experienced and thoughtful judge who had the advantage of seeing and hearing the parties may have seen something which we have not).

190. However, that does not inevitably mean that it is fair to give the agreement its full weight in the circumstances as they now are. We would not, for example allow this wife to cast the burden of supporting her husband onto the state. More relevantly, the agreement did not cater for the fact that they might have children together. It is common ground that provision must be made for their two children. His Honour Judge Collins CBE decided that it is in their best interests to spend time living with each of their parents. These are the children of an extremely rich mother, although she did not want the family to have an unduly lavish life style. Nevertheless, since there are ample means available to enable them to do so, the children

should be able to enjoy the same standard of living while they are with their father as they have when they are with their mother. Hence it was accepted that he should have a home for them, not only in England, but also when they were spending time with him in Germany or (now) near the mother's home in Monaco, and also the means to support them generously in their homes with him.

191. The issue is whether this should all come to an abrupt end when the youngest child grows up. When unmarried parents separate, the court has no power to make provision for the parents. It can only provide for the child and indirectly for the parent by taking the child's need for care into account when making provision for the child. Provision for the child has to cease when the child ceases education or vocational training, unless there are special circumstances (Children Act 1989, Sched 1, para 3(2)). And the courts have held that capital payments, or property settlements, to provide the child with a home should revert to the other parent when the child grows up. There is therefore no power to provide for an unmarried parent whose financial position has been irredeemably compromised by the demands of bringing up children or looking after the family. Married parents are different, in that the court has power to make provision, not only for the child, but also for the parent. There is no reason in principle why the court should limit its support in the same way that it has to limit its support for the unmarried parent. Quite the reverse: this is what distinguishes marriage from cohabitation in our law. Where parents are married, the court can look beyond the needs of the child while growing up and look independently at the needs of the parent, and in particular those generated as a result of parenthood. Not only this, these days parents often expect to continue to be a resource for their grown-up children, a base to which they can return and a source of the unconditional love and support which is what parenthood is all about.

192. That may well be why the wife agreed to discharge most of the husband's debts and also acknowledged before Baron J that the husband should have a house, not just while the children were growing up, but for life. The Court of Appeal appeared so anxious to disagree with the *obiter* views of the Board in *MacLeod* that it decided to treat these parents as if they had never been married. That cannot be the right approach. This couple were married in England. They intended to make their matrimonial home in England. They had been advised that their agreement might not be effective under the laws of another country where they chose to live. The main concern

of the wife and her family was to ensure that the husband acquired no proprietary claim to shares in the wife's family companies – which might then become forfeit. This was in no way prejudiced, as the judge made clear, by a lump sum order which the wife could readily meet out of her cash income.

193. In my view the Court of Appeal erred in principle in treating a parent who has been married to the other parent in the same way as they would treat a parent who has not. If, for example, a parent has irredeemably compromised her position in the labour market as a result of her caring responsibilities, she is entitled to at least some provision for her future needs, even after the children have grown up. It would not be fair for an ante- or post-nuptial agreement to deprive her of that. Where parents are not married to one another, there is nothing the court can do to compensate her. But where they are, there is. A nuptial agreement should not stand in the way of producing a fair outcome.

194. I would therefore have varied the judge's order so that the husband was entitled to his English home, or any home bought to replace it, for life. I would also have asked myself whether there were likely to be any continuing support needs attributable to his parental status after the children grew up. The answer to that is probably "no" although I also consider that the husband's decision to leave his lucrative career in banking and acquire further qualifications with a view to changing direction was not as completely selfish as some may have thought it to be. The wife appears to have agreed with it at the time. And why should she not? The couple were rich enough each to be able to pursue their own dreams. She had not been happy in New York and perhaps she understood why her husband was no longer happy in banking. If the decision was taken for the good of the family as a whole, this would have been for the benefit of the children as well as their parents. Happy parents make for happy children. Discontented parents make for discontented children. The judge found that, once that step had been taken, there was no going back.

195. It may be that the case should have gone back to the judge on this basis, as well as on the cross-appeal, for we are not in a position to make findings of fact which she did not make. But while I am clear that she did not give enough weight to the agreement in this case, I am equally clear that the Court of Appeal erred in equating married with unmarried parenthood. Marriage still counts for something in the law of this country and long may it continue to do so.

# Index